THE POWER OF MIRACLES

THE POWER
OF MIRACLES

The Truth Behind
Spiritual Healing

Rochelle M. Gibler

HEADLINE

Copyright © 1998 Rochelle M. Gibler

Photographs © Miracles and the Extraordinary magazine

The right of Rochelle M. Gibler to be identified as the Author of
the Work has been asserted by her in accordance with the
Copyright, Designs and Patents Act 1988.

First published in 1998
by HEADLINE BOOK PUBLISHING

10 9 8 7 6 5 4 3 2 1

British Library Cataloguing in Publication Data

Gibler, Rochelle M.
    The power of miracles : the truth
    behind spiritual healing
    1.Spiritual healing
    I.Title
    615.8'52

ISBN 0 7472 1921 4

Typeset by
Letterpart Limited, Reigate, Surrey

Printed and bound in Great Britain by
Mackays of Chatham PLC, Chatham, Kent

HEADLINE BOOK PUBLISHING
A division of Hodder Headline PLC
338 Euston Road
London NW1 3BH

This book is dedicated to my mother, Romayne Gibler, whose love and friendship I will always cherish, and to the loving memory of my father Edward Gibler.

Also to my friends who art in heaven:
Jesus, King of All Nations and Mary, Queen of Peace.

Contents

ACKNOWLEDGEMENTS

I would like to give special thanks to Pastor Simeon Kayiwa,
Maria Esperanza di Bianchini, Father Peter Rookey,
Dr Kenneth McAll, Revd John Hampsch, Myles Dempsey,
Dr Raphael Gasson, and Father Benedict Groeschel.

I would also like to thank all the people who shared their
remarkable stories of healing with me.

Introduction

Why Should We Believe in Miracles?

We all want to believe in miracles. Deep in our hearts we hope there is a force for good, a righter of wrongs, a bringer of peace, a fighter for those less fortunate than ourselves. But the modern world addresses the head, not the heart. We have been told so often and for so long – by scientists, politicians and, especially, businessmen – to reject faith in favour of what is called the 'real world'; we have been lured into the belief that only commerce counts. There is nothing wrong with commerce, of course, but its new form is devoid of all sense of community and compassion: the only god is money and the only religion is the market. This insistent message has led people, particularly in the West, towards a crude individualism and materialism.

We have been educated in disbelief. Nothing can happen, unless we make it happen. God has been sidelined or, just as bad, reinterpreted, in such a way that He no longer resembles the God we first met in our Bible. Many people now prefer to see Him as a force, like gravity; or a blanket notion of the universal mind; or even as a kind of potential within all of us, which we can realise without prayer, without effort, without sacrifice.

Even the great Christian Churches have attempted to play down the significance of God's works. In so doing, they have smuggled out from his teachings the very measure that makes God the Supreme Being, the notion that He alone has the power to perform wondrous acts. So the very concept of miracles has been scorned.

1

The clergy are as vehement in their opposition to miracles as non-believers. Most of the Protestant denominations of Christianity deny their existence, and many Roman Catholics agree with them. The Church hierarchies are very hostile indeed to miraculous events. They seem to find miracles embarrassing, viewing them as archaic hangovers from the supposedly superstitious Dark Ages. They warn people against believing in the supernatural, which, if you think about it, represents a total denial of the essence of all Judaeo-Christian teaching and its scriptures. These religions were founded on supernatural events and their scriptures are testament to those happenings. They tell us that God communicated with His people on His earth. Why should people who affect to believe in those scriptures deny that God has gone on communicating with us ever since?

Given this anti-supernatural propaganda, it is not surprising that so many people are sceptical about the idea of the 'iron-clad' laws of nature being subject to interruption from a greater being. No wonder they find it hard to imagine a personal God, like a friend, acting on their behalf. Having been led to the conclusion that nothing is real if they cannot touch it, feel it, see it – or, more likely, buy it – they find the concept of a supreme power beyond their comprehension. They cannot fathom that there might be a power capable of listening to their thoughts – the feelings of their hearts; a power that is aware of – and also understanding about – their faults and weaknesses. They find it still more difficult, of course, to imagine that this power is interacting with people on earth as never before in recorded history.

Yet all is far from bleak. There has been a reaction against this ungodliness. Though many, many people have been persuaded to turn their backs on God, and on organised religion, in recent years there has been a widespread recognition of a spiritual void. People have sought in increasingly large numbers to find new routes back to spirituality. It is the failure of science to answer all the questions, and the failure of commerce to offer a genuine and lasting satisfaction, which have convinced people to seek answers elsewhere. For many, these paths have proved to be dead-ends, because they have tried to take shortcuts, or tried to avoid God altogether. But the positive point here is that more and more people are, at last, opening themselves to spiritual and even supernatural ideas.

One key area that has opened their eyes to science's failures is medicine. In the fight against cancer and Aids, or the struggles with depression and alcoholism, people have been moved to take matters into their own hands. They are not only searching for physical cures but for inner peace, an emotional healing after years of isolation or memories of abuse. Our spirits have become heavy and desensitised to the harshness of life's problems. But where can one find relief?

Alternative health therapies certainly seem to provide common-sense answers and people are spending more and more money to try such options. They often choose experts in homeopathy, chiropractics, acupuncture and nutrition, rather than orthodox doctors who routinely administer drugs. We have come to understand that we are what we eat. Studies also show that our will plays a vital role in the battle against disease. A positive mental attitude and the power of the mind are being taken seriously, so unlike the situation twenty years ago, when it was thought that pharmaceutical companies could provide cures for everything, given time and money. Now the study of psychoneuroimmunology – the way the mind influences the immune system – is fast becoming a valuable field of medicine.

The more broad-minded among us, even within the medical profession, are embracing the ancient wisdom of healing from past civilisations. The paradigm is shifting: Newtonian scientific thinking is no longer considered to be a great fount of answers. For the first time what has too often been derided as nonsense – the art of healing and the supernatural – is being taken seriously and the evidence is generated through systematic research.

Recent developments include the emerging field of energy medicine, or PSI healing, which incorporates a variety of disciplines: clairvoyance, clairaudience and channelling. These are defined as the spiritual capacity of inner vision, inner hearing and contact, with that which lies beyond or behind the veils that mask spiritual reality from the material world of the five senses. In this realm we find an interesting interface of 'paramystical phenomena',[1] such as faith, prayer, meditation, relaxation techniques, faith healing, the power of Jesus, apparitions, spirit guides, psychic healing, South American shamanism, Native American medicine men, witchcraft, trance-induced healing, hypnosis, astrology and spiritualism.

For centuries, these spiritual beliefs or traditions have been considered the domain of religion, and it was the job of the

3

Church to scrutinise their acceptability. Yet the Christian Church, despite its good will and good intent, has failed miserably to rise to the challenge, with attendance plummeting to 10 per cent in England and 30–40 per cent in the USA. Unfortunately, many people are suffering, and have suffered, because of its inadequacies. Too many doubt the existence of God and reject the idea of His place and His authority. The hope and high-mindedness so characteristic of a healthy, morally prosperous society have dissipated.

In this vacuum, we find health-care professionals embracing meditation, philosophy and spirituality, announcing themselves as 'experts' in these 'new' techniques. Mind-and-body institutes across America and Europe have generated funding to explore, and substantiate, the overlap in healing and consciousness, which is now referred to as 'inner space'. Many brave doctors diligently tackle the quagmire of emerging theories to determine what may help or even save us. But are they really equipped to bridge the gap that exists between religion and science? By whom are they guided? Not by the wisdom of theologians, for science has long been the atheistic enemy of faith and belief in God.

Those who seek spirituality are being offered a rather mixed bag: astrology has been incorporated into hypnotherapy; occult spirituality is now considered a form of prayer; channelling and shamanism have been woven into psychology. However valuable these approaches might appear, their content demands a more discerning eye.

But who is equipped to pass judgement, when religious practitioners have succeeded in alienating the modern populace, and when good and evil have become accepted as part of the same cosmic whole? The idea of faith in God as the Creator has been subordinated to the idea that there is a god-like power latent in all of us. The central moral concept of right and wrong has been swept aside and downgraded into a nebulous relativism, while the notion of sin has been dismissed altogether as outmoded. So the remaining question is: can science continue to make a reasonable assessment of spirituality, without the wisdom of religion? Surely scientists can, if only they are willing to look.

The spiritual world is brimming with evidence of the miraculous. There is proof that events have taken place, and are still taking place, which are extraordinary and cannot be explained away as figments of people's imagination. Across the world there

4

are people with supernatural gifts who put Einstein in the shade. Sadly, there is no publicity about them, no spreading of the good news, because an atheistic media chooses to ignore them, robbing us of what we need most today: *hope*. All sorts of uplifting stories about God's work – of healing, for instance – are hidden from the majority of us.

In this climate it is not surprising that there is so much confusion and scepticism about spirituality. The purpose of this book is to look behind the myths, to explore the facts, to tell the truth, to end the confusion. *The Power of Miracles* is about to take you on a miraculous journey. I will present documentary proof – doctors' reports and medical records – of God's healing power at work today. He can save people from Aids and cancer; He can reverse paralysis; He can cure individuals and nations. (When you read about the miracles of Uganda and then realise how that country has been transformed from the ravages of civil war to a new prosperity, you begin to grasp God's power.)

But to appreciate this you will need to clear your mind. Put your preconceived notions and your scientific education on hold, while you indulge yourself in the world of the miraculous. I have travelled the world in search of miracles and I have not accepted what I have been told at face value. I could have written a book four or five times as long as this one, but I have restricted myself to miracles that I could prove. In the light of my research, and my own experiences, I am giving you a chance to read a variety of real-life accounts, which offer a fascinating and compelling insight into the world of the supernatural. But, of course, it is for you to make up your own mind.

Notes

1. The term 'paramystical phenomena' is used by Father Benedict Groeschel, in *A Still Small Voice* (Ignatius Press, San Francisco, 1993).

1

Miracle-Worker Extraordinaire:

Pastor Simeon Kayiwa

This is a truly powerful story that many will find difficult to believe. I can well understand that. Even I, who have witnessed and experienced the miraculous, often found myself awestruck by the facts that I present here. But I must stress the factual accuracy of what you are about to read.

I too had difficulty coming to grips with the extraordinary accounts of healing. They are – not to put too fine a point on it – of biblical proportions and you could be forgiven for thinking that the man responsible for them is the Second Coming. This is not blasphemy, nor is it wild exaggeration. Mark the name Simeon Kayiwa, for he is a special man.

Sadly, the world of miracles is always open to the wiles of the deceitful and the deluded. Fraudulent claims are common, engendering a scepticism that convinces people to set their hearts and minds against all such supernatural phenomena. The eyes shut; the ears close; the soul hardens, robbing people of the hope they rightfully deserve. We encounter televangelist preachers with their questionable methods greedy for money and hungry for fame. They help to perpetuate the process by which the truly miraculous, the real works of God, are discredited. But here, I tell you from my heart, is the genuine article.

I first came across Pastor Kayiwa's story four years ago. Then it seemed just that – a story. Now I cannot think of it like that. After a dozen trips to Uganda, a thousand hours of conversation, countless interviews with doctors, nurses, businessmen, politicians and even a king, and days of travelling in the bush to document the most difficult of stories, I have made a judgement call. Simeon Kayiwa does not lie.

Twenty years ago from the depths of Africa he received a gift from God, which even today shines as brightly as the sun. He was initially granted this gift at a time when Uganda was suffering the tortuous reign of Idi Amin, a bloodthirsty murderer and well-known Satanist, who used the powers of darkness just as Hitler did, to advance his relentless domination over his own people. He all but killed the spirit of an entire nation.

But more than Simeon Kayiwa's astonishing capacity to heal the sick and rehabilitate the minds of men, this is a story of a personal God, who could not shut his eyes to the fact that hospitals were not functioning, medicine was scarce and people did not have food to eat. Just when darkness was overshadowing human existence, a God of tremendous power intervened, devastating our laws of nature, defying all scientific principles. And he chose a sinner, just like you and me – a man with nothing but the clothes on his back – to crack the hardest rock of all, the human heart. That is why, today, there are an estimated two million Africans who now consider miracles to be a way of life.

I urge you to read Simeon's story with an open mind. I can confirm that the healing taking place is not restricted to the Third World or to a people whom some may believe are easily led. My own beautiful niece, Hilary (aged four at the time), was healed in front of my own eyes, with my family as witnesses. Her face was covered with dreadful hives as she was about to start school. 'Mummy,' she would cry, 'what's wrong with my face, and what will the other kids think?' She had a severe milk allergy, and keeping a child away from all milk products – cheese, chocolate, yoghurt, and so on – was close to impossible, especially when there are other children in the house. One sip and her face swelled. I took Simeon home to the States and he met Hilary who even at four understood who Jesus was. He asked her, 'Do you believe that Jesus can heal you?' 'Yes,' she replied, with amazing confidence, not the timid doubt you might expect. He touched her, and that was enough. The next morning she started to drink milk, and later she ate some chocolate. This act of healing may appear slight to you, but for a family that has a suffering child, it was extraordinary. It was not achieved by chance or by coincidence; Hilary's healing was received after prayer. It was a miracle.

On another occasion my friend Lisa rang Simeon because her sister-in-law was due to have surgery for kidney stones. Lisa wanted Simeon to pray for her, for she was frightened. Simeon said to Lisa, 'Can I use your hands?' Lisa replied, 'Yes.' He told Lisa to put her hands on the small of her sister-in-law's back, then told her the words to say. Within hours Lisa had done as instructed. The stones passed by the next morning and the surgery was cancelled.

Then there was Jean, who had been married for years and could not conceive. She was distraught, spoke with Simeon over the phone and two months later – after years of strain on her marriage – she became pregnant. Some may say this was coincidence. But how can such extraordinary things happen after the prayer of just one man? I now prefer to think of coincidence as God's way of acting anonymously in life.

Then there was the time I was talking on the phone from the United States to Simeon in Kampala. It was early morning for him, but just after midnight for me and I was sitting in the dark, drinking a glass of milk, which is unusual for me because it is a beverage I would normally have only in tea. Out of the blue he said to me, 'So you're drinking a glass of milk.' Even someone in the same room would not have been able to identify what was in that glass. I asked him why he thought that had happened, and he said, 'It was a sign from God for you to believe in the power of miracles.' These are just a couple of the amazing situations in which I have found myself, due to my friendship with the remarkable Simeon Kayiwa.

Rumours of healing abound, but documentation about them is rare. I wanted to find a story so amazing that even sceptics would take note. I know that miracles happen every day – after all, I have experienced them at first hand. I also know that people, in their excitement at being healed, rarely go back to their doctor for confirmation of their healing. So trying to prove to a world of disbelievers that the laws of nature are subject to change through divine intervention is far from easy.

My hopes were lifted when a friend, well connected in religious circles, heard of a man who was healing people of Aids. I was sceptical, but I did some checking and was told that tests were taken before and after the healing, which naturally limited the possibility of error. My breakthrough had arrived. I was eventually introduced to a contact in London who had met this man in Uganda with an extraordinary ability to heal the sick. Most importantly, this contact felt that the story could be properly documented, although it would be difficult – nothing is easy in Africa. Intrigued by the claims, I made more inquiries. 'He's called Pastor Simeon Kayiwa,' I was told. 'But he doesn't have a telephone, and he's very busy. I'm afraid the chances are that he won't be able to see you.'

Undaunted, I obtained his address and sent him a letter, by Federal Express, to a PO box in Kampala, the Ugandan capital. Since FedEx does not normally deliver to PO boxes, I was not very optimistic that I would receive a response, but I need not have worried. Three days later Simeon phoned me and confirmed what my contact had told me: there *was* documentary proof that people had been healed of full-blown Aids. Why didn't I come out to Uganda to see for myself? I wanted to send someone else to do the groundwork, but Simeon pleaded with me to come. I had never been to Africa and had no idea what I was getting myself into. I did not know this man. I had only spoken to him twice for about 20 minutes. I kept thinking: I must be out of my mind just to get on a plane and go. But I felt an incredible peace about it. I ignored the pleas of my friends to take phials of my own blood to a country riddled with Aids, and off I went.

When I arrived, Simeon was late. For forty-five minutes, as I paced the arrivals hall, I kept asking myself what I was doing here. Would I be putting my life in jeopardy if I got into a taxi with one of the locals? Finally, he turned up, a slight man, neatly dressed, greeting me with a broad smile. His casual, sincere manner immediately put me at ease. He was amazed that I had made the journey alone. I said that I was surprised he had responded so quickly to my letter, when I heard he was always so busy with visitors. Only later did I discover why he had called me.

His wife, Celia, told me that Simeon had a dream. 'In this dream,' she said, 'an angel told him that he would receive a letter in three days' time, in a white envelope [most envelopes in Uganda are brown]. The angel said, "Do not reject what's in that envelope." ' For Simeon, this was important. He knew that the Lord meant business when he sent an angel (as you will see

10

later). I rather liked the idea that I was announced by a heavenly messenger. And, apparently, Simeon himself had no say in the matter.

On the journey he urged me not to stay in a hotel, for he had arranged for me to stay with one of his choir members. Her home turned out to be a small bungalow, fringed by banana trees, set in the lush tropical surroundings of Kampala. Betty was a lovely, friendly woman, who insisted that I take her room during my visit. Simeon's influence was becoming more apparent to me.

It took barely an hour before I started to hear reports of an amazing man, gifted with the power to change lives. Betty remembers a story that gave her hope when she needed it most. She and a few others were watching television with Celia, while Simeon was resting in the next room with the door open. Betty, who was in the process of getting her life together, was depressed and needing encouragement, so she made a silent prayer: 'Lord, if you are really with me, please give me a sign.' At that very moment Simeon called out, 'Betty? Where is Betty?' He got up half-asleep, gave her a piece of cake and went back to bed. Was this a small sign from a God who was listening?

I was given a grand tour of the compound (as it is called in Uganda) where Simeon and Celia live. There were lots of jokes and much laughter. Poverty did not prevent people from having a sense of humour. Simeon's white stucco house is very modest. It sits alongside the church and a few makeshift shelters for those unable to afford housing. When the heavy tropical rains fall on its roof of aluminium sheeting, the noise explodes, as if nature is going wild. The house is furnished with burgundy-coloured velvet sofas and a large dining table, similar in size to the one shown in *The Last Supper*, the painting that hangs on the wall. The sitting room is more like Grand Central Station in New York than the quiet refuge of a home, for there is a constant stream of visitors in and out. But it is a place of comfort and peace for all those who come. Simeon and Celia live here with their seven children, aged from five to eighteen.

I was taken outside to look at the church, which is always referred to as a fellowship. Its close proximity to the house prevents Simeon and Celia from ever having a private moment. Their dedication to the needy is profound. On that first visit I thought the church very rustic, with its barn-like doors, dirt floor and wooden benches. Somehow, the rustic qualities of the buildings appealed to me: it was easy to imagine greatness hidden under the unassuming exterior of the surroundings. Since then there have been many changes: it now has a brick front, a cement floor and scores of white chairs, but it remains humble.

For Simeon, life is hard, but the amazing miracles that imbue his life give him great endurance. The difference between him and many other well-known personalities, who claim that they can heal the sick, is that he actually has the ability to do so. In a world of miracles, the powers given to Simeon are truly extraordinary. No effort is required to find testimony to his success. People in their thousands flock to tell of the remarkable man who has turned miracle-working into an everyday event. He cures and comforts millions with appalling diseases through the power of God. He foresees the future and he explains the past. He is a man of great wisdom and understanding of the mysteries of life.

On my visits to Uganda I have come to regard Simeon as a friend, a rare man of God and a truly unique human being. He has healed at least thirty people diagnosed with the HIV virus, some of them with full-blown Aids. He has commanded the crippled to walk, the blind to see and the earth to quake, confirming to the world that he is a true prophet. He has baffled doctors, astounded the unbelieving and converted the sceptics. And, after years of knowing him, I have come to believe that Simeon's Namirembe Christian Fellowship may well be a place where heaven touches earth.

As we settled down to a meal of traditional African food, another heart-warming story was told to me. Simeon had been out in front of the compound when he saw a young woman walking by who looked distressed. So he motioned to her to enter the compound. She was pregnant, without a penny to her name and did not even have a blanket to wrap around her expected baby. What would she do? Simeon asked her to stay at Namirembe for a while and to inform her family. She helped with the chores and gained solace from the experience. One day, while she was sweeping the yard, a car drove by, bumping over the potholes, and a large bag tumbled out of its boot. She chased the car but to no avail. Dutifully she brought the bag in and handed it to Simeon, not giving it another thought. A radio appeal for the owner stated that the lost goods would be held at Namirembe for a week.

After that week had passed and no one had collected the bag, Simeon told the young mother-to-be, Mary, that she could keep the contents, whatever they might be. As she opened the bag, her heart melted. It was brimming with baby clothes, blankets, nappies – everything she could ever need. This was the beginning of my miraculous journey in the depths of Africa, observing a man who deserves to be recognised throughout the world.

Simeon's successful case histories include several patients ravaged by full-blown Aids, which has been reversed; a doctor who suffered from leukaemia; and a nurse struck by hyperthyroidism (better known as a goitre). Then there was the King's cousin, whose son endured years of epilepsy, but suffers no longer. A former Ugandan President under house arrest escaped after a single prayer. One man even claims that it was through Simeon that his poverty disappeared. And the pastor has forewarned many of punishments to come if people ignored advice to change their lives before God. Among a people all too easily lured by the powers and traditions of witchdoctors, the power of the Holy Spirit invested in Simeon stands out as a beacon of light in a country – and a continent – darkened by dictators and disaster.

Often Simeon sees more than a hundred people in a single day. He does not ask for any payment to cover his expenses. Though he is far from rich, he and Celia raise their seven children uncomplainingly on the meagre income from donations from a largely impoverished congregation, who come faithfully every Sunday to hear him speak.

Now forty-two, Simeon was born in what he calls a 'humble up-country Christian family' in western Buganda, the kingdom in which Kampala is situated, with seven brothers and three sisters. Well educated at the International University in Nairobi, Kenya, and later at Makerere University in Kampala, he went on to become a successful artist and an art teacher in a secondary school. It was during this period, in his mid-twenties, that he was given his gift of healing. He admits that at first it confused him. 'I was not a believer in anything supernatural. I deeply despised those who believed in God. So the changes that occurred in me were not really of my own making.'

In his pre-Christian days, Simeon was similar to any other single man, enjoying the attractions of women and the comforts of life. He was quite the man about town. Little did he know that his life was about to change, for ever. After a late night out, he

13

was lying on his bed, when Jesus appeared before him. 'It startled me; my heart almost stopped. I thought He had come to punish me. And then Jesus said to me, "Bring my people back to me. Tell them to leave witchcraft. I am the greatest power in all heaven and earth. Read Isaiah verse sixty; you will perform miracles and wonders wherever you go in My Name." ' After he stopped shaking, Simeon hesitantly said, just as Moses did, 'Lord, I am a sinner, send someone better, like the bishop or the sheikh,' but He did not listen.

At about this time Simeon had a dream in which he found himself at a mass given by Pope John Paul I in St Peter's Basilica in Rome. 'I was in front of the Pope. He held out the chalice before me and said, "Take this cup and serve. I can no longer continue." I heard people shouting from outside the church. They were calling out, "Simeon, are you a Catholic now?" I told them, "I have no religion. I am looking for Jesus!" '

The next morning he awoke and went into the adjacent room, where his cousin was sleeping, and told him about the dream. Oddly Simeon's cousin did not doubt the dream, but thought that it was a premonition of the forthcoming death of the Pope. Later that day – 28 September 1978 – while they were listening to the news, the death of Pope John Paul I, who had served for just thirty-two days, was announced.

Although Simeon is certainly similar in standing to a Pope in his own country, he remains non-denominational to this day. But one wonders about the meaning of the symbolism in that dream. It was at about that time that the miracles began to flow. It was the vision of Jesus that most disturbed Simeon. Was it, he wondered, simply a figment of his imagination? Why would the Lord be interested in him? He mentioned the vision to some of his relatives and they questioned his mental faculties, until an uncle had a remarkable experience. He was in desperate need of money and asked Simeon what he should do. Nonchalantly, Simeon directed him to the taxi rank. Following his instructions, the uncle went and, much to his amazement, found a friend there who ended up giving him the money he needed.

But Simeon was still bothered by his divine intrusion and sought out his closest friend at the time, Robert Saidi, a lecturer in French and philosophy at Makerere University. Explaining this unusual encounter to Robert, Simeon asked his friend if he thought it was merely his fancy. Robert was not a religious man,

14

and Simeon was surprised by his response. 'I certainly don't think it was your imagination,' Robert said. Then he added, without any apparent reason, 'I am working at two jobs just now, and I still can't support my family. Do you think you could pray for me?'

Though amazed by Robert's confidence in the validity of his experience, Simeon told his friend to affirm his faith by resigning from both jobs. He asked Robert to bring him the resignation letters as proof that he had done so. Within a week Robert handed over the letters to Simeon. 'We prayed together on several occasions about it,' Simeon told me. 'Then one day I simply told Robert to go into town and get a job.'

I quizzed Robert about these events. 'In town I stopped at the post office to get my mail and ran into a friend of mine. He told me that he was opening a business and wanted me to run it. He asked me how much I made as a teacher and said that he would give me three times that amount. He even offered me furniture for my house and, later, I received a car. At that moment, I just couldn't believe it. I was awestruck. How could this have happened without the power of God? I actually felt fear of God. I knew then that He really existed. That day changed my life. When you work with God, your life is full of miracles.'

At the time that Simeon became aware of his gift, war-torn Uganda was suffering under the dictatorship of Idi Admin. The country was in a parlous state. Many hospitals and schools were closed and the rest were barely operating. Medicine was in desperately short supply; supermarkets had little, if any, produce to sell. Everything appeared to have come to a standstill; the country's infrastructure had broken down. Gunfire could be heard everywhere; houses were raided nightly. Anyone who could afford to had left the country. Millions of Ugandans were suffering perpetual anguish.

It was at this moment, with despair running deep, that Simeon, despite his lack of belief in God, was empowered to heal the sick, when there was no other way for them to be cured. He was able to offer the people a safe haven from the ravages of dictatorship. For, as the situation worsened, Simeon's compound seemed to be under a sort of angelic protection. It was never raided. Soldiers entering early at dawn got down on their knees to pray, in fear for their own lives. As people began to realise this,

15

they arrived in droves. Even the current Minister of Finance, Maganja Nkanji, slept on Simeon's floor.

A desperate need had required the ultimate act of divine mercy and somehow, even in his own sinfulness, Simeon's heart was a place where God could dwell comfortably. In two other war-torn regions, Rwanda and Bosnia (for the latter, see Chapter 4), there were supernatural warnings for people to change their lives, but the response there was weak. Through God's gift to Simeon, Uganda was more fortunate. As word spread about his gifts, people came from all around to hear him speak. A lame woman was carried into his church on a stretcher and was later able to walk back home. To show her gratitude, she had her son present Simeon with the keys to a new car, which he drove for many years afterwards. Dreams now began to play a significant role in Simeon's life, enabling him to see into the lives of people, as well as into the future, as you will see from the following story.

Dreams seem to be one of the ways frequently used by God to communicate with Simeon, as with the prophets in the Old Testament. In one of the earliest examples, Simeon was taken to a room in heaven, which he describes as an administration area, and encountered a creamy-skinned angel in white robes standing behind some files. The angel told Simeon, 'You are here to be told what I am going to do to someone you know, Mr Lusuwata, for being disobedient to Me.' (Mr Lusuwata is an uncle of Simeon's wife Celia.)

When I asked Simeon whether 'Me' referred to an angel or the Lord, he replied that on the many occasions when angels have spoken to him, they have always spoken in the first person singular, as if they were speaking for God.

The angel opened a huge book, six feet square, and said, 'This is how I sent him to earth.' Then the pages began to speak: 'Go to the world and build many churches for me.' The angel turned another page, to where there was some scribbling, and pointed to the marks. Simeon told me, 'It looked to me as if they were dead birds. Somehow it was symbolic. I knew it meant that Mr Lusuwata had done nothing.'

The angel went on, 'He will die within one year, but he has the opportunity to live longer if he will agree, when you ask him, to let you lay hands on him and tell him what I have said.' Then the angel said, 'This is how he will die – he will be standing in the

16

front door of his house with his son, James, and will be shot dead. His blood will splatter on the left sleeve of his son, who will be dressed in white, with short sleeves. I can see his wife coming many times to church to pray, therefore she will not die, she will escape. I will return to you, Simeon, one month prior to his death.' Then Simeon woke up.

He told me, 'I was very sure this dream came from above, that someone had spoken to me. The impression it left me with was so deep. It was just too real not to be true. From the first day I heard God's voice, I learned how to recognise what comes from Him and what is from me. Like a baby who knows the voice of his mother.'

Naturally Simeon told his wife about the dream and they discussed it over and over again. They prayed that God would forgive Mr Lusuwata, a member of the Anglican Church, if he would not listen to Simeon. Simeon's Namirembe Fellowship was newly founded and people were being warned – as a way of keeping them in their own churches – that Simeon was a false prophet.

Mr Lusuwata's wife was informed of the dream and told her husband of it. But he replied, 'I belong to the Anglican Church. I will pray for myself.' Later his wife noticed that he had noted in his diary for that date, 'Some people want to kill me.' It is unclear whether he was taking the threat seriously, but certainly not seriously enough to do as the angel suggested.

Before the year end, the angel returned to Simeon in another dream. This time he was not in heaven. He said, 'Look at Mrs Lusuwata. She has taken the children to school and has gone to the hospital, but her husband is not there to help her.' Then he showed Simeon an instrument that looked like a gun and told him to look through it. 'I saw young women at a distance,' Simeon told me. Then the angel continued, 'These are all his girlfriends. Even though I blessed him, he is not living a holy life. In one month he will die. But even now he has the opportunity to live longer, if he agrees to be prayed for and to do the work assigned to him.'

Simeon went on, 'I told his wife about the second dream. She told me she thought the instrument I had seen was a gun and that it would be used to shoot her husband.'

Late one evening at the end of the month, Mr Lusuwata was shot dead, for no apparent reason. Two young men were said to have shot him while he was standing at the front door of his house. His blood splattered on the left arm of his son, who was standing in the doorway with him, just as the angel had predicted.

Simeon was immediately informed. Only he, his wife Celia, Mrs Lusuwata and a small group who arranged to pray together knew of the dreams. The horrible prediction foretold had come to pass. Simeon was indeed a prophet. In biblical times were not predictions such as this always associated with the prophets?

At Mr Lusuwata's funeral, the bishop declared that God's son had been taken home to heaven; but, in Simeon's view, it looked as if the man had been judged, for his wrong actions, as well as for not using his God-given talents. It appears that all of us have been assigned some special task or duty, to which the Bible refers as 'good works'. If we neglect this task, as Mr Lusuwata did, we may run the risk of putting our eternal life in jeopardy. As it says in 1 Timothy 6, 17–19: 'Tell the rich . . . not to rely on so uncertain a thing as wealth but rather on God, who richly provides us with all good things for our enjoyment. Do good . . . be rich in good works . . . be generous, ready to share, thus accumulating as treasure a good foundation for the future, so as to win a life that is true.'

From those early days comes another unusual story revealing to us more about the nature of God, the God of justice. War was raging, and the Chief of Staff of the Ugandan Army, Oyite-Ojok, was known to be a brutal murderer, who was randomly killing civilians. He was speaking in Kampala to the local people about the insecurity in the country. In a beguiling manner he told them, 'If a soldier comes to your house with a gun and desires to take your wife, or your property, you should realise that he is human. Cooperate with him and the other soldiers and you will have security. You are the ones who cause the insecurity, not the soldiers.'

Oyite-Ojok had imprisoned many innocent people he believed were a potential security threat. One of them, a bishop who was a friend of Simeon's, had written him a letter. He said that the Army Chief of Staff had come to the prison, to inform the prisoners that he intended to kill all of them. There was not enough money to waste on bullets, so he was going to command his guards to whip them into the lake until they drowned.

Everyone in the country was deeply disturbed about the

human suffering experienced at the hands of this man and Simeon was enraged. He had a premonition that Oyite-Ojok was going to be punished; if he did not repent, something terrible would happen to him. Simeon told this to the people in his Fellowship, which, at the time, included an informer, planted by the regime to spy on them. Simeon felt so strongly about the premonition that he wrote the Chief of Staff a letter, which was delivered by the informer. When Oyite-Ojok heard what Simeon had said, he became angry and threatened to burn the church to the ground. Cunningly, he sent a message to Simeon saying that he was on his way to Tanzania, but, when he returned, he wanted Simeon to appear on national television with him, for prayer service. Simeon did not believe that this gesture was sincere, but agreed to appear. However, on the Chief of Staff's return trip from Tanzania, his plane exploded into flames in mid-air. The punishment had been executed, again as foretold.

It was during these horrendous days of bloodshed, when food was so scarce, that Simeon felt powerless. There were many staying at the church and Simeon was overcome with worry, for there was no way to feed them. He had approached other churches and the few businesses still operating, pleading for help, but all he received was stale bread and rotten fish. Nursing mothers were crying out to him, in desperation. His conscience was tortured, so he prayed.

The Lord said to him, 'Go out to the mango tree and command it to produce fruit.' This request Simeon thought absurd, but of course he obeyed immediately. 'I went out to the mango tree in the yard and said to it, feeling odd but with faith, "I command you in the name of Jesus to produce fruit." Within a week the fruits were falling off the tree.'

That tree produced fruit until the war ended, but since then not one mango has been seen. While even believers may find this story difficult to digest, I encourage you to read further. This is a man whose life is shrouded in the mysteries of the supernatural. He does not lie, or even exaggerate. After extensive investigation, I am certain that the events happening at Namirembe are not grounded in the imagination, the hysterical workings of the needy or the questionable powers of witchcraft. No matter how unlikely it may seem, they are the truth.

Here is another even more astonishing story, which has

19

attained almost legendary status among those who know of Simeon. A woman who was being threatened with brutality by her husband came to Simeon for help. The husband wanted to end their relationship, so he set a trap for her. He had given her all his money to keep safe in a small purse. While she was out one day, he took the purse and, intending to blame her for misplacing it, actually lost it while swimming in the river. When she arrived home that night, he became angry and threatened her, demanding the return of the small purse. She would be out of the house for good, he shouted, if she did not recover it.

Desperate, she went to see Simeon, crying and pleading for him to do something. He prayed over her and sent her home, telling her that it would be all right. It was evening, and one of the typical Ugandan boys who cycle around selling fish came into the compound. Eager to assuage her husband's temper, she bought a large fish for their evening meal. Later, as she began to clean it, she slit open the belly. What did she find, but the purse? She could not believe her eyes and burst into tears.

When her husband came home, she quietly gave him the purse. He was mesmerised, then looked intently at her, wondering how she could have retrieved it. When she told him the story, he immediately set out for Namirembe to see Simeon. When he got there, he fell to his knees and asked for God's mercy. From that day he became a believer.

All of Simeon's miracles seem to have a biblical connotation. Matthew 17, 27 says, 'Jesus said to Peter, "Go to the sea, drop in a hook and take the first fish that comes up. Open its mouth and you will find a coin worth twice the temple tax. Give that to them, for you and for me." '

Simeon's fame eventually forced him to give up schoolteaching. He told me, 'People used to come running into my classroom yelling, "Simeon, Simeon, I have been healed." It was rather embarrassing and a bit disruptive to the class. Finally, the headmaster called me in and suggested that I choose between God and the school. It was an easy choice.'

His mother-in-law, Julia Lule, told me of those early days. 'Simeon collected petty thieves and young people on drugs and brought them home. He fed everyone from the proceeds of his paintings. He started a small prayer room, which he used daily. This was his first church. Little by little, from his example, the

20

kids began to listen and then slowly the miracles began.'

Simeon did not set out to create a new Church. 'There are many faiths and religious organisations nearby, so they took care of the need for sacraments and services,' he says. 'People come here from neighbouring countries because they have heard about the miracles. We feed the visitors who don't have money. I want them to see, through the miracles, that Jesus is active today. In general, after people have received healing, I tell them to go back to their church, but they keep returning to Namirembe anyway.

'In the beginning, when the churches heard about the miracles, they started claiming I was dangerous, a false prophet. Then slowly, when their own members began to come, they took the position that I should form an allegiance with one of them. I told them – the Anglicans, the Catholics and the rest – that if I did that, people would think that Jesus belongs to one group or another. He doesn't. He belongs to everyone.'

Given Simeon's amazing track record, it was hardly surprising that word about him soon spread, not only across Uganda but throughout central Africa. Meanwhile, that first abandoned building at Namirembe – its windows blown out, doors off their hinges, weeds grown high – grew to be a substantial, airy church, with twenty-foot-high ceilings. It now serves as the Fellowship's headquarters. The surrounding Kayiwa village now has about 500 residents. One church led to two, then twenty-two and then 220, spawning the building of hundreds more meeting places. The Fellowship now has more than 2,000 affiliated churches, with an estimated two million members. Their belief in Pastor Simeon's gifts is remarkable.

While documenting a cure for an Aids case in Entebbe, I visited one of the Namirembe churches, where I heard that Simeon had asked all his followers to fast only on water for three days before the Ugandan election of April 1994. When I asked how many had fasted, the entire church congregation raised their hands. I was totally taken aback, for he had moved these people to such an extreme that they were willing to endure suffering. In fact, the fast culminated in a national day of prayer, in which the leaders of every faith – Moslem and the two main Christian Churches, Catholic and Protestant – joined together. Christian tradition has taught that sacrifice is the most powerful form of prayer. It brings to fruition our requests. God governs the world, but prayer may govern God.

Simeon always stresses that his Fellowship is not linked to any particular denomination. 'I am a non-denominational follower of Jesus, because I believe I'm dealing with a Creator who cares more about men and women than about their different theologies. All religions are trying to find the path to God. The barriers between them are man-made. Faith is about a relationship between man and his God. Every religion struggles to define that relationship in its own unique way.'

He does not see this as a theological debating point, but in purely personal terms. 'My relationship with God is due to the fact that I actually met Jesus. When he appeared to me, He told me, "Bring my people back to me. I am the greatest power in heaven and on earth." He told me to read Isaiah verse sixty: "Arise and shine for your light has come and the glory of the Lord has risen upon you . . . But the Lord will arise over you and His glory will shine upon you."

'Remember, I knew nothing about the Bible at that time. I didn't know what was in Isaiah verse sixty. It was His manner and His authority that made me believe immediately that it was indeed Him. The signs began when I did things in His name, using His authority. And because the sick received healing and the demonic were freed, and people repented of their sins, I knew it was Jesus of the Bible, and this was his normal routine.'

It is this foundation of belief that gives Simeon enormous strength to tackle any problem. Like the time he heard that the Ugandan President, Yoweri Museveni, was planning to outlaw the cutting down of trees, in a national preservation campaign. Simeon understood the dilemma: the President wanted to conserve the country's dwindling tree crop, but most of the country's people used firewood for cooking. 'How will these people eat?' he worried. That night he prayed and the next day he wrote a letter to the President, explaining how this new regulation would affect people's lives, and delivered it personally to the President's office. A compromise was reached, and later that day President Museveni apologised on television for his harsh actions.

This was proof of the respect in which Simeon is held by the ruling classes in Uganda. He is well connected and his influence is strong. In 1980 there was a coup and the President, Godfrey Binaisa, was placed under house arrest. He sent for Simeon, who took his mother-in-law, Julia Lule, with him. When they arrived,

Simeon asked President Binaisa, 'Your Excellency, what do you want, sir?'

The President replied, 'I would like either to die in peace or to escape.'

Simeon told him to kneel and he prayed over him. Then Simeon said to President Binaisa, 'Tomorrow morning, at exactly ten a.m., God will allow you to escape. Have a car waiting and go directly to the border!'

I spoke to former President Binaisa: 'It was definitely a miraculous escape,' he said. 'I was held in a bungalow near Entebbe airport. There were about 100 Tanzanian troops guarding me. The conditions were atrocious. Three of them slept in the same quarters with me. There was no hope of escape. I had seen Pastor Kayiwa on Christmas Eve. The next day was Christmas and I requested to spend it with a friend in Kampala. It surprised me when the commander said yes. That morning the guards escorted me to Kampala.'

When they arrived, President Binaisa began to appeal to their human side. During wartime, people were stripped of everything, and very few even had food. He told the guards that his friend had no food, and they had nothing to eat for Christmas. 'After some time, they actually left me to go and fetch some food. This was a real God-send. It gave me breathing space to plan my escape from the country. My friends were able to secure a vehicle from the Ministry of Defence. Off we went, with my young daughter and wife. People thought we were government officials, so we had no problem driving through the country. We heard there were lots of guards at the Kenyan border, so we had to abandon the car and travel on foot to the village town of Busia, which lies both in Kenya and Uganda. As we got out of the car a young boy appeared who had been a messenger from one of the law firms in town, who dealt with the State House. He recognised me immediately and offered to help my wife and I carry the few belongings we had managed to escape with. He could very easily have turned us in. Once we were over the border, we were safe. And the rest is history,' said Binaisa.

The day after Christmas the headlines read: GODFREY BINAISA'S WHEREABOUTS UNKNOWN. When asked whether he believed in God, he said, 'Oh yes. I was raised to believe, my father was a minister in the Anglican church.' As Simeon had foretold, President Binaisa had escaped – what a Christmas present!

During the presidential election in June 1996, President Museveni asked Simeon to come to his house to pray with him. While touring the countryside with the King of Buganda (pronounced 'kabaka' in Loganda, the local dialect), Ronald Mutebi told me, 'If there is any help we can give Pastor Kayiwa and the work he is engaged in, we are happy to do so.'

As a regular on television and radio talk shows, Simeon's voice and face are now familiar to millions. He is a musician and has composed over 200 songs and seventeen albums, featuring his popular Calvary Cross Choir.

He has a magnetic personality. He is funny and entirely without conceit. In the best spiritual tradition, he takes no credit for the healing that occurs through him. He is relaxed, casual, welcoming to anyone and, despite administrative duties that roughly combine those of a bishop with those of a mayor, he takes time to have fun. Yet fun has been in short supply, as Uganda tries desperately to recover from thirty years of destruction.

When the land is so beautiful and seductive, it is hard to imagine the bloody eight-year reign of terror of Idi Amin. The area around Kampala, for as far as the eye can see, is fertile and abundant, with the wavy leaves of banana trees swaying over the neat, green, rolling hills of tea and sugar cane. Almost every fruit and vegetable known to man grows in the deep-red earth. They say that if Uganda was well organised, it could feed all of Africa. Around noon you see school children walking home for lunch in their smart, tailored, red and blue uniforms. Almost everyone looks amazingly well dressed, their clothes brightly coloured and neat, no matter what their economic situation – even the people who live in mud houses manage to look fashionable.

I witnessed a richness in Uganda that can never be taken away. It showed in the bounty of the land, but I noticed it most in the people – in a gentleness, a purity of spirit, like spring water. There was not an inkling of hearts hardened from years of war, which you find in our Western world. After my time with Simeon and his people, I knew something of what was meant by 'the Kingdom of God is among you'. Nevertheless, these people go on suffering, for the legacy of Amin has been replaced by a new terror.

In 1981 (before this terror was identified) Simeon had a dream of rain falling on the map, in every country. 'When this rain touched the skin of people, dark spots appeared, then a voice told me there would be no cure for this disease but Me, meaning God. This disease will touch every home.' The parallel with Aids is obvious. And Aids does indeed touch every home in Uganda. Statistics reveal that 35 per cent of the Ugandan population of nineteen million is HIV-positive. Approximately 160,000 children have been orphaned. There is virtually no homosexuality or drug addiction in the country. In the 1800s, the King of Buganda at that time forbade homosexuality and the educational system reflected those values, so it never took hold in the Ugandan culture. Heterosexual sex can now be a death sentence. Ugandan doctors see evidence that even condoms sometimes fail to prevent the spread of Aids.

If you are beginning to wonder about Simeon's claims, then let us hear from just a few of the people who have benefited from his miracles – people who have been delivered from the death sentence of Aids, like Juliet, Robinah, Grace and Wilson. I have not accepted their stories at face value – I have checked them thoroughly, demanding authentication; I have interviewed their doctors extensively, checked their medical records and spoken to their families and friends. These people have been tested not just once, but many times both before and after their healing, to be certain that there was no mistake.

Everyone in Uganda is familiar with the symptoms of Aids, just as you or I might be with measles or flu. The disease devours the body, and when the symptoms disappear there can be no denying that something highly unusual has taken place. Not by willpower or by might can you recover from full-blown Aids; but only through a direct act of God. Together these stories provide unequivocal evidence of the fact that Jesus is in the world today and is working through a rare man named Simeon Kayiwa. I present them individually so that you, the reader, can properly judge this modern miracle-worker and his success.

Juliet: 'Prayer is the best medicine.'

One balmy summer night in 1989 Juliet was walking home through the streets of Masaka, a small town close to the outskirts of Kampala. She was an attractive, well-dressed seventeen-year-old doing part-time relief work for the American Immunisation Team. She was a virgin, a young woman from a respectable middle-class home, where sexual habits are not dissimilar from those of a suburban English or American family. (At the time she was reluctant to reveal her name because of her desire to marry; she has since married, but I have agreed not to publish her surname.)

That fateful night Juliet did not even hear the footsteps behind her, before she was knocked to the ground. Her attacker brutally raped her. 'I will never forget his face,' she told me. Nor has she ever been able to forget the outcome of this appalling crime. A few months after the attack she began to notice what she thought was a rash developing all over her body. It was, in fact, Kaposi's sarcoma, the classic symptom of Aids. Chronic headaches began, along with symptoms of malaria. Eventually her tongue was covered with sores that prevented her from eating or drinking without extreme pain. After six months of suffering quietly, she sought medical advice and was told that she was HIV-positive.

'I was distraught and all I could think of was suicide and how I was going to do it. I didn't want to experience that horrible death,' she remembers. While she underwent further tests, she refused to tell her family. She feared that the pain and disgrace would send her mother over the edge.

People commented on her weight loss. She had lost half her weight and was down to just under six stone (83.6 lb), but her family did not link this with Aids, because Juliet did not have a boyfriend. She wore long-sleeved blouses and longer skirts to hide her infected skin. She thought her life was over, believing, with good reason, that people never recover from SLIM (as Aids is known across Africa). Around her, people were dying of the disease every day. It had killed her brother, her sister and many of her friends. Doctors told her there was no hope.

In desperation, grasping the faintest of hopes, Juliet remembered a story about a deaf person cured through Pastor Simeon's prayers. 'I didn't know if he prayed for Aids victims, but I just wanted to die in peace,' she told me in a low voice, as we sat on old wooden crates in Pastor Simeon's garage, so that no one could hear us. 'I was embarrassed to tell this man of God about my illness. What would he think? Finally, after I let it all out, I collapsed in front of him. When I recovered, he told me that God was my answer. And that I would be healed and would not die. He explained passages in the Bible, where Jesus promises healing to those who believe in Him. I didn't believe him, but I had no other hope.

'Pastor Kayiwa told me to come back the next day and I did. "You will see, Juliet, within six months there will be no sign of Aids on you – no rash, no headache, no malaria, no sores on your tongue." I thought: could Pastor Kayiwa be deceiving me? How could he say such things? It couldn't be possible. He said prayer was the most powerful unused weapon against destruction. He told me, "I will pray and fast and seek God for you. You pray and fast too, Juliet." He told me that God is not a religion. God is a person and He listens to his people.'

The next day Pastor Kayiwa told Juliet his dream of the night before. 'God showed me a mountain and the mountain started to decrease and it eventually disappeared. Juliet, God told me this is how Aids will disappear in you.'

'When I heard this, I rushed to the doctor, but my test was still HIV-positive. I had three tests altogether and all were positive. I couldn't stop the thoughts of death, the suffering was immense. I went back heartbroken and asked the pastor, "Please, just pray for me."'

'He said to me harshly, "I am serving the living God and you will not die. I will pray three times and then you return to your doctor for another test." I went back three more times to see him, and then had my test done again.'

It was negative. The doctor was amazed and insisted on repeating it, in case of an error. Again it was negative. Juliet recalled, 'I couldn't believe it. I went back and told Pastor Kayiwa. We were both so excited, we started praising and thanking God.'

'She hugged me like a mad woman,' Simeon told me.

Juliet continues, 'Now I pray continually in thanksgiving. Pastor Simeon asked me to go back once more and to bring him the test results. I went back three times, and each time the results were negative.'[1]

In the following weeks and months Juliet's sores began to heal and she gained weight. Puzzled doctors took more tests, but she was entirely clear of the Aids virus. It was, by any standards, a miracle – the first real, documented proof of a full-blown Aids patient being cured.

27

'I still can't believe I've been healed, but I feel great. During this whole time I didn't tell anyone about my problem, except my doctor and Pastor Simeon. I believe many more people would be cured, but their friends and relatives say, "It might be possible to be healed of most things, but not Aids." When my mother saw my weight return, she asked me what was going on with me. I just smiled and said, "Jesus works." She laughed, but didn't understand what I meant. My only living sister also couldn't believe the change in me. She asked if she could come with me, to see Pastor Simeon. She had high blood pressure at the time. She was healed as well and now goes to the hospital two days a week and prays for the sick. Prayer is the best medicine I know of. Jesus is the doctor of all doctors, and I'm living proof.'

I interviewed Juliet's doctor (who prefers to remain anonymous) at the S & B Health Care Clinic in Kampala. He confirmed her illness as Aids and her current tests as HIV-negative. 'I have my opinions, but I would just as soon the medical community not know exactly what I think,' he told me. 'The main thing is that Juliet has been healed. Sometimes an Aids test can be mistaken for another, and this is why we sent Juliet's tests to Entebbe for final confirmation. Many patients with malaria or yellow fever can test positive for HIV. At one stage in the evolution of the virus, you can have a negative test because it does not produce antibodies, so several tests are required.'

He described Juliet's weakened body as encrusted with sores and told of how they began to disappear. 'We don't have Aids drugs here, so we try to give comfort, treating the symptoms. Juliet has gained weight. She now weighs nine stone eight pounds and there are no signs of Aids on her body. *Where science stops, God begins.*'

To combat the growing problem of Aids, Simeon has a simple solution, as a young woman explained to me. Elizabeth Balirwa, an agricultural lecturer at Makerere University, told me, 'Pastor Kayiwa insists on abstinence, or marriage with a partner who has been tested, as our only options. It isn't difficult when you look at the choices. People drink to forget their problems – no money, sickness, etc. Waragi, the local drink, is distilled from bananas, and it's lethal and cheap, about forty pence a glass. It's dangerous because it makes people lose control. They don't care whether they are sick, have sex and infect someone. It can spread the disease quickly.'

'Miracles are a way of life here in Uganda,' Simeon says with gentle simplicity, as if denying his own key role in the process. 'Everyone has witnessed or experienced them. We have had thirty or more cases of Aids, that I know of, that have been healed.' His reticence is understandable, because he sees himself only as a conduit for God's work. He knows that prayer heals, but he also knows that sometimes it does not.

'There are instances when I have taken only a minute for prayer and God has answered,' he explained. 'Other times I must pray over people for a year. It is also true that some people receive healing and others don't. Not being healed doesn't prove that God does not exist, but rather that He has a choice about what He does. He may decide suffering could shape that person into a better human being; He may decide to heal them, after they have developed humility. God views our life from the standpoint that this world is not our permanent home. There is another place where His power is omnipresent. In this world there will always be suffering, but in the next world we will be restored.' In John 16, 33 it says, 'In Me you have peace, in the world you will have tribulation. Be of good cheer, I have overcome the world.'

Must a person have faith, then, to be cured? Simeon concedes that faith can play a crucial role, and even Jesus did not perform miracles in Nazareth, because there was no faith. He points out that 'God is sovereign and can act without anyone's efforts. This is how babies and animals are healed.' In these cases, God uses the faith of the parents as a channel for the healing. Faith is the 'substance of things hoped for, the evidence of things not seen'.

Some people believe that, because they have done terrible things in their lives, God will not listen to their prayers. But this simply is not true. Simeon has seen the prayers of sinners answered as often as those who lead close to perfect lives. God is hoping that all of us will some day want to know Him more intimately. It is as if a small divine imprint was placed on our hearts at birth, an urge that one day grows into a desire to know the answers to the important questions in life. It may not come until a deathbed illness or the loss of a child, or until times of financial crisis or divorce. But, for most people, it will come.

When we embark on this search and begin to pray, if we look carefully we will notice signs that our prayers are being heard. And it feels pretty good. It is not about coincidence, but about a response from a personal God, who is familiar with every thought in our mind and aware of every hair on our heads. Often we will want more and, only then, slowly, do we begin to change our lives. God will always take this opportunity to nurture us. It is like the story in the Bible of the prodigal son coming home – no sin is too great to be forgiven.

Robinah: 'People who are that ill with Aids don't recover without divine intervention.'

There was, it seemed, no hope for Robinah Serunkuuma. She lay in a coma after contracting the Aids virus from her husband, who is now dead. As soon as she recovered consciousness, doctors at the cash-strapped hospital were so convinced she would die that they sent her home, in order to avoid paying the transport costs for her body. Instead she was taken, by stretcher, to Pastor Simeon. That, she now believes, saved her life.

Robinah had been working for the International Red Cross for five years when, in 1989, the staff were immunised against TB. Mrs Juliet Mugab Nakamanga, her supervisor and a registered nurse, recalls, 'Robinah's tests were not satisfactory, so we instructed her to have another one. Then she developed a cough and did not respond properly to treatment. We tested for Aids and the results were positive. At that time she was pregnant with twins and her condition started to deteriorate. She was able to deliver both babies full term, but one died soon after.

'Within a month both Robinah and her daughter were ill. Her lungs were filled with fluid which is one of the last stages of the disease. By this time we had lost eighteen people on our staff to Aids, and none of them was as sick as Robinah.'

Simeon heard about her case while praying for others among those sick in the hospital. 'I went to Robinah, who had been in a coma for a month and a half,' he explained. 'I could see that her case was desperate. But I had to take my eyes away from the circumstances and believe in their survival. I prayed for both her and the baby.'

I found Robinah working at the Red Cross office. Her face was lined and visibly hardened by her suffering. She was fragile, but grateful to be at work. She told me, 'The hospital, realising I would never get well, discharged me. My aunt took me straight to

Pastor Simeon's church. I was so weak I had to be carried in on a stretcher. I couldn't even hold my baby at the time. Pastor Kayiwa arranged for a car and driver to bring me to the church about four times a week. He told me to fast on fluids and pray. There was an immediate change. After a month, I regained my strength and could walk by myself. I was even able to go back to work. And my baby was cured as well.'

Robinah's case was remarkable. To be so desperately ill, in a coma and near death, and yet for both her and her baby to recover astonished doctors. Her body was too weak for the healing to be explained by the powers of the mind. It was obvious that this was an act of God, whose power knows no limits. Nurse Nakamanga told me, 'Robinah was sick from time to time, but she always carried out her activities well. Many of the men who were also ill used to take turns driving her to church. They have all since died. Yet Robinah was the first to become ill and now she is healthier than people who never had the virus. After a year we tested her and the baby again. They tested negative. We continued to test and, I can confirm, her results are HIV-negative.'

I asked Nurse Nakamanga what Robinah's doctor thinks about all this. 'He has always told Robinah he believed she would be healed and, confidentially, he has advised other people to go to Pastor Kayiwa. But he fears for his job, so he keeps his opinions to himself. I know Robinah has been healed through the power of God. There is no question about it. *People who are that ill with Aids don't recover without divine intervention.* Pastor Kayiwa has a wonderful gift from God and I feel very fortunate to know him. He is a blessing for our country.'[2]

Grace: 'I just knew I could have a miracle.'

The Aids test was a formality for pilots in the Ugandan Air Force, so Godfrey Rubanga was hardly concerned when he went for his six-month check-up in March 1991. But this time around he got a heart-stopping shock. His blood tested HIV-positive. He could not believe it. Worse was to come the following year when his wife, Grace, was also found to have the virus.

She told me, 'I was so upset because we have small children. Immediately I went to Namirembe for counselling and prayers.

Elizabeth, my sister, knew Pastor Kayiwa well and was aware of the miracles. We have lost another sister to Aids, but I just knew I could have a miracle. Elizabeth told me she had a dream that I would be healed, but that my husband needed prayers. The dream gave me a lot of hope. At the time, my husband didn't believe in God and we felt that, if he didn't turn to God, death was certain. And, sadly, Godfrey is now dead.'

Grace's wish was to be healed before the end of the year, and she had set this goal for herself. She was very ill, had lost a lot of weight and was down to about six stone six pounds (90 lb). Kaposi's sarcoma, covering her neck, was already visible. She was distraught at the thought of leaving her two children, both under five, and was angry at Godfrey, who had contracted the disease from another woman. Everyone in Uganda knows how dangerous unprotected sex can be. The couple quarrelled constantly about how the children would suffer because of his carelessness. He lost his job shortly after the Air Force found out that he had tested HIV-positive.

For Grace, the only hope was prayer. She saw Simeon several times a week, but Godfrey was embarrassed to have his wife announce that she believed in the power of God to heal her. He resented the time she spent in church, when she could have been at home cooking and cleaning, even as sick as she was. On her first visit to Simeon, the pastor told her, 'Jesus has the power over all diseases, including Aids.' He gave her a lot of encouragement to believe that she could receive what the Bible promises. After a year of continual visits, her symptoms began to disappear. Simeon told her to go and have another test, but it was still positive.

Like Juliet, it was a constant battle for Grace, with voices in her head telling her that she was going to die, especially in the face of another HIV-positive test result. She believed this was the devil trying to confuse her, telling her that it was all nonsense – that it was not possible to be healed. Later on, she had another test. She told me, 'The doctor said my blood count did not coincide with someone who had the virus. He told me to get tested again. I did, and it was negative. This was just before Christmas. My wish came true.'

Grace is softly spoken, with a manner that reflects her name, but now she was exuberant, ready to tell the world she had been healed. But Godfrey, full of disbelief and anger, rejected the fact that she had been cured. So intense was his resentment that he forced her to have unprotected sex. He thought that if she contracted the disease once more, she would definitely not be healed and he would be right in his claim that the healing was a fake. Grace did not contract Aids from him again. She has now been tested a total of thirteen times, with four positive results and nine negative ones.[3]

Godfrey did not live much longer, but towards the end he found faith. I interviewed him in hospital shortly before his death and asked him if he believed in God's power to heal the sick. 'Yes,' he said. But one wonders whether his life would have been spared if he had changed his attitude earlier.

Irene: 'I was a Christian but I never believed in miracles.'

Irene Najja's description of her illness sounds terrifying. In 1988 she suffered an extreme case of hyperthyroidism, commonly known as a goitre, and generally due to iodine deficiency. 'I felt a small gland in my neck that was enlarged. It grew and grew. I couldn't eat because it was difficult to swallow. Things got worse, the whole front of my neck was three times its normal size. It was hard and so painful. My left eye protruded – it was coming out of its socket. At night I used to think that, when I woke up, I would find my eye out on the bed.' This is not merely the exaggeration of an ordinary patient. Irene may be a petite, rather shy person, but her medical knowledge cannot be doubted, for she has been a nurse in Kampala for thirty years.

Her neck eventually swelled to the point where she had no chin. She could not swallow without acute pain. She was told that surgery was the only option. Dr Mary Kiwanuka, a surgeon at Mulago Hospital, told me of the normal procedure in such cases. 'If the goitre is not surgically removed, it can press on the trachea and the oesophagus. This causes difficulty in breathing and restricts swallowing. Without an operation, the eyes will protrude. In surgery we remove most of the gland, leaving one-eighth for the production of the hormone. Once you reduce the bulk of the gland, the eye gradually returns to normal.'

Irene had heard about the miracles at Namirembe, through her children. Even though she was a Christian, her medical background was an obstacle to a belief that miracles were possible. But with the pain, her deteriorating condition and the constant urging of her children, she decided to visit Pastor Simeon. 'I remember every detail exactly,' she told me, as we sat in the office of Dr Jane Bosa, director of Makerere University Hospital. 'It was 21 June at 9.30 p.m. when I went into his counselling room. At first, I was frightened. He asked me what was wrong with me and I told him. He looked at me and said, "Your goitre is healed." I touched my throat and it had completely disappeared – no pain. At that moment I think he was as astonished as I was. I was overwhelmed and so grateful. It took a couple of weeks or so for my eye to return to normal. He told me to continue praying. *Medicine had failed to heal me but, through prayer, I was healed.* I was a Christian but I never believed in miracles.'

Dr Bosa nodded. 'I remember it well. Her neck was enlarged and it was serious. Then the problem disappeared after she went to see Pastor Simeon for prayer. One day she was scheduled for surgery and the next time I saw her it had completely gone.'

I asked Dr Bosa whether, as a medical professional, she could offer an explanation? 'I really have no answers. I have wondered about this myself.'

The surgeon, Dr Mary Kiwanuka, was also baffled. 'I was amazed when Irene came to me after her experience with Pastor Kayiwa. The goitre had occupied the whole of the neck. I saw her within a week and her neck was normal. The goitre had vanished, except for the eye, which took a little more time to return to normal.'

Could this have been a case of natural spontaneous remission? 'No,' said Dr Bosa firmly. 'Spontaneous remission could have occurred at one stage, maybe. But why did the healing occur only after Irene went to see Pastor Simeon, and not before? That is where we have problems. Why did she first need to have prayer? The disappearance of the goitre is bewildering to all of us.'

Irene's scepticism stemmed from her medical education and experience, but she was desperate for relief, and not quite willing to resign herself to surgery. With just the smallest bit of hope, her prayers were heard. No matter how drastic the situation or how desperate we become, there is still, according to Simeon, reason to believe that healing and miracles will happen. There is no degree of despair over which God has no power. Mark 10, 27 states, 'With men *it is* impossible, but not with God, for with God all things are possible.'

But Simeon's ability to heal is not restricted to those who believe. Even sceptics have been the beneficiaries of his gift, as the stories of Wilson Birungi and Dr Kiyimba illustrate.

Wilson: 'I went to the pastor but I was not even a Christian.'

Wilson Birungi was delighted when his uncle arranged a marriage for him, to a Dutch woman. But Wilson was not aware that his wife had once lived with a man who had Aids. Months later, in 1991, after noting signs in her that looked like SLIM, he too began to feel weak. 'The pain in my lungs felt like open wounds,' he told me. 'I was vomiting and I knew something was wrong. I thought it was time I went to Kampala to have a blood test. I knew I would test positive. After all, at that time my wife was on her deathbed.'

He heard rumours from people in Masindi, where he was living, that Aids could be healed at Pastor Kayiwa's church. 'When I arrived I was told not to be afraid. I was so ill. He told me to fasten my eyes on Jesus. I was not even a Christian. Pastor Kayiwa repeated the scriptures in the Bible that speak about healing. When he began to pray for me, I felt relief right away, especially in my chest. It was like experiencing an inflow of life: my weakness was leaving and my strength returning.

'During the next year, at the request of the pastor, I lived on the church premises. My health returned and I decided to have my blood checked. There was no trace of the Aids virus. My wife had died. A year later I wanted to remarry and told Pastor Kayiwa about it. I found a nice woman and we fell in love. The pastor wanted to be certain that Aids was a part of my past.

'I was tested six times and was found negative.[4] I showed the results to Deborah Nakayiwa, the woman I wanted to marry. She took the results to Pastor Kayiwa and pleaded with him for consent to the marriage. Last year we were married and now we have a baby girl. There isn't anything I wouldn't do for God or Pastor Kayiwa.'

Dr Kiyimba: 'Prayer should go hand-in-hand with medicine.'

'I was hoping it was clinical malaria or any other treatable disease. Then the test came back and I knew I had primary leukaemia.' Dr Joachim Kiyimba is recalling that awful moment when he discovered that he had what the rest of the medical community regards as an incurable cancer of the blood.

Dr Kiyimba is a general practitioner and the medical superintendent of St John's Ambulance Mission Hospital. He is also an attendant physician at Mulago Hospital – Uganda's national hospital – and at Biva Clinic. As an experienced physician, he is fully aware of what he is talking about. 'Leukaemia is a malignant disease, where increased numbers of certain immature or abnormal leucocytes are produced. It leads to a higher rate of susceptibility to infection, anaemia, bleeding and enlargement of the liver, spleen and lymph nodes.

'People die from this disease,' he says. 'There is no remedy.' His haemoglobin count was strikingly low in the first test, so he ordered more comprehensive tests. He sent a sample of his blood to Nairobi for a second opinion. At each stage his fears were confirmed.

'Then one day a friend came to my home. He told me about a man called Pastor Simeon Kayiwa and about the sick who were being healed. He insisted that we should go and see him. As a medical professional, I didn't believe these things. But, to please my friend, I went along. Fortunately I was ushered in right away to meet Pastor Kayiwa and told him my problem. He assured me that, through God's grace and mercy, I could be healed. I said, with little faith, "OK, let us see." I mean, you can see how difficult it was for me to accept what looked like point-blank nonsense.

'He told me I should return for more prayer. That night for the first time I slept comfortably without pain. I had been experiencing a lot of pain. Initially, I thought it was probably psychological. Maybe my mind was playing tricks on me. When I went back the next day, he asked me how I felt and I had to admit I felt better. I asked if he would give me another dose of prayer. He continued to pray for me and I started to improve rapidly. My haemoglobin count rose to normal and never dropped again.

'I went to see him on several occasions, whenever I had time. Within a few months I went back for a complete examination. It was negative – there were no signs of leukaemia. Now I am a strong believer that the power of Jesus is at work in the world.'

Asked if he was a Christian before meeting Simeon, Dr Kiyimba says, 'I was a Christian but I didn't believe miracles were possible today. As for my colleagues, some believed my story, some didn't. Most couldn't believe, even coming from me, that it was possible to be healed of a malignant disease through prayer. They said perhaps there was a mistake somewhere. But there couldn't be. I told them I was very ill and now my health is perfect. It happened to me, not to one of my patients. Those who treated me said they couldn't understand or believe it. But I am well. As a doctor, it is easy for me to recognise those terrible symptoms, leukaemia is a dreadful disease.'

I asked Dr Kiyimba if he thought there could be a role for prayer within medicine. 'Prayer should go hand-in-hand with medicine. As a human being, no matter how scientific you are, you must be guided by God's power. If God's power is really there, things will work. Sometimes we doctors get stuck, like anyone else, not knowing what to do. My colleagues have had patients with a variety of cancers. All those patients are now dead and I'm alive. You can see the difference prayer can make. I think Pastor Simeon is a man who has a gift. He gives it freely. I didn't pay anything for it. He is trying to tell the truth. *Through prayer anything is possible.*'

Princess Nalinya: 'My son is healed and he is happy.'

'We were all so worried. Ian, my son, was having four epileptic seizures a day. He couldn't eat or walk and his vision was bad. We were desperate,' said Princess Nalinya (which means Princess Royal). 'Ian was born a normal baby. After three years he began showing symptoms of epilepsy. At first the doctors thought it was malaria. The medication they gave him didn't work. We had never seen epilepsy, it is very rare in Uganda. It wasn't in the family.'

Princess Nalinya Irene Ndagire is a cousin of the Kabaka (the King of Buganda), Ronald Mutebi. She accompanies him on official engagements or represents him when he is unable to attend. She is also an adviser to President Museveni on matters of poverty.

'I said to God,' she continues, ' "This is my first-born and you gave this boy to me. Then why are you allowing him to be so ill? If you want to take him home, take him now." Then a friend of my husband told us about Pastor Kayiwa and the miracles that were happening. I didn't believe it, but I said to my husband, "Let's at least give it a try. What have we got to lose?"

'We went to see Pastor Kayiwa and he told us we shouldn't worry. He prayed for Ian for only a couple of minutes. I didn't understand why his prayer was so short. But I said to myself, "Let's see what happens." The seizures came again. My husband wanted to take him back to the pastor every day. I think he had more faith than me. So we did for a week. Then the seizures occurred less frequently, once a day, or once every two days. After three or four months they stopped completely. When we took him back to the doctors, they were amazed to see him well and walking.

'Ian is now twelve and has had no more seizures. His brain suffered during this time and he is in a special school. But my son has been healed and he is happy. We are all happy. That's what's important.'

But Simeon is not only credited with curing people of disease. In an unprecedented deposition, one man even claims that his rags-to-riches life story is directly attributable to Simeon's prayers.

John Buyinza: 'I rolled in the dust and became rich.'

At sixteen, John Buyinza joined the Ugandan Army. He could barely read or write Loganda, his native language, let alone speak English. The following year Idi Amin was finally overthrown and young John, like many soldiers, found himself in prison. 'I had been in a cell for six months when my sister met Pastor Simeon,' he recalls. 'She went to the church to pray for my release and he gave her a handkerchief for me.'

Simeon explains, 'I blessed the handkerchief and said, "In the name of Jesus, you release him." If Jesus used dust to heal a blind man, I can use any object in His name for miracles. The dust is as lifeless as the handkerchief I prayed over. It is the authority of God that creates the miracle.'

One week later John was indeed released. 'When I went to the court to face the witnesses who were going to testify against me, they mysteriously didn't turn up,' John told me.

Freedom was all very well, but John desperately wanted to make something of himself, to make a success of his life. After trying, without any luck, he decided to return to Simeon for advice. 'I had nothing to lose and I thought God was the only one who could help me. When I arrived all I had was a one-thousand Ugandan shilling note.'

Simeon took hold of the note (then equivalent to about US $1/60 pence) and asked John if he believed that he would see a miracle. The young man nodded. He also asked John if, when he became rich, he would serve God. John replied, 'Yes.'

Simeon says, 'In the Loganda dialect, I then said to this one-thousand-shilling note, "I command you in the name of Jesus to go and bring your sisters and brothers around." '

That was ten years ago. John learned English with uncanny speed and has since accumulated a small fortune. He now lives in a house worth £250,000, owns several buildings in town, runs a clothing company and a taxi firm, has about £200,000 in working capital and says happily, 'I travel all over the world trading.'

As I was to discover, John's relationship with Simeon seems to be built on miracles. John says, 'I began by selling used clothes by the pound, collected from other countries. Little by little, the business grew until I began to import my own clothes and now I'm successful. As I saw things getting better, I went back to Pastor Simeon. He told me to roll in the dust. I said, "What?" I thought he was out of his mind, but I obeyed him. He was laughing and having fun with the whole idea.'

Simeon smiles at the memory. 'John was beautifully dressed that day. I told him, "For every grain of dust you have on your clothing, that will be the amount of money you will have in your life." '

John jokes, 'I immediately asked Pastor Simeon if I could roll in the dust again. The funniest part is that I don't think there is one person who knows the pastor who wouldn't have rolled in the dust, if he had asked them to.'

With his new wealth, John can live wherever he chooses, but he prefers to stay close to the pastor in Kayiwa Village and, as the next story illustrates, it appears that is where he belongs. John had stopped to see Simeon on his way home from work one evening, just to have a chat. As he was about to leave, Simeon began to feel very uncomfortable. The feeling grew and he tried to persuade John to stay, but John could not. Simeon became more adamant in his request. John tried to reason with the pastor: his wife and children were at home and what would they think, as he was needed there? Unable to fight this logic, Simeon conceded and reluctantly let John go.

At 3 a.m. that morning the pastor and his wife heard fierce pounding on their door. It was John. He had been bitten by a poisonous snake while asleep in his bed. Simeon prayed over him and sent him to the hospital. The doctors told him he was lucky, as the bite could have easily killed him.

When I asked John why he thought he had been so blessed, he replied, 'Maybe God knew that one day I would have to support seventeen children. Two of my brothers have died and I now take care of their children.'

The miracles continue. John had a client who owed him £35,000, and whom he feared was about to go bankrupt. He asked Simeon to pray about this and promised that, if the matter was resolved, he would cement the floor of the church. I was with Simeon in England later when he announced, out of the blue, 'Oh, someone has just brought ten bags of cement to the church.' He had not had a phone call, letter or fax.

I didn't think much of this until, two weeks later, I travelled back to Uganda with Simeon and discovered a new cement floor being laid. Later, John told me that his client had paid him the money just weeks before going bankrupt.

Simeon explains, 'Money is not the root of all evil. It is our attachment to it, or the way we use it, which can become evil. It is a tool God gave us to use. The Bible says that all the silver and gold in the world belongs to Him. If we use it badly, neglect our taxes and pile up debts, or if we love money, it can have a negative effect. If God wanted to change a person's soul, and money was the only means He had available to reach him, well why not? Many people who have heard about the miracles that God did for John Buyinza have had their faith strengthened.

'When the Lord sent me out into the world for Him, all I had was a pair of trousers and sandals, and of course I knew how to paint. The changes in my life have come about through God. When I look at all of life, it suggests to me that there must be an intelligent mind who is behind the existence of all things. This is the one Jesus called His Father and the one the Bible calls God.'

If one believes in miracles, in the power of good, then it follows that there are also darker forces at work in the world. After my own experiences of evil (see Chapter 4) and interviews with people who have been the victims of witchcraft, I have come to believe that the powers of evil are also at work today in the world. Initially, I considered the following story a fantasy. But, as I heard of many similar examples of such manifestations, a pattern began to emerge. Too many rational people had become victims for it to be due to hysteria or the imagination. Simeon is always conscious of the devil's role in life, even when it is the disguise of good.

In 1980 and 1981, at a peak of insecurity in Uganda, people were powerfully influenced by witchdoctors, who preyed upon the fear of the many, even the ministers. People were told to carry the relics of sacrifice, claiming that it would provide them with protection. But, on entering the church, Simeon could see, through the power of the Holy Spirit, the amulets and charms inside the clothing of the people. One woman standing in the service wore the traditional Ugandan dress, which includes a wide sash around the waist. Simeon told her immediately to hand over the witchcraft she had underneath her sash. This X-ray vision continued until the people realised that there would be no witchcraft at Namirembe.

'In many cases when I was faced with serious disease or problems, and when I commanded the devil to leave, to stop afflicting them, their condition improved. This has happened in hundreds of cases. The fact that the disease or problem began to disappear was proof, for me, that there is a negative supernatural force at work. I have seen too much not to acknowledge an evil being, one that is highly deceptive and intelligent. For example, in my country people go to witchdoctors – the Western equivalent of psychics or shamans – not knowing that the power they use is demonic. People believe that they can see the future or heal the sick, but involvement with witchcraft or the occult can create a lifelong curse, whose roots can go undetected and whose manifestations remain unconnected with the underlying cause, which is evil.

Simeon explains the nature of a curse. 'Curses are a form of imprisonment, either emotionally or psychologically, financially or physically. The demons can influence the mind to become criminal or perverted. Few would ever connect this type of problem with the devil. I'm sure there are many cases, on every continent, where medical doctors are baffled: when their patients

41

receive prayer, the demon is rebuked and there is an instant change. One might say this was the power of the mind, but I disagree. A positive mental attitude can reduce disease caused by stress, but the demonic can often superimpose on a weakness, creating a condition that can only be healed through deliverance prayer. This is a specific type of prayer, in the name of Jesus, to combat the intervention of evil. Instead of rejecting this evidence as non-scientific or religious, the medical community should take it onboard and integrate it with their existing treatment.'

One of the many stories of Simeon's work illustrates this point. Mr Nabongo, a Ugandan businessman, had asked Simeon for his help. He and his family were, he said, suffering from a curse placed on them at the request of a house-girl whom he had fired. Shortly after she left the house, the family witnessed a series of mysterious events: glasses broke by themselves, dishes would levitate, clothing and curtains caught fire spontaneously. This is usually referred to as poltergeist activity.

At first these things happened during the day, after the children had gone to school and Mr Nabongo had gone to work, so that only his wife experienced them. When she told her husband he did not believe her. Eventually, the children saw these manifestations too and were so frightened that they urged their mother to let them stay with relatives.

Mr Nabongo continued to be sceptical about his wife's reports until, one afternoon, he arrived home from work unexpectedly. As he walked into the house, he saw stones flying around, yet there was no wind and the windows were not open. Then furniture ignited by itself. He was shocked, but not in the way that people in the West might be. In Kampala, as in many African countries, people aren't totally disbelieving when they hear reports of the supernatural. I've seen them written about in newspapers. Mr Nabongo had indeed become the victim of a curse.

He interrogated the former house-girl, who confessed that she had paid a witchdoctor to put a curse on the family, as revenge for being fired. Mr Nabongo went first to his own Anglican church and asked the vicar to rid them of the supernatural disturbances. He did so and the activity decreased, but only for a short time. Next he tried the Baptist church, but once again the disruptive activity came back with a vengeance.

Then a friend, Dr Nsubuga, who said he had had a similar experience, told him about Pastor Simeon. So Mr Nabongo went to Namirembe and pleaded for help. Simeon said that he would come the following day, and added, 'You tell the devil, I'll be there at exactly two o'clock to kick him out of there.'

Mr Nabongo did as he was told and, to his amazement, the activity worsened. But as soon as Simeon set foot in his compound, it stopped. The pastor prayed with the Nabongo family and commanded the devil to leave. The same day Simeon got his Calvary Cross Choir to come by and sing songs of praise to Jesus. According to Simeon, there are few things the devil hates more than praise to Jesus. He warned Mr Nabongo that the spirits would try to return in a small way in seven days, but the family now had the power and knew how to drive the demons away. In seven days, just as Simeon had forecast, the activity began again. The Nabongos carried out the same procedure and this time it worked for good.

As the Bible says in Matthew 12, 43–5, 'When an unclean spirit goes out of a person, it roams through the arid regions searching for rest but finds none.' It goes on to say, 'I will return to my home from which I came. But upon returning, it finds it empty, swept clean and put in order. Then it goes and brings back seven other spirits more evil than itself. They move in and dwell there, and the last condition of the person is worse than the first.'

Simeon told me that he saw this in a vision – one day for each spirit. 'I have never driven out spirits and had them return. Only if they are very powerful may they come back on the third day, or the seventh day. I don't know why exactly this happens, it is just my experience. I don't want anyone to misinterpret this as a concept of magic – which I am against – or even as theologically based. But I have seen the activity come back on these days, before it is rebuked for the last time.'

Sometimes Simeon does not need to have people arrive on his doorstep with their problems. He learns about trouble even before the victim. In the next case, he foresaw in a vision what would happen.

Vida: 'Thank God I had been warned or I might not be here to tell this story.'

Vida had been a member of the Calvary Cross Choir at Simeon's Namirembe Fellowship years before, and has since moved to

43

another part of the city. It had been a long time since she had attended his church. Yet Simeon had a vision about her, in which God said to him, 'You need her here. She is going to be struck by lightning.'

Next morning Simeon sent a few choir members to look for Vida. He said, 'When they found her and brought her back, I told her to fast for three days, during the day only, so that God would protect her. I explained that it was best for her to stay at the church during this time.'

Vida told me, 'Naturally I was surprised when the choir members came to tell me I was in danger and that I must return to the church with them. Pastor Simeon told me that the devil was planning something awful and that he had been forewarned, so I fasted. On the fourth day he told me I could go back home. That afternoon I was washing my clothes outside and lightning struck in the very place where I was standing. I was thrown a few feet, but I was not harmed. The grass where I was standing caught fire. It was terrible. Thank God I had been warned or I might not be here to tell this story.'

Simeon explained to me, 'The Holy Spirit can warn of impending danger so that we may pray and fast, in order that it may be overcome. It appeared that the devil was planning to kill her, and it was divine intervention that saved her life. I have seen from this and many other experiences that it is the devil who often plans destruction.'

It can be dangerous if family members are actively involved with witchcraft or the occult in any way. This can affect the entire family – especially the children, who cannot fight for themselves – as you will see from the next story.

Pamela: 'I was pregnant and the pastor could see there was something wrong with the baby.'

Pamela is a very attractive, regal-looking woman, with creamy mulatto skin and long dark hair. She is married to one of Uganda's wealthiest men, a Moslem, who has more than one wife. Pamela could not conceive, while another wife had also not yet conceived a son. (In Uganda, the son inherits the father's fortune upon his death.) But the two wives acted in very different ways: Pamela visited Simeon; the other woman visited a witchdoctor, although Pamela was unaware of this at the time. Nor did she know that her husband was also drawn towards the black magic practised by witchdoctors.

Pamela became depressed after failing to conceive during four-and-a-half years of marriage. She told me, 'When I met Pastor Simeon, the things he said really touched me, so I decided to become a Christian. Within a year I was pregnant. I was delighted, and my husband was so pleased he was reduced to tears. But weeks later he suddenly appeared to change his mind. He told me to have an abortion. I couldn't understand why, because I knew he had desperately wanted a child. It didn't make sense. Eventually I agreed to the abortion, but insisted that it must be performed abroad. It was a trick on my part to escape. I had no intention of having an abortion.'

'By then, Pastor Simeon had become a good friend of mine. One evening he said he saw something wrong with the baby, something around the nose. I was so happy with the thought of having a child that I really didn't pay much attention. He suggested that we pray about it, so we did. I didn't give the matter much more thought – not because I didn't believe in prayer, but because I had faith my child would live. I was convinced that God had answered my prayer when I became pregnant. I couldn't possibly believe my baby was in danger.'

'I knew my husband's other wife was very jealous of me. She had no intention of sharing my husband's good fortune with anyone else. At the time I had no idea that she was actively involved in witchcraft, nor about my husband's interest in it. It was only later that I discovered that, during one of his visits, a witchdoctor had told him I would never have a child. And if I did, it would be deformed. So when I told him I was pregnant, he became frightened. That was why he ordered me to have an abortion. I now suspect that the other woman had seen the witchdoctor and put a curse on me.

'I travelled to London and went into Hammersmith Hospital. The first scan did indeed show a deformity: a diaphragmatic hernia. This is when there is a hole in the diaphragm and the intestines cave in, preventing the lungs from growing. She was born with two lungs, and neither worked. One was so small that it wasn't functioning, and she had to be put on a respirator.

'At that point, I understood what Pastor Simeon meant when he had said there was something over the nose. The pastor was so

45

kind and wonderful. He came to be with me in London and even stayed in the hospital. My mother shared the same room with us. My husband was to come later.

'About four-thirty one morning Pastor Simeon woke up with a scream that scared us all. He told us, "I had a dream of a ruthless woman, searching for the heart of the child. During my prayers for the baby to be healed, I held the heart of that child in mine. This woman couldn't take my heart, but she took the child's. I felt so bad."

'We rushed down to the child and called the doctors. They told me there was no hope and said I had better hold her, so that she would be able to die in my arms.'

When I asked Simeon why prayers had not worked for Pamela, he replied, 'The Lord had warned me about the problem. The situation needed much more prayer. Pamela was just so happy to be pregnant that she dismissed what I had said. I felt so bad for her. The prayer of the mother for the baby is very important.'

The following year, back home in Kampala, Simeon's wife, Celia, gave birth to a little girl named Deborah. Pamela said, 'When I went to Namirembe and saw this beautiful baby, all I could do was cry.'

Simeon recalled, 'When I saw her crying, I prayed quietly to God in my heart to give her a child more healthy and beautiful than mine.'

When Simeon told Pamela about his prayer, it brought about a dramatic psychological change. 'At that moment, the bad feelings left me – the depression, everything. Afterwards Pastor Simeon called me to say that he had had a dream about me. He said he had dreamt that I was pregnant again. Sure enough, I went to hospital and they confirmed that I was.'

It was not entirely good news, however. Simeon told her, in the fifth month of pregnancy, that she would give birth to a boy, but there would be something wrong with his private parts. Pamela says, 'I don't want to say anything that will harm my child's future, but when he was born he had the problem that Pastor Simeon described. But he is a healthy little boy now. I realise it took a conversion to conceive my children. And I also realise that, since my husband did not renounce witchcraft, my children suffered. He feels the witchdoctors have power and that they know best, but to me the truth is obvious.'

In this case, Pamela's Moslem husband and one of his other

wives were seeking prosperity and personal security through witchcraft, so they became deeply enmeshed in the occult. In Uganda, witchdoctors have a practice of dedicating small items to demons and then require their clients to carry them in a pocket or small purse at all times. They claim that these demons are ancestral spirits, who will protect those who carry the charms. In reality, according to Simeon, these demons replace our guardian angel, leaving us at the mercy of demonic power.

The Bible says that demons were once angels, serving God under the archangel Lucifer. Together with Lucifer, they rebelled against God and were thrown out of heaven to earth. Many of them operate on earth today, to deceive and deprive man of the good things that are meant to belong to him.

'I have concluded from my experiences that the devil is real,' Simeon told me. 'He can listen to our conversations, he can influence our thoughts to think in his direction. He only responds to the authority commanded over him in the name of Jesus, by believers.' As it says in Mark 16, 17: 'Believers will be given the power to perform miracles, they will drive out demons in My Name.'

While demons operate outside the laws of nature and have the power to provide people with money or health, they will always rob them of something precious, like fertility or happiness in marriage. Simeon argues that there will always be a curse, with devastating results.

It was in 1990, while Simeon was in London praying for Pamela's child, that a friend of his, Mrs Simbwa, asked him to visit her sister, Florence, and pray for her husband, Barry, who was suffering from arteriosclerosis. She was a Ugandan Christian, while he was a Jewish official in a synagogue. Simeon wondered how her husband would react to prayers said in the name of Jesus, but Mrs Simbwa assured him that it would be all right. By chance, the chosen day was a Jewish feast, with special festivities at the synagogue.

Barry was proud of the synagogue and showed Simeon around, pointing out ancient scrolls, which he was asked to kiss. In Jewish tradition, it is customary when leaving to walk backwards from these scrolls in reverence. Simeon found this hard to understand. To him, these scrolls were mere paper and ink, and he would not walk backwards in the presence of the Bible, even though he had become what he is today through its inspired words.

As the tour continued, Barry took Simeon into a room that was dedicated to a large candelabra, dating back to 1910. After the service there was a reception, which Simeon joined. He began to speak to a woman who told him about her beliefs. She was not sure if there was an afterlife like the one Jesus had described, she said, and they were waiting for Elijah to show them the way. Simeon asked her if she believed in Jesus. She replied that she had been a Catholic but got fed up with it. The very mention of Jesus in fact gave her brain damage.

Simeon considers Jesus to be not only his Saviour but his friend, and was deeply offended by this comment. Depressed at the memory of the Jews' involvement with the crucifixion of Jesus, he went into the library to pray and to read more about the Jewish religion. 'In that mood, I felt it was wrong to have a candelabra as an object of worship. The idea of worship and celebration of God's works without respect for Jesus bothered me.'

Suddenly there was a loud bang. Mrs Simbwa's husband came running into the library and screamed at Simeon, 'What have you done? You are the only one here who believes in Jesus. We know of the miracles of Jesus. Come and see what you have done.'

Simeon told me, 'I explained that I had done nothing. I had been sitting quietly in the library reading. As we entered the room, I could see that the whole candelabra had been shattered. The rabbi's wife had been standing at the door. She said, "I saw it collapse, and fall by itself. I was standing right here."

'They were angry with me, but had no evidence. Years later this man travelled to Uganda and came to visit me. He had begun to believe in Jesus, in His power of salvation and that it was He who was going to come back to the world, as the Messiah. He asked me, "Is this because you have been praying for me, to change my mind? You know, since the day you prayed with me, my arteriosclerosis has not bothered me." '

As I was about to leave Uganda on the last occasion, and – as always – with enormous reluctance, I asked Simeon if he could explain why people are healed. He told me, 'People must come to terms with how they have turned their back on God. When you believe you can live your life better without the care and wisdom

48

of your Creator, trouble begins.'

That trouble, in Simeon's view, is evident in the developed countries of the West. 'A miracle depends on many things, but it is most important for a person to expect it. What I notice most in the West is the amount of scepticism. This is very bad. It makes it impossible for miracles to happen. If a person says, "Let's wait and see if it will happen," then it won't. But if one says, "I will see a miracle happen. I'm expecting it. I must see a miracle and I will tell others about it," the chances of it happening are far greater. It is important to remember that even Jesus could not perform miracles in Nazareth, because there was no faith.'

Jesus heals the sick and the evidence we have seen here indicates that He continues to do so today. Unfortunately this is discounted or ignored by the media, due to the tremendous scepticism in our developed world. With the complexities of our personality, our intellect and our background, we can miss the answer to a prayer and the simplicity and manner in which it has always been available to us.

Notes

1. Test results for Juliet: HIV-positive 20 March 1990 at St James Clinic. HIV-negative on 21 January 1994 at S & B Health Care Clinic, Uganda.
2. Test results for Robinah Serunkuuma are confirmed by her superior, Nurse Juliet Nakamanga, at the International Red Cross, Uganda.
3. Test results for Grace: HIV-positive 22 June 1992 at Taso Entebbe Centre (Aids Support Organisation). HIV-negative 15 December 1993 at Joint Clinical Research Centre, Uganda.
4. Test results for Wilson Birungi: HIV-positive 27 May 1993 at Aids Information Centre. HIV-negative 23 March 1994, Republic of Uganda Ministry of Health.

2

Greatest Mystic This Century:

Maria Esperanza

Of all of the unusual stories I have tracked down, I think the most astonishing has been that of Maria Esperanza Medrano de Bianchini. Her life experiences break all the laws of nature; her story defies logic. Sceptics will argue that it is too unrealistic to believe. But there is overwhelming proof from hundreds of people concerning what has happened to Maria. Even the most unbelievable occurrences in Maria's unparalleled life have been documented by experienced doctors, senior policemen and leading clergy. She is, by any standards, an extraordinary and unique woman, around whom a whole constellation of startlingly mystical events has been happening for twenty-two years.

Though I do not speak any Spanish, and I have only been able to talk with Maria through interpreters, she is truly captivating. I see sincerity in her eyes, dignity in her manner and godliness in her works. The events that surround her are nothing short of profound. She has suffered from debilitating illnesses most of her life, yet she has put herself in God's hands, as you will shortly discover. Maria Esperanza is modest to the point of shyness. Whenever she is asked about the phenomenal events that have marked her life, and which continue to do so, she stresses how embarrassed she is to talk about them. Yet she may well have been graced by greater contact with supernatural happenings than any other human being in the twentieth century.

She is sixty-nine, a grandmother and somewhat frail, with a

51

touching inflection in her voice, almost as if she is about to break into tears. But she has an indomitable spirit and her children testify to her refusal to rest. In spite of her age and poor health, as her fame has spread beyond South America, she has recently begun to travel the world to satisfy the hundreds of thousands of people who want to see her. What is most memorable about her appearance are her bright, clear eyes. That cliché about piercing eyes that look through people is apt. Many people have claimed she was able to see through them, with a sort of X-ray vision that was also associated with a man who acted as her spiritual director for years: the Capuchin monk Padre Pio. There is an aura about Maria that is noticeable the instant she appears in a room. Yet she is not distant. She is warm and animated in conversation and enjoys the laughter generated by her family, who are always with her.

Maria is far from poor. She lives in a luxurious sprawling home in the hills overlooking the Venezuelan capital of Caracas. Her husband is a successful businessman and the family does not want for money. Her children are all college-educated. She is surrounded by their wives, husbands and friends, all of them professionals, all of them convinced of Maria's God-given gifts. She also receives visits from scores of independent people, many of them initially sceptical, who have proved credible witnesses to extraordinary phenomena. On her farm in the mountains outside Caracas, for example, is a spring that is known to have healed many people – cures that have been meticulously documented by the priest, Padre Otty Ossa Aristizabal, who regularly says mass at Betania, and his bishop Pio Bello Ricardo.

When I first visited Maria, I was expecting to hear about the people who have been healed through her prayers and the stigmata that she suffers annually. I had not anticipated the multitude of astounding events that she has seen and experienced throughout her life. Padre Otty says he has witnessed her levitating. Others have testified that she can bilocate: in other words, appear in two places at the same time. And, on fifteen separate occasions, Maria has 'given birth' to roses from between her breasts. Difficult though this phenomenon is to believe, it has been witnessed and investigated by sceptics, including doctors and television journalists. I have come to believe that Maria Esperanza may be the greatest mystic of this century.

The other important factor about the supernatural incidents in

Maria's life is that so many of them have been witnessed. Since her first sighting of the Virgin Mary near her home, thousands of other people have seen the same vision and been healed by bathing in or drinking the spring waters on her farm. Hundreds of people attending a church service also witnessed the communion bread bleeding, a fact later proved in police laboratories.

It fell to the Bishop of Los Teques, Pio Bello Ricardo, to investigate these claims, after hundreds of people started to tell him that they had seen the Virgin Mary. He could be forgiven for having thought they might be hysterical or deluded. Maybe they were being deceptive. Having trained as a psychologist, he had some insight into such matters. Then an old friend from Rome, whom he regarded as an impeccable witness, visited to tell him the same story. Bishop Ricardo says, 'General Tarre Murzi, who was the military attaché to the Venezuelan ambassador to Italy, had been at Betania on 25 March 1987, when close to 130 people saw the apparitions. So he came to give me his official testimony and his story was the reason I decided to take it seriously and carry out the investigation myself.

'The General and his wife saw four of seven apparitions. He was so overwhelmed. He told me that she appears in human form. It is just like looking at you right now. The same wind that blows through your hair blows through hers.'

The Bishop refused to take the easy way out by appointing a commission to investigate. Instead he decided to find out for himself, and took testimonies from 490 people. He dedicated 500 hours to the subject in the following months, questioning about 200 people and studying 381 declarations. He has now devoted years to investigating and documenting the web of extraordinary events in Betania. He says, 'Although the first apparition was only seen by Maria Esperanza, many others on that day saw something like a cloud coming out of the hill and movement of the sun. Since that time she has given me over 550 declarations about her visions of the Virgin Mary and other phenomena.'

Thousands of people have seen the apparitions and have been cured by the waters. However, Maria Esperanza remains the only person to whom the Virgin Mary has spoken during the visions. People flock to Betania, especially on vigil days, hoping to see and pray with Maria. 'Many miracles have happened here,' she told me. 'Our people are very faithful and they bring their sick.

Many people have been cured, people who have suffered multiple illnesses, people in wheelchairs, children on stretchers.'

One case from Bishop Ricardo's archives involved a senior surgeon. Dr Vinicio Arrieta, director of the medical school at the University of Zulia in Maracaibo, Venezuela, was diagnosed with cancer of the prostate, which metastasised to his spine in 1987. He had taken two courses of chemotherapy, which had not removed the cancer, and was told he had not long to live. With his wife and a cousin, he set off for a prayer vigil at Betania.

'I felt very bad and was sweating a lot,' recalled Dr Arrieta. 'I woke up around five in the morning and prayed. About three hours later a solar phenomenon began. There were about 500 people there to see the sun lose its light. The centre part turned green and it began to spin on the inside. I felt heat within my body. I grabbed my wife and began to scream. They thought I was crazy, but I was screaming, "I'm being cured." My wife wiped the sweat off my face and said I looked pale and very bad. But that's not what I felt. I felt healing: first, my spinal column and then my prostate.

'Immediately after this, the Virgin appeared above some trees, looking like a real human being. Her hair was moving in the breeze. She had a beautiful face. In her right arm she carried the child Jesus. From her other arm a rosary hung down like an illuminated pearl. When I saw her, so did hundreds of other people.'[1]

Dr Arrieta, who studied medicine at Harvard, returned to his own hospital for an examination by Dr Vinicio Paz, a university professor and chief of nuclear medicine with twenty-two years' experience. Dr Paz and his team were baffled. There was no medical logic for the transformation in Dr Arrieta's health. 'My impression is that only religion could have done more for Dr Arrieta than science, because there is no scientific explanation for what happened to him. At certain times things happen within a human body that science cannot explain and this, apparently, is one of those cases.'[2]

The incomparable life of Maria Esperanza began on 22 November 1928 with a special prayer. Her mother, anxious to find expert medical facilities to deliver her expected child, set out on a voyage to the United States. The cruiser was still off the Venezuelan coast when her labour pains accelerated and she realised that she was about to give birth. So she prayed to the Virgin Mary for the safe delivery of her baby and promised, if it were a girl, to name her Maria Esperanza (Esperanza being Spanish for 'hope').

When we met at her home in Caracas, Maria told me all that has happened in her life. She was only five when she had her first mystical vision, again associated with her mother and a voyage. Her family was gathered at the port of Bolivar City, at the mouth of the Orinoco River. She told me, 'I was saying farewell to my mother, who was about to leave on a ship. I was a quiet girl, and I walked away from the rest of my family and began to look into the river at the movement of the waves. Suddenly I saw St Theresa, known as the Little Flower, rise from the water. It was a vision, but she was real, like you or me. I loved her so much. I had her prayer card. She threw a red rose to me. I tried to catch it, but it fell. Then I picked it up and ran back to my family. "Mother," I said, "St Theresa sends you this rose so it will accompany you."

'My mother said, "How did you get this rose?" I told her about St Theresa throwing it to me and she just thought it was a childish fantasy. I took a petal and kept it.' Maria put it in a locket, which she wore around her neck, against her heart, for years afterwards. 'That rose stayed fresh and I had it with me until just recently, when it was lost in a misplaced trunk.'

It is possible to view that initial vision as nothing more than the vivid imagination of a small child, just as her mother did, but later events show how important it would become. Her vision of St Thérèse the Little Flower was the first reference to the flower theme that has played a significant part in Maria's life of mystery.

At twelve, Maria developed pneumonia, the first of many illnesses she has suffered. She told me, 'The doctors said my lungs were closed and I heard them say, "I don't think she will live." Then the Virgin Mary appeared right in front of my bed. She said she was my mother and that she had come to alleviate my discomfort. She told me to copy down what she said and go to the pharmacy. I was shocked to see her but honoured to feel she cared enough to come to me. The things she told me about were natural oils and roots. When I heard these words, all I could think of was that I had to kneel, but I was too ill. From then on, I began to improve and I was well again within a couple of days.

'From that time on I could see the future. I knew when people

55

were coming to visit. I knew when friends had hurt themselves or when they were ill. I also went to mass daily, through rain and storm.'

Maria Esperanza suffered a heart attack at fourteen. It was from this point in her life, six decades ago, that the Roman Catholic Church began investigating and documenting her visionary experiences. At seventeen, she had to appear before an ecclesiastical jury. This was not a pleasant process, recalls Maria. 'It was so horrible that I just wanted to escape and become a nun. Things were very hard on me during this time in my life. My health was never good. One of my doctors told me that he had seen three other cases like me in the world – someone to whom supernatural things happen. He said they had all died, but if God gives you life, you may change the world. The responsibility of those words was frightening.

'Then unusual things started to happen to me. I entered a convent and I saw St Theresa again, this time during mass. She threw me a rose. I tried to catch it, just as I had done when I was five. As I tried to catch it, something pinched my palm and my hand started to bleed. She told me to leave the convent, that I was meant to be a wife and mother. It was very difficult to follow these words and actually leave the convent.

'On 1 November 1954 I was told in a vision that I would meet my husband at the Vatican. I didn't want to marry. I thought it was a joke. In another vision I was even told what day I would marry him. Anyway, I did meet Geo. We did fall in love and we were married on 8 December 1955, in the Vatican chapel where Michelangelo's *Pietà* is now behind bullet-proof glass. No one had ever been married in that chapel before, but we had permission from the Holy Father, Pius XII. Now we have six daughters, one son and fourteen grandchildren.' Laughter breaks out among the family gathering when Geo Bianchini Gianni interrupts to say they had seven children in eight years, 'and no television'.

Geo told me, 'I felt from the beginning that Maria had something in her that was very interesting, beyond her own humanity. About a month after we married I began to see things that weren't normal. I have never doubted her mission for a moment.'

Even the site of Maria and Geo's farm in Betania was determined by a vision. As Maria showed me around, she said, 'I

56

was told in a vision in 1954 there would be an old sugar-cane mill, a grotto and a fountain from out of the rock. We searched for the place for years. Then I recognised it. At first we couldn't see the grotto. Then, once we began clearing the bush away, there it was.' The water from that rock fountain was the subject of Maria Esperanza's first sighting at her farm of the Virgin Mary, on 25 March 1976. During that apparition, said Maria, 'The Holy Mother told me the waters of the cascade would heal the sick.'

It was eight years later when Geo also saw the vision of the Virgin Mary. He said, 'It was on 25 March 1984 and it lasted three and a quarter hours. The Virgin appeared seven times.' He added, 'I think Maria has been called to wake up the hearts of men. People should think about how they behave towards each other. There will come a point when there won't be any more time left.'

This is a common theme – the view that time is growing short – which echoes through the countless reports of apparitions of the Virgin. Mary's interventions in our world are a desperate attempt to persuade us to reconsider how we live, and how offensive it is to God. They warn us that it will be our own actions that will bring down the hand of God.

Maria's God-given gifts of healing and counselling, and her personal charm and warmth, are given entirely without charge. The successful Bianchini family business is linked to Venezuela's dominant industry, petroleum, which has made it the wealthiest country in South America. Maria's husband and son provide petroleum maintenance services for major oil companies and have won several lucrative contracts. Maria comments, 'Every time I tell them how much to bid for a contract, we win. When my son bids, we often lose. God has given me something special.'

Giving birth to roses

There is nothing more unique, more mystical, more extraordinary, than the phenomenon of the roses to which Maria has given birth from between her breasts. 'It is very hard to talk about this. Can you imagine that the roses are born from here?' she said, pointing to her chest. 'I cannot understand it. Nobody can. The Bishop [Ricardo] has investigated all the data, on all the saints, and there has never been a miracle like this one. You really

57

have to live this in order to believe. I am so embarrassed because I am an older person and yet I have had to uncover myself for doctors and priests, for them to see for themselves.'

The first time it happened was in 1986. Since then it has occurred on fourteen more occasions and Maria seems to believe that the fifteenth occasion, on 15 August 1995, will be the last. She said, 'Our Lady told me it will be my fifteen mysteries.' There was a long gap, of about three years, before the last one. In 1993 it happened three times. 'On one occasion, a rose came at 5 a.m., but the stem broke off. Two hours later, I had to give birth to the stem, thorns and all.'

Maria has little warning that it is about to occur. She told me, 'Usually, I feel a bit nervous, and so I walk around. It comes on like a heart attack. I feel a pain in my chest, then contractions, as if I'm giving birth. But instead of a child, there is a rose. It happens very fast, in about fifteen minutes to half an hour after I first feel it. My chest gets swollen and I feel something going on inside. Then my skin opens and a small button pops out, which is a tiny bud, and it immediately blooms.'

After the rose has formed, Maria breaks off the stem. There is little blood, she says, and no scar. It heals rapidly. She keeps the largest petals and gives the rest away, usually to family members and close friends. People who have been given them report that they do not dry out, but remain fresh; some claim they have healing powers. Maria keeps the centre of the flower for Bishop Ricardo. She told me, 'Although it is painful when the rose is being expelled, afterwards comes an inner joy, the tenderness that you feel when your child has been born. There are no words to describe it. I know the rose is hard to believe, but, you see, roses have always had such significance for me. The rose is a rose of love, and the chest of a woman is her most sacred area.'

For independent evidence of this phenomenon we must turn to three unimpeachable sources: Dr Luis Gutierrez Burgos, a Harvard-educated Venezuelan surgeon; Dr Juan Succar, an obstetrician, academic and director of several hospitals, based in Lima; and television journalist Carolina Fuenmayor, who was allowed to film on one occasion.

Dr Burgos is a military surgeon and director of the Military Hospital in Caracas. He studied medicine at Harvard, then worked at Massachusetts General Hospital as a postgraduate. He told me he had met Maria seven years before, through a lawyer friend. 'I was a sceptic then,' he recalled. 'But the first time I met Maria Esperanza she looked into my mind and told me everything about myself and my family.

'I have seen her give birth to the rose from between her breasts three times. It begins like a heart attack. Her pulse speeds up. Her blood pressure goes down. Her face becomes very pale and she sweats profusely. There are muscle contractions around the thorax and the lungs expel something. She refrains from food that day and has only a glucose drink for energy. Then a small button of flesh protrudes between her breasts. Immediately she uses her arms to try and eject it. It is similar to the delivery of a baby.

'The rose, always a dark red, breaks through the skin and blossoms immediately. It has dew on it, very fresh. Many times I have seen glitter on the rose. The stem can be up to six inches long with thorns, just like any other rose. But there is only a single drop of blood. When the rose appears, Maria is happy. A smile appears, just like a woman who has had a baby. Once the petals come off the rose, Maria gives them to her family and friends. Many people have reported cures with these petals. Unaccountably, they remain fresh.'

Dr Burgos says that on one occasion his grandson was very ill with a high fever. He had just received an urgent call from Maria to come, because she was going to give birth to another rose. Dr Burgos, an astute man, had by now accepted that Maria Esperanza's life was directed by God, so he rushed the child into his car and headed for Maria's home. He reached there in time to witness the moment when a small opening appeared on her chest. He saw the bud burst through. Then it blossomed and was covered with glitter. Maria reached out to him and the glitter immediately appeared all over his arm. He knew this substance was of heavenly origin. According to the Bishop, it had been examined at the laboratory and was found to be organic. It was alive! The doctor took hold of his grandson and the glitter transferred instantly to the boy. His fever vanished and the boy recovered completely from his illness.

Dr Burgos can only categorise what happens to Maria Esperanza as a medical mystery, although he realises the inadequacy of the phrase. 'What I have witnessed defies all scientific explanation. After thorough examination of Maria, I am convinced these events cannot be faked. The only explanation I can give is that something more powerful than the laws of nature, something of a divine nature, has occurred.'

He is supported in this view by Dr Succar, who witnessed the same event with his daughter, Kathy Chebly, who now acts as one of Maria's interpreters. Dr Succar wrote a lengthy description just hours later. 'Around 5 p.m. Mrs Esperanza began presenting physical signs of thoraxical pain. Her hands were pressed to her chest. Her breathing altered, she had difficulty walking and was visibly fatigued. I observed her facial expression as one of intense malaise.

'She was helped into her house, where she sat on a chair with her back to the wall, hastily unbuttoning the blouse she was wearing. From inside her brassière, which she also undid, sprouted an untouched red rose. While it was sprouting, Mrs Esperanza was praying. There was a multitude of purplish red-coloured petals, some with a golden glitter and even with dew. She ingested some petals until her face assumed a pinkish colour and she began speaking of love, words that were recorded and filmed.

'Minutes later she began to talk naturally and said that more petals were going to come out, and searched under her breast and more were indeed obtained. She allowed me to examine the rose. It consisted of a green stem of two segments. At the joint of these I noticed five small, fresh green leaves. Mrs Esperanza's husband stayed by his wife, apparently confident that she would not suffer any harm, although showing signs of some apprehension.'

Dr Succar's daughter, Kathy, said, 'My father was amazed. He explained that it is impossible for a human cell to produce plant cells, because the DNA is incompatible, with different chromosomes. It would be impossible to do it with the power of thought, because the genetic information in the cells precludes it. He said it had to be a miracle and he sent a testimony about it to the Vatican. My father has studied paranormal phenomena and doesn't take things at face value. In Peru, he unveiled a fraud by some crafty Brazilian doctors, who said they could operate without opening flesh. But what happened to Maria Esperanza happened in front of his eyes. He concluded that it couldn't be faked medically, and so it must be a supernatural occurrence.'

The filming that same day was carried out by Carolina Fuenmayor, a broadcaster for Venezuelan television. She said, 'Maria and I were walking down the hill when she started to have pain. I thought maybe she was having a heart attack. When we got to the house she sat down and I couldn't help staring. She opened her blouse and I saw this little rose coming through her chest. Many people had told me about it, but I didn't believe them. I have the footage, but she told me not to show it to anyone until she dies.'[3]

The stigmata

Both Dr Burgos and Ms Fuenmayor have also witnessed Maria's annual suffering of the stigmata. Her hands bleed from wounds that resemble those of the crucified Christ. This happens to her every Good Friday. Maria told me, 'From the Wednesday before Easter I feel pain in my whole body, on my shoulders, my feet, my hands. But it isn't constant. It comes and goes. On Good Friday, around 3 o'clock, I feel the pain increasing. Then the wounds begin to open.'

Dr Burgos first witnessed this phenomenon nine years ago. He said, 'It starts around 1 p.m. on the Friday. By 2 p.m. each wound can be two cubic centimetres. She feels tremendous pain in both hands, in her feet and over her ribs on her right side. Before the stigmata appear, her whole hand and arm is full of glitter.'

Maria says that several doctors have studied the event, as have priests. Yet she remains largely unaware of what is happening. 'I am in the hands of my Mother,' she says, 'as a child who knows nothing.' In recent years she says that, instead of blood gushing from the wound, oil pours from her hand. 'I think it happens in this soft and delicate way because the Lord doesn't want me to suffer. Now it is always mild.'

Maria's long-time spiritual adviser Padre Pio, the Capuchin monk, had the longest known running case of the stigmata, which he suffered for fifty years. A few days after his death it was reported by his physicians that all visible signs of the wounds had vanished completely from his body.

Maria understands pain, because she suffers so much herself. 'I carry this pain and then it passes. Rather than send His wrath, He asks certain souls if they will suffer for the sins of mankind. When they have said yes, as Jesus did, they must endure tremendous physical pain. It's really hard, but God gives me the

61

grace, and tells me that while I am giving of myself, He will give to me. It is true, if you give, then you have the right to receive.'

Maria and others who suffer in this manner are thought to be victim souls. She has taken on herself the suffering of others, often absorbing their symptoms. It is a supernatural phenomenon that even the devout do not understand. Apparently, it is through suffering that offences against God are forgiven. These days, as the world turns its back on Him, these offences mount.

Maria has also embraced fasting. Many of the prophets, mystics and saints fasted for an answer to prayer, viewing it as purification of the spirit. 'I've hardly eaten anything in the last four years,' she explained. 'I only have juice and soup, no meat. Small amounts of food nourish me. I don't feel food is for me.'

The glitter mentioned by Dr Burgos in relation to the stigmata is one of the regular phenomena associated with Maria Esperanza. It is also linked to the rose petals that appear so often in Maria's presence and are reported to have healing qualities. When Maria was taken to hospital in Caracas for a heart operation six years ago, one of her god-children happened to be undergoing surgery there too. She told me, 'I was sitting beside the sick child with her mother, Aida, when petals suddenly began to rain down everywhere. It was beautiful. One of the physicians at the doorway asked, "Where are they coming from?" while the nurses shouted, "Roses! Roses!" My god-child soon recovered.'

The medal of the Mother of God

One might expect the medical community to be sceptical about Maria, but she says, 'They have grown to be so fond of me. Often, when they are going to operate on someone and it's a very delicate operation, they call and ask for my help. The chairman of the Caracas Clinic and I are friends. I once gave him a medal of Our Lady Reconciler of Nations [as she has identified herself at Betania, Maria's farm] and told him, "It's going to be useful for some case when there's no hope."

'Many months later an anaesthesiologist gave a boy too much anaesthetic and the child went into a coma. As chairman of the clinic, he was responsible and would, of course, be sued. The father went mad with rage. He told the doctor, "It's said that this is the best hospital in Venezuela. If you do not cure my son I will kill you afterwards." So the doctor called me and asked, "Why am I undergoing this situation? I told the man: we are not God, we are scientists, and we'll do all that is possible to save your son." '

Maria replied, 'From this night I'll be with you spiritually. Be calm.' She said the doctor heard a voice saying, 'The medal I gave you. What are you going to do with it?' She continued, 'The doctor went home, found it, gave it to a nurse and said, "Place this medal given to me by Mrs Maria Esperanza close to the boy's head. Let no one know of this."

'They stood watching the boy for a reaction and, after fifteen minutes, he noticed the boy move one leg. Some time later he moved the other one. Eventually he saw the boy lift each arm in turn. The doctor was unable to sleep that night. In the early hours of the morning, the nurse called him and said excitedly, "Now the boy is breathing unaided without the oxygen apparatus."

'The next day the doctor and the boy's father reached the clinic at the same time and, when the doctor told him his son was getting better, the father looked sceptical. But by noon the boy was able to see, and able to acknowledge people. The father later told me, "I will never forget this. I have told my friends too. They will really believe what God can do." He acknowledged it had all been a mistake and never sued.'

Maria says, 'These things show the influence of Our Lady and of Jesus, because what can I do with a medal? It is the medal of the Mother of God, and it is her intercession that makes the miracle take place. The important thing in all of this is faith.'

At the same hospital, Caracas Clinic, Maria once had an operation for a bad knee. After she had bathed, ready for surgery, her physician, Dr Sanchez, came to see her and was immediately struck by the perfume of roses in her room. Then he exclaimed, 'Why do you have all this glitter on your leg? Is there no way to take it off?'

The nurses had tried to scrub it off before surgery. Maria recalled, 'This doctor didn't believe in anything supernatural. His next surprise was that an anaesthetist gave me an epidural, which had no effect. "This lady is so strange," Dr Sanchez said. Then he looked up and saw the Blessed Mother. He said, "Am I going mad?" Our Lady smiled at him and then disappeared. He said he couldn't even breathe. After the vision he turned to the nurses and asked, "Who is this lady?" One said, "Don't you know? It is Mrs Maria Esperanza." '

The healing of a boy with spina bifida

Ryan Hulick was born on 2 October 1992 in Middletown, New York, with the most serious type of spina bifida. His spine was open to the air and all his body below the base of the spine was affected although, unusually with this disease, he could still move his legs. On the day of his birth he was flown to the County Medical Center in Valhalla, New York, for emergency surgery. The lamenectomy went well, but within twenty-four hours Ryan was showing symptoms of water on the brain. The next day his tiny body was back on the operating table for a procedure called a ventricolostomy, in which doctors drill through the skull to siphon off excess fluid backed up from the spinal column into the brain.

A week later came Ryan's third operation, when surgeons installed a spaghetti-like shunt around his abdomen to release the excess fluid. Within two weeks the shunt began to malfunction. Ryan cried inconsolably. Then came the fourth operation in the first month of his life.

His parents, teachers Pat and Casey Hulick, were naturally distraught. Casey takes up his son's story. 'Three months later the area behind Ryan's ear where the shunt was implanted swelled up like a football. There was a terrible snowstorm and we panicked, afraid we'd never make it to the hospital in time. Later the neurosurgeon told us that if it had taken one minute longer, Ryan would have had brain damage. The same thing happened again five months later.

'Pat was terribly depressed and felt she had done something wrong. We had heard about Betania, about the thousands of people who had seen the Virgin Mary and about the hundreds who had been miraculously healed. So on 12 August 1993 we took Ryan to Maria Esperanza. She prayed with Pat and told her that Jesus would heal Ryan, if it was God's will. She warned that we must always be resigned to God's will in our lives and that many times we are called upon to suffer. She told Pat that the whole family should continue to pray for Ryan's healing.

'The next day Pat and I, along with hundreds of other people, saw two apparitions of the Blessed Virgin. We also saw a statue of Jesus shedding tears of blood.

'A month later, we took Ryan and our other son, Evan, to meet Maria Esperanza when she travelled to the States. We prayed with her in the lobby of the Sheraton Hotel in Lowell, Massachusetts. She went into ecstasy, then reached back to touch the sacral region of her spine. "Here, this is the place," she said, indicating the location of Ryan's injury. She said she could feel the spine straightening out. She assured us, "Jesus is healing your son, and the healing will be in three parts. The first part is happening at this moment."

'Pat brought the boys down to the lobby to pray with Maria. She said she could feel the power of Jesus healing Ryan. A week and a half later the physical therapist noticed that Ryan's spine had straightened out and that the muscle tone of his legs, which had been consistently low, was now in the normal range. Three days later several doctors at the Spina Bifida Clinic at Westchester County Medical Center in Valhalla were impressed with Ryan's condition, especially with the surprisingly positive reaction in his shunt reservoir.

'Next spring, in April 1994, we again took Ryan and Evan to see Maria Esperanza, this time at the Valley Forge Sheraton Hotel. Maria prayed with Ryan and told us he had received the second healing she had predicted. The following day the physical therapist noticed what he called an unnatural leap in Ryan's condition, when compared with the previous week. We asked the neurologist to check Ryan's notes against those of six months ago. We could all see the changes were remarkable, considering that nerves don't regenerate.

'We went back to Betania in August, hoping for the third part of the healing. On the bus from Caracas, Ryan stood on Pat's lap laughing euphorically for fifteen minutes. He couldn't be interrupted. People sitting nearby believed he was having some sort of spiritual vision. On the bus he rotated his ankles in ways he never had before. The next morning he tiptoed in his sneakers for the first time in his life.

'When we got home he bolted up the stairs and jumped up and down happily in his crib. The physical therapist noticed his ankles were now straight when he stood, rather than rolling under, as they had before. He also noticed an increase in body strength. Ryan's doctors said he had far exceeded any of their expectations.

'Ryan has entered the Brookside School in Cottekill, New York, three days a week, where he receives physical therapy, occupational therapy and speech therapy. The neurosurgeon, orthopaedist, urologist and psychiatrist at Westchester County Medical Center were astonished to see Ryan walking. They were all exceedingly pleased with his improving condition.

'In December 1994, Ryan had a urodynamics test at the medical center, where the technician reported that his bladder behaved in a normal manner for a child of his age. The neurosurgeon reported that in a Magnetic Resonance Image test, which looks into the body without radiation, Ryan appeared stable. No new problems had developed. In short, he was doing just fine.'

In a letter to the delighted Hulicks, Marilyn Baeckelandt – marriage and family counsellor at the Rainbow Hospice, Park Ridge, Illinois – charted the difference in Ryan before and after a visit Maria Esperanza. She wrote, 'When I first saw him in your arms, Pat, he lay there placid and made no movement, his eyes weren't completely focused on any one object and he looked like a retarded baby. I was so surprised when you told me he was twenty-three months. He acted more like a six- or seven-month-old baby. After you two returned from being with Maria, the change in Ryan was startling: his eyes focused on whoever was speaking to him, he was jumping up and down on your lap, Pat, laughing, attempting to talk and acting like a normal 23-month-old child. He clapped his hands and repeated gestures shown to him by other passengers on the bus. It was as if he was going through all the development stages between six and twenty-three months right before our eyes. I was utterly fascinated and astounded at the dramatic change.

'Normally, a child at this stage, after enduring being stuck all day in a stroller with crowds of people around, would have been tired, cranky, fussy, whining. Ryan was delightful. It was as if he was going to show all of us his newly gained muscle strength; plus his manner was purely angelic, as if he had just come from seeing a saint. He acted like a small child that had just awakened from a nap refreshed and ready to play. I will never forget the dramatic

66

change in Ryan. I also felt a peace and goodness surrounding all three of you.'

'Spina bifida is a devastating disease, it affects the brain, the spinal cord, the nervous system – anything from the head down,' said Dr Rifkinson, Ryan's neurologist. 'I think he has excelled beyond what is objective analysis – the pictures: the MRIs, catscans, X-rays – might have led us to believe.

'The art of medicine 100 years ago was holistic, in that we didn't have the technology and capability of correcting anatomical abnormalities. We've forgotten about faith, we've forgotten about hope and positive thinking.'

Cases of instantaneous healing are very rare. Most 'miracles' are gradual, taking place over a period of weeks or months, like Ryan's. When you see the first signs of healing, prayer and resignation to God's will become vital.

The day the host bled in Betania

There have been several occasions in history when, during mass, the communion host has been transmuted to a substance later proved by laboratory tests to be human flesh or blood. Historians of the Roman Catholic Church argue that the most notable example occurred in Lanciano, Italy, in the eighth century, authenticated in recent years by modern scientific methods.

A priest undergoing a crisis of faith was celebrating mass in the church of St Longinus, named after the soldier who pierced the side of Jesus during his crucifixion, around AD 700 when, as he consecrated the host, it began to drip blood. The blood and a bit of flesh were displayed on a side altar for centuries and, in 1902, transferred to a marble altar. Neither container was hermetically sealed. Then, in 1970–1 and again in 1981, two professors of anatomy examined the flesh and a portion of the blood, which had coagulated into small pellets.

They concluded that the flesh was human, with the same blood group (AB) as the blood. It had not decayed in the way that blood and flesh removed from a corpse would have done. They identified the flesh as human heart muscle (striated muscular tissue of the myocardium). But they could not explain how, after twelve centuries of exposure to the atmosphere, the tissue and blood had remained in such a good state of preservation.

In 1994 another Eucharistic miracle was verified in Worcester, Massachusetts, in the bedroom of a young girl, Audrey Santo, who has been in a coma-like state, known as kinetic mutism, for over a decade. At the age of three, in 1987, Audrey had nearly drowned in the family pool, and since then the most bewildering manifestations have occurred in the bedroom of this young girl.

It all began with signs of the stigmata, which appeared in the presence of her nurse. Wounds appeared on her forehead and opened on the palms of her hands. They corresponded with an increase in her respiration and heart rate. Even her body became rigid, as if experiencing tremendous pain. Then a statue of the Virgin Mary in Audrey's bedroom began to weep oil, so much so that a small dish had to be placed beneath it. Over the years Audrey's room had been inundated with religious mementoes and was full of statues. Now a statue of Jesus began to cry tears of blood. By the time the Santo family called for advice from the Roman Catholic Church, twelve icons were weeping profusely.

Father McCarthy of Chicago was selected to sort out this extraordinary activity. He said, 'There was a smell of roses with the oil. I have had sinus problems and, for all practical purposes, I hadn't smelled roses in thirty years. Oftentimes when you have a case like this, people will look for a tangible presence of God. So I looked for fraud.'[4]

Most clergy are not spiritually impressionable and do not race to promote such phenomena as miraculous. Their usual reaction is to wonder why God has not chosen to communicate with those who have given their entire lives in service to Him. Their caution and prudence are generally similar to that of any sceptic.

As the priests tried to come up with logical explanations, more and more unusual phenomena occurred. More statues wept. Items used at masses, kept in the Santo home, were also affected: the chalice developed pores and perspired oil; a dish used for communion bread was found to contain oil; even the Bible dripped with oil. The volume of oil kept increasing.

Then the Eucharistic miracles began. On four occasions, communion hosts bled during mass. A brownish substance was found on the bottom of the tabernacle in Audrey's room, which was used to store consecrated hosts. A reddish substance dripped from a crucifix. The Santos, and spiritual directors of the Roman Catholic Church, realising the spiritual implications, thought it critical to send the evidence for laboratory scrutiny. Both the HS

Research Laboratory in Cambridge, Massachusetts, and a Californian laboratory of forensic science concurred: the substance was human blood.

This exceptional situation was captured on film. There were three priests present at a mass led by Father George Joyce of Springfield, Massachusetts. He noticed a small host changing texture and people in the front gasped as they watched it bleed. The priests were visibly shaken.

Father Joyce says, 'I don't recall whether it occurred before the consecration or not. But I know when I looked down at the consecration, I saw something that was not on top of the host, but apparently was "in" it. So I sensed that something was going to happen. And when I came to "Behold the Lamb of God", I lifted the host up and the first two rows of people said "Aaahh". I knew something had happened. I looked down and there was a small drop of blood on the host concentrated on the centre . . . it had an indented cross on it and the blood was right in the centre, where the beams met . . . It was quite heavy, so the blood seeped out through the indentures of the cross.'[5]

Betania witnessed a similar transformation of the host on 8 December 1991. I interviewed Presbyter Otty Ossa Aristizabal, the man who held the bleeding host in his hand, and his Bishop, Pio Bello Ricardo. I have also seen two of the hundreds of eye witnesses talking about it, as it was captured on film.

Padre Otty told me, 'I had two assistants helping me with the mass, one of whom was an engineer. My assistant said, "Padre, look at the host. It is bleeding." I told him I had already seen it. I was worried that people would rush the altar if I acknowledged the bleeding.'

But people did see it. Tom Rooney, a tourist from New York who filmed the event, said, 'It was red. It was real blood. I filmed it for a couple of minutes, while Padre Otty stopped and held it steady for me. I could see the blood flowing out of the host and collecting in the bottom of the glass.'[6]

Tourist Pat Stamandolini agreed, 'I was on the altar not two feet from it. I saw a red dot on the host. It just couldn't be fake. Ever since that mass I go to church every day.'

Bishop Ricardo, who has become something of an ecclesiastical detective because of the mystifying events that thousands of people have experienced in his diocese since 1987, spoke to me at length about what happened. But he summed it up most authoritatively when he wrote on 12 February 1992, in an official communiqué to the press, declaring that the host had indeed bled.

'It was midnight on 8 December 1991 and the chaplain of Finca Betania, Presbyter Otty Ossa Aristizabal, was celebrating mass. When the moment for the communion arrived, the chaplain divided the Eucharistic bread into four parts, as usual, and placed one of the pieces on a paten or communion dish.

'Moments later he was amazed to discover that a small red dot had formed on a fragment of the host and that a red substance had begun to ooze, rather like blood from a wound. This continued until a surface area of a square centimetre had been covered. This same phenomenon was observed by the Lay Minister of the Eucharist, Guillermo de Jesus Padron, who was assisting at the altar.

'My first action, on learning about this case, was to order Padre Otty to bring the fragment to the Cathedral of Los Teques so that it could be subjected to initial tests at the bio-analytic laboratory here. The analysis was carried out by trained experts, Josuae Zubizarreta and Rosa Da Silva, on 12 December. Their conclusion, based on the cytological evidence obtained, suggested the existence of blood, but they recommended a more thorough analysis.

'As a result, I requested the help of the Caracas police forensics department. The Director, Dr E. Aponte Viloria, assumed responsibility. In the ensuing haematological test, the sample underwent microscopic analysis to determine its physical properties, and biochemical tests: the Teichmann and Takayama tests. The analysis revealed the substance to be blood. The resulting report had been signed by Dr Raul Ramirez Pinto, head of the criminal division, and Daisy Canizales de Bolivar, head of the microanalysis department.

'Therefore I feel confident in saying that there is sufficient evidence to recognise the miraculous bleeding of the host in Finca Betania.'

Bishop Ricardo's verdict

Thin, with a calm and circumspect demeanour, Bishop Ricardo is a distinctly cerebral man. He explained, as a psychologist, just why the Betania sightings of the Virgin Mary are so distinct from others witnessed around the world. Most officially recognised Marian apparitions in the twentieth century have been seen by an individual, as at Lourdes, or by a small group of children, as at Fatima and Medjugorje. But in Egypt in 1968 an estimated 250,000 people did see Our Lady as a radiant light on top of a Coptic church. She appeared in different forms and postures two or three times a week for two years. The visions lasted from a few minutes to eight hours. The other mass sighting was in the Ukraine on 26 April 1987, the anniversary of Chernobyl, when a schoolgirl saw Mary on the back of a church. She has continued to appear to thousands of eye witnesses at open field shrines in the Ukraine up to the present day.

It was also in 1987 that Bishop Ricardo conducted his investigation. 'There have been false apparitions, of course, at least four or five,' he told me, puffing away on his cigarette. 'In Lourdes, two hundred were reported to be false. Many people come to Betania thinking they will see the apparition. From listening to hundreds of people, I know right away who is speaking from imagination.

'The Church generally does not declare the authenticity of apparitions. It is usually the conformity of the apparitions with the faith on which they will rule. I can guarantee these apparitions are authentic. Before I even started my investigation, I had interviewed 108 people who testified to seeing the apparition of the Blessed Mother. I questioned them rigorously while trying to remain open-minded, though I maintained an attitude of doubt and scepticism.

'I was interested in determining the credibility of witnesses, their condition as human beings, their sincerity, their common sense, their capacity to reason, their sense of criticism and their emotional balance. Once the credibility of witnesses was established, I tried to decide how much the witnesses could have been influenced by collective or personal suggestion.

'Since her first appearance, the Blessed Mother has presented herself as the Reconciler of Nations, but she only speaks to Maria Esperanza. She is seen with a white dress and a blue waistband. Some say she extends her arms out in a welcoming or saluting gesture. She wears a veil and you can see her hair.'

As a result of his role as chief investigator and the repository of knowledge about the apparitions of Betania, Bishop Ricardo has amassed a vast collection of stories about what happens to people who visit Betania. Over 1,500 people have sent him written depositions.

'A 23-year-old atheist came to give me his declaration. He had only come to Betania because his mother and sister pestered him. While they went to mass, he went to a small house near the grotto to drink a few beers. Then the apparition began. At first he joked about it to those around him, but he saw the Virgin.

'Another woman came to Betania only for a picnic, and had no knowledge of the apparitions. When she went to fetch water from the cascade, she cried out to her sister, "There is the Virgin Mary! What is this?"

'Then there was a woman of twenty-four who was finishing her PhD thesis on the petroleum industry, who brought me a ten-page document about her experience. She was a practising Jew and was invited to Betania by a Catholic friend. She kept saying that she did not understand why she saw the Virgin, because it had no meaning for her. She kept asking what the meaning of this experience was. She then began to fast. At the end of the fast she decided it was important for her to go to the synagogue more and develop a better relationship with God. Her family was quite orthodox and she was fearful of what they might say if they found out she had seen the Virgin.

'I suppose I will have to reconcile myself to not seeing her, while thousands of others do,' Bishop Ricardo concluded. 'Perhaps it's best that way, since I seem to have been chosen to evaluate.'

Bishop Ricardo is evaluating for the toughest group of miracle sceptics in the world. The Roman Catholic Church in the twentieth century retains its traditional arm's-length attitude towards visions and mysticism. Nonetheless, as a result of his report, Betania has become the fourth apparition site to be approved by the Church this century. The others are Garabandal in Spain, Fatima in Portugal and Lourdes in France.

In an open letter on the apparitions in November 1987 Bishop Ricardo wrote, 'By earlier this year, 500 to 1,000 people had reportedly seen the Virgin Mary. She does not appear in any established frequency, but generally on Saturdays, Sundays or Marian feast days. Many people mentioned that their apparition came as a surprise. These people initially looked for natural explanations, reflections of light, tricks, suggestions etc. She usually appears in the vegetation around the cascade near the little parish house or by the river. There is no sense of reality loss, mystical state or trance, as in other visionaries throughout time.'

The Bishop listed the six phenomena that generally accompany the apparitions: fog that seems to come out of the trees; intense luminosity that brightens the hill; an invisible choir; a profuse scent of flowers, especially roses (water from the cascade acquiring the same perfume); and movement of light from the sun.

Bishop Ricardo continued, 'There have been cases of exaggerated emotion and hysterical reaction, but the general environment has been balanced. Very few people faint during the apparition.' He commented on those who have seen the apparitions and how they were affected: 'People who never pray have begun and receive a strong injection of spirituality. People who didn't attend church do so. And there are remarkable conversions. All experienced an interior change towards God.

'Since the beginning of my investigation, I realised this was not another case of craftiness, collective suggestion or a promotion of the interests of a person or group. Relatively soon in the course of my investigation, I acquired the certainty that the character of the phenomenon was definitely supernatural.'

The final words must be Maria Esperanza's, her special message for everyone: 'We must learn to be more humble. I always say that humility is the crystal bridge that leads us to heaven. Without humility we can do nothing. Let us be small, and God will give us all His graces.'

Notes

1. 'Marian Apparitions of the Twentieth Century', video by Marian Communications, Lima, Pennsylvania, 1991.
2. Ibid.
3. Ibid.
4. 'Audrey's Life,' video, USA, 1996.
5. *Queen of Peace* newspaper, Pittsburgh Centre for Peace, 1997.
6. Op. cit., note 1.

3

Healing the Family Tree

Although it is routinely said that we are all born equal, we really know that is not so. We have come to accept that inheritance in all its forms is a deciding factor in who we are and who we are to become. In the material sphere, for instance, we may be born into affluence or poverty. In the physical sphere, we understand that the shape of our bodies, the colour of our eyes, the composition of our facial features are all circumscribed by the genetic make-up of our parents, and their parents and so on, going back through generations. We acknowledge that we inherit certain talents for say, music, or sport. In the same way, we accept that emotional characteristics such as shyness, charm or aggression are passed on, as are behavioural attributes like eating disorders or alcoholism. It is also suggested more and more often that we inherit illness too. But the reasons for what we might call 'negative inheritance traits' are not immediately clear.

However, there is one area of inheritance which has been entirely overlooked: spiritual heredity. Yet this is a major factor in our heritage because it is the one that provides reasons and, most importantly, it is the one that we are able to 'cure'. But I must not race ahead. First, let me explain the concept of spiritual heredity.

Many of us are uncomfortable with aspects of our own behaviour, or with that of close members of our family. We are aware of unwanted tendencies or addictions, like drinking, smoking, drug-taking and over-eating. Then there are those who lead questionable lifestyles: from the sexually promiscuous to the compulsive liars, gamblers and spendthrifts. Perhaps we look aghast at these peculiarities, wondering why they occur and, especially, why they occur in our own family.

Some scientists would have us believe that it is all genetic. Others argue that it is caused by our environment. Still more fuse the two, taking our genetic make-up modified by our environment. Nature and nurture are inextricably linked, they say, and that explains everything. But this misses out the spiritual sphere entirely and therefore cannot offer a rational answer to the problems so many people and their families face.

For example, the geneticists cannot explain why some genetic patterns go wrong. They are aware that a tiny error among the three billion sub-units providing the information for the chromosomes that create our genetic code can cause disease. What the scientists do not know is why the errors occur. Then we see idiosyncrasies emerge, maybe anti-social habits, possibly small things like rudeness, critical or negative attitudes, excessive cynicism or cold-hearted bitterness. When this behaviour becomes apparent, if it is abnormal or exaggerated we may label it eccentric. However, if we examine the family heritage further, we may find the same trait in a grandfather or great-grandmother, which apparently has been passed on, though we cannot grasp the mechanism of this transmission.

In one study a man is three times as likely to become an alcoholic as an average person if his grandfather was a heavy drinker, but not necessarily if his mother or father were. Furthermore, this particular type of alcoholism is not reflected in the genetic structure. There is a certain subtlety in the transmission. This kind of example indicates that there might be something more at work here than genetics or environment. Experts agree, it is something that is transmitted through the human spirit.

There are dozens of family disorders that have come to prominence in the last couple of decades, manifesting as psychological problems: eating disorders, attention deficit syndrome, phobias, panic attacks and schizophrenia among them. Unfortunately, we grow to accept these problems in our families, taking these unfortunate facts for granted.

But we no longer need to live in darkness. The Reverend John Hampsch, a Catholic priest, skilled psychologist and college professor from Los Angeles whose works have appeared in the *Journal of Neuropsychiatry*, has studied the question of spiritual heredity in depth and come up with many rather dramatic insights. And Dr Kenneth McAll, surgeon, psychiatrist and Anglican vicar, who pioneered the field of 'healing the family tree', has found that prayer has had remarkable results, when fellow psychiatrists were at a loss. Together they have built up a body of information that might possibly shed light on these unwanted hereditary habits and problems.[1,2]

Before we explain the most unusual and profound observations of these two men, it might be useful to draw upon what we have developed thus far in the book. We have seen, through the amazing gifts of Simeon Kayiwa and the supporting documentation of healing, that the God of the Bible more than likely does exist. He can and 'does' cut through the laws of nature when it suits Him. We have also seen unprecedented mystical phenomena in the life of Maria Esperanza di Bianchini from a very early age, with highly credible witnesses that would also stand up in any court of law. From her experiences, and those of Audrey Santo (see Chapter 2), we could conclude that God, author of all life, can, if we allow Him, use us in a way we could not even presume to understand. In short, the forgotten God we met as children just may be the greatest power in heaven and earth, as it suggests in scripture.

From my own personal experience, I am convinced that the popular description of God as a universal mind – with all things being one, mankind, nature and the universe, endowing man with 'divine potential' – simply is not true. Those who subscribe to this theory believe that since 'we are made in God's image', according to scripture, we are not separate but the same. Therefore, it is possible for us to evolve into an ideal state and become gods. They believe the power is within – there is no external power as God the Creator. Human potential becomes the key, faith in oneself is the answer.

But one cannot accurately quote scripture and empty it of true meaning to promote more fashionable, modern spiritual assumption. We are God's creatures, made in His image but separate from the Creator and subordinate to Him. The God I have experienced and come to know is a personal God, all-powerful, who could rip continents apart with his little finger, should He so desire. I have felt just a drop of that power and have concluded that He is one to be respected and feared, because we have no defence against Him. He controls nature and the very air we breathe and certainly is not someone whose justice I care to see. But this is not a judgemental, vengeful God, as many would like to believe. It is more likely to be as a consequence of human error that there is so much evil in the world, rather than as a result of God's actions. By ignoring what one might call the basic 'operator's manual' on life, given to us centuries ago, we could be creating our own suffering. This is a realisation that I have come to accept gradually, after many years of searching and many mistakes. And it is difficult today to have strong convictions about anything, in the face of such widespread disbelief.

Spirituality is a path but, contrary to what many believe, not all spirituality leads to God (as we will discuss further in Chapter 5). Wisdom and truth in popular spirituality seem to be more a matter of opinion today, and so are the rules we were given to guide us in a healthy existence. It appears from the evidence in this chapter that it may be our inability to acknowledge the importance of those rules as the most basic prescription for health and survival that could be responsible for much of the disease and hardship running rampant in our world. There is a delicate balance in our relationship with the Creator and when we dismiss its importance we become rather like the woodcutter who saws off the branch on which he is sitting. The answers to life's problems, according to the experts, may be more simple than we think. It is only the problems *we* create that can continue to haunt us for generations.

The power of the family

The family, as scripture tells us, is the entity that God uses to shower us with grace. It has been referred to as a cluster of grapes, in which one rests upon the other and acts as the avenue of influence. The family is organised by marriage and blessed before God through matrimony. This vehicle, according to Revd Hampsch, was designed not only as a channel of grace but as a channel of healing for every kind of psychological, emotional and even physical disorder. But it can also be the bearer of bad news, as well. Past indiscretions can create a negative spiritual environment, which then creates what Revd Hampsch refers to as 'transgenerational bondage'. 'Problems such as disease and disorder can result, which are then passed down to us, and become our spiritual heredity,' he says. 'In the past ten years, I would estimate that roughly eighty-five per cent of all diseases – emotional, spiritual and physical – occur as a result of the dysfunctional lives led by our ancestors.' It is hard to imagine that our deceased forebears could have any bearing on us today but, according to the theories of Dr McAll and Revd Hampsch, so can family miscarriages, stillbirths and abortions.

Revd Hampsch stresses that we are all interdependent, part of a society that has responsibilities towards each other: parents towards children, employer towards employees, and politicians towards our community and country. We rely on the 'social constellations' in our life – our families, our workplace and social networks – and consequently we influence those around us, for good or for bad.

As we draw up our family tree and analyse our ancestors, we may see somewhat eccentric or dysfunctional patterns, and often uncomfortable information may be revealed, which we would prefer to keep hidden. But it is precisely these skeletons that are the root of the problem. And if you want to deal with the root of a problem, instead of alleviating the symptoms, then it has to be revealed in the full light of day and washed clean, so to speak. With specific prayer, dramatic healings have resulted in virtually thousands of cases, ranging from physical problems (from arthritis to asthma) to mental problems (such as schizophrenia) and a range of psychological and family disorders. Sometimes healing is instantaneous, but usually it is a gradual process. People generally resort to this method out of desperation, after both conventional and alternative medicine have failed.

But such supernatural healing of the family tree is not new. It dates back to the early days of the Old Testament, where prayer for disease was understood as part of tradition and, to grasp the theory fully, we must go back to the scriptures.

What does the Bible say?

According to Revd Hampsch, there are fifty-six places in the scriptures that refer to the concept of transgenerational bondage. Let us give three examples. In Exodus 20, 5: 'The sins of the parents are visited upon the children to the third and fourth generation.' In Lamentations: 'My forefathers have sinned and I am suffering for it.' And in 1 Kings, Elijah speaks: 'The Lord will bring disaster upon you and your descendants.'

Revd Hampsch points out that in biblical times people often lived with their parents, grandparents and great-grandparents, in what was referred to as a household. It seems that God felt it was important for us to see how offensive sin was, and in this manner the effects of sin would result in disease and disaster and not go undetected. He wanted us to realise the importance of our actions, and grasp how we could cause disease and disorder right under our roof. But, as urbanisation developed, the punishment of disease for offensive behaviour before God went unnoticed.

The Bible talks about wasting diseases: 'Because of their father's sin they will waste away.' (Leviticus, 26, 39: Deuteronomy, 28, 15–21). 'Wasting diseases . . . will destroy your sight and drain away your life' (Leviticus 26, 16). Today Aids, cancer, tuberculosis, cirrhosis of the liver, anorexia and ME could all be considered wasting diseases; cataracts, glaucoma and *Reddenitis pigmentosa* are diseases that can destroy eyesight.

Apparently the bad deeds of world leaders can also affect people individually. This is easy to appreciate from the errors of Communism or the horrors of Nazism. While the concept of responsibility for personal sin is purely a private matter today (and subjective as well), it is fair to ask whether the misconduct of those in authority has a more wide-ranging effect.

As far back as David in the Old Testament, punishment for sin was recognised: David had become captivated by a married woman and was so obsessed by her beauty that he murdered her husband, Uriah. God told him that murder would threaten his family ('we reap what we sow'). Seven days later, David's illegitimate son was found dead. God then sent a terrible plague on Israel, killing 70,000 people. David, acknowledging punishment for his sin, questioned God's judgement. 'I am the one who sinned and have done wrong things, these are but sheep. Oh God, let your hand fall upon me and my family, but do not let the plague remain on your people.' He was hoping that the widespread effect of God's punishment would be diminished by his prayer, which it was – God halted the plague. According to Revd Hampsch, this illustrates that leaders of cities or nations have a responsibility for the larger community.

The good news is that blessings are passed on in immeasurable amounts to those who struggle to behave and live by their conscience. God promises to those who love him, 'I will bestow blessing for a thousand generations.' In Psalm 112, 'The offspring of virtuous parents will have a very special heritage, including salvation.' In the book of Sirach 4, 7, they 'will have wisdom, the highest of the non-charismatic gifts, they will have holiness'; in Sirach (44, 11–14) it is 'prosperity'; in Ezra (9, 12), 'fertility'; in Deuteronomy (7, 15), 'increased capacity for love' and (29, 29) 'wealth'. As for the New Testament, Romans (11, 8) promises 'revelation of God's secrets'. In Jeremiah (31, 16–17) it says, 'Stop your weeping, dry your eyes; your hardships will be redressed . . . there is hope for your descendants.'

The evidence, over centuries of recorded testimony, seems to indicate a personal God at work in the universe. A God who gave the reins of free will to mankind, with very specific guidelines that we must use to break ourselves of bad habits and morally suspect behaviour. The problem is that if discipline was not integrated into our personalities at a young age, it is almost impossible to achieve as an adult. Hence the importance of the family. If the seeds of our own misfortune have us singing a rather needy tune, only then is the heart humble enough to ask God for help. Revd Hampsch says that we have no power over sin, on our own; it is actually a blessing which is only achieved through prayer.

The wrath of God does not sound terribly appealing. And God is quite specific on the ramifications of inappropriate behaviour in Samuel 15: 'I will punish men, women, children and cattle. I will wipe out the whole tribe because of their sins.' (One could be forgiven for wondering whether BSE – mad cow disease – is part of His justice, a type of community or corporate punishment.)

We also find evidence of this tradition being carried on into the New Testament. Jesus says, 'Upon you Pharisees, the blood of Abel on to Zacharia, will come upon this generation, fill up for yourselves the sins of your forefathers because you haven't disengaged yourself for those sins.' It appears that repentance and forgiveness are important to clean the slate of past indiscretions.

There are even clear-cut disorders and afflictions assigned to specific sins. 'The offspring of those who commit adultery are

81

often infertile and die young' (Book of Wisdom, 3, 16). In Job 4, 8–11, adulterers' offspring will suffer. Descendants of those who practise bribery may suffer from defective eyesight (Job, 17, 5). Loss of prosperity is quite a common punishment for ancestral sin.

In some cases, the punishment is more severe than just three to four generations: conceiving or giving birth to a child outside marriage carries a punishment of ten generations, or 400 years. There is even a special punishment for those who do not bother to teach their children the basic principles of religion.

It appears that God has always maintained punishment as a means of guiding us to a healthy and prosperous life, similar to the method we use with our own children. But over the centuries we have overlooked the potential consequences of human error and His threats of divine justice. Modern society has discarded even the possibility of divine retribution in the form of disease, even though it is clearly spelled out in the Old Testament. There is no real incentive to live by the rules. The benefits of being virtuous are not spelled out in convincing terms. But if this theory on healing the family tree is accurate, it is our actions which can cause disease and disorder in our children. Will this be enough to get our attention?

Revd Hampsch tells a story, related to him, of a man – an atheist – who had written a book that held Christianity in great contempt. Consequently none of this man's descendants was normal. His children were born with crippled legs, or were accidentally crippled later in life or became crippled as a result of illness. Some children were mentally retarded, as were some of his grandchildren. All of his descendants had a certain moodiness and seemed to suffer from depression. And – mark this – all of them were profound atheists.

Revd Hampsch says, 'Such consistent patterns are often found among descendants of people who set themselves against God and fall into the hands of His enemy. Forces of evil then interface in a person's life. The pattern sanction is quite common. To explain such patterns as mere coincidence would ignore the fact that such disorders are statistically related to the immoral behaviour, or perverse beliefs, of an ancestor. The pattern sanction is repeated with great consistency, not just in a few family trees, but in thousands upon thousands. The case for the intergenerational or transgenerational bondage theory becomes quite tenable, almost irrefutable, just on the basis of statistical probabilities.'

Today, suffering is not recognised as inherited punishment. 'The morally infected family lineage is often submerged and not recognisable, until it surfaces by happenstance. Jesus made a great point to stress that "delayed punishment is now hidden from your eyes" ' (Luke 19, 42–4). 'It is often shown to be true,' says Revd Hampsch, that 'even from birth the wicked go astray, from the womb they are wayward' (Psalms 58, 3).

Of course we know – and the experts agree – that not all disease and disorder stems from ancestral sin. It can result from bad diet, poor hygiene, genetics or environment. But from the statistical results obtained, spiritual heredity plays a greater role than may seem plausible.

Prayer can break the bondage which acts to transmit the inherited punishment between the living and the dead members of a family tree. Many Christians have a hard time with this concept, which is widely misunderstood. According to Revd Hampsch, there are 300 scriptural references for its use. Part of the problem may lie in distinguishing between associating with spirits of the dead – as in seances or channelling, which is called necromancy and is prohibited in scripture – and praying for the dead. For those wondering about the theological correctness of praying for the dead, consider it was Jesus who prayed to God to raise Lazarus from the dead and then thanked his Father: 'Father, I thank you for having heard me (His prayer)' (John 11, 41), thereby giving us the opportunity also to care for the deceased. As I see it, when you pray for the dead, you are asking God to help them when they are no longer in a position to help themselves. Praying for the dead had been a common practice among the Jews for the better part of a century before the time of Jesus. As it says in Maccabees 12, 4: 'It is a holy and wholesome thought to pray for the dead that they may be loosed from their sins.' Relatives would stand at the graves of their loved ones and plead with God for mercy. Revd Hampsch feels that it is useful to understand the accepted teachings at the time of Jesus, for 'it is this framework which makes His work understood'. And while it is obvious that this teaching was not rejected by Jesus or the apostles, many still have trouble with the idea of praying for the dead.

In Baruch it says 'Pray for the dead and their children who have sinned. Remember not the sin of our forefathers, we have turned away from their evil, we suffer for their sin.' In Leviticus

26, 40, it says: 'Confess the sins of your ancestors.' 'Invoking the dead and invoking God's mercy for the dead are two very distinct and different matters,' says Revd Hampsch.

Others believe that we are all part of the body of Christ and give support to one another into the next life, and vice versa, on the guidelines presented in scripture. We intercede before God on behalf of the dying and deceased. Those considered saints in heaven also intercede before God for those of us on earth. There are many mediums who seek the counsel of spirits, who therefore violate this dictate, not fully understanding that the reason it exists is for our own protection. Evil can interface with disembodied spirits to deceive us. Even when they appear in seances disguised as a relative or familiar person, we can never be certain who, or what, is really present. We will discuss the nature of evil at length (see Chapter 5), but, based on the study of demonology, we are told that the intelligence of these beings is far superior to that of man. So, rather than subject ourselves to the vile and cunning nature of evil, everything in the occult area is considered off-limits.

In his psychiatric studies Dr McAll found that bondage or a harmful link could exist between members of the living and members of the dead. This condition can also exist among the living, when one person in a relationship becomes totally dependent on another. Often the passive partner is unaware of the loss of his or her own identity and is unable to break away from the other's control. This is called 'possession syndrome'. Traditionally, psychiatrists have found it beneficial to try to break the link between the controlling person and the partner, both sides being fully aware and cooperative. Obviously this is not possible if one member is dead. But Dr McAll has taken a different route, bringing about the break by transferring control through prayer to God. Along with the 'gift' of release, he believes that this brings about an acceptance of God's power and will in the situation and in the lives of his patients.

Dr McAll's breakthrough presents great difficulties in diagnosis and in effecting a cure. He has identified several forms of such bondage, not only from ancestors but resulting from miscarried and aborted babies and even a person unrelated. Problems will often manifest in siblings which are born to replace that child or just after the deceased infant, as we will see. But the most dangerous and evil form of all, and the most difficult to unravel, is the bondage and accompanying problems stemming from occult practices. Dr McAll has found that this type of bondage may even skip a generation. Of course, every method of psychiatry should be used to integrate the personality, Dr McAll believes, but when it is used in conjunction with prayer (especially the Eucharist), there is a particularly strong dynamic at work. The power of prayer is able to break the destructive control of the bondage and psychiatry is essential as a means of support to maintain the healing.

Dr McAll considers Claudine one of the most dramatic healings of his career.[3] She was fifty years old at the time and had spent twelve years under hospital supervision suffering from chronic schizophrenia. Neither treatment nor drugs had improved her violent temper, which was coupled with a delusional state of mind. Considering that she could not deteriorate any further, her doctors decided to operate on her brain in a London hospital. The operation failed and she did deteriorate further, losing both the power of speech and sight. Claudine was then left in a vegetative state in a mental hospital, lost her hair and became obese. About eighteen months later the family obtained permission for her to spend a night at home and she was brought to see Dr McAll.

'She gave no indication of understanding and, after a quick check-up, I confirmed that there seemed to be no hope for her and I could recommend no therapy. The damage was indeed irreversible. At the time I did not understand the influence of the family tree, or even realise the extent of the healing power of the Eucharist. Not knowing what else to say or do, I prayed aloud, simply trying to listen for the Lord's guidance and seeking His forgiveness for man's destruction of a human being. We said the Lord's Prayer together, with its final plea, "deliver us from evil". Our prayer was that Claudine might be left in peace.

'My patient and her family returned to their own home, where Claudine was to remain overnight. The next morning, the whole household was awakened by Claudine shouting, "Come in and look at me." Not having heard a word from her since her disastrous operation, her startled parents rushed into the room. Claudine was gazing at her reflection in the mirror and shouting, "Look at my hair." During the night, a quarter-inch of hair had appeared all over her head. She could speak, she could see, she had hair.

'Later that day Claudine was taken back to the institution. Astonished by the change in her, doctors questioned her for several hours. Repeatedly she explained simply, "They prayed with me." The doctors could not understand what had happened. It was almost beyond belief that a patient who had suffered such disabilities could be healed so suddenly, and so completely, that she could be re-admitted to the normal world outside.'

Both Dr McAll and Revd Hampsch rely heavily on the healing power of the Eucharist, which it may be necessary to repeat several times before healing is evident. And, as we have seen previously, there is forensic evidence for the transition that occurs during this service (bread has changed to flesh and blood), and therefore it is this power left to us by Jesus that these men rely on to effect such dramatic healings.

Abortions, miscarriages and stillbirths

Abortion is a highly controversial and sensitive issue. According to published statistics, there are about fifty million abortions per year. Many Russian women use it as a form of birth control, undergoing up to ten or twelve terminations in their lives. Today in many countries women are allowed to abort up to their sixth month of pregnancy. Doctors acknowledge that the foetus feels pain during late-term terminations and suggest anaesthesia. Pope John Paul II is strongly opposed to this practice and says that we are now living in a culture of death and that countries which authorise such practices may one day be held accountable. Given that we have established scriptural reference on the plausibility of 'corporate' punishment, as in the case of David, we might want to review what it says about the child in the womb. 'Can a mother forget her infant, be without tenderness for the child of her womb? Even should she forget, I will never forget you. See upon the palms of my hands I have written your name' [Isaiah, 49, 15–16]. Or Jeremiah, 1, 5 and Psalm 139, 13: 'Truly you have formed my inmost being; you knit me in my mother's womb . . . Before I formed you in the womb I knew you.' And Matthew 18, 10: 'See that you do not despise one of these little ones, for I say to you that their angels in heaven always look upon the face of my heavenly Father.'

Mother Teresa was also quite vocal on the subject: 'The seed of abortion is nuclear war,' she said. Many people did not understand what she meant by this comment, or how abortion could possibly result in such massive destruction. In light of the evidence on the nature of evil (see Chapter 5), and after listening to the experts on healing the family tree and their views on evil, it appears that if this action is offensive before God, it will result in a negative spiritual environment in both the life of the father and the mother. It then becomes possible for a negative spiritual force, or in reality a demonic force, to superimpose onto the emotional scar that can result through abortion. Parents, of course, remain unaware of its destructive nature, but this negative spiritual environment can create all types of misfortune and disorder in life. It is analogous to a wound that has become infected. (The plausibility for a demonic spiritual force will be dealt with later in this chapter as well as in Chapter 5.)

And if these people are accurate in their view that abortion is offensive to God, it would mean that most countries in the Western world which sanction this practice could be subject to corporate punishment, jeopardising the security of their people, just as David did with his people.

Dr McAll has extensive experience in this area and his conclusions are interesting. He says, 'Medical studies show us that a foetus from about fourteen weeks will have formed a memory area in the brain, which records sounds coming from its parents. This can be proved and the information retrieved in the adult life by the technique known as drug abreaction.' He cites a study of pre-natal experience which was presented in a paper in 1978 at Loyola University, in Chicago, by clinical psychologist Andrew Feldmar.[4] Patients were studied who annually attempted suicide and it was found that the dates, oddly enough, did not correlate to family deaths, holidays or any important event in their lives. Instead, it was the exact date that their mothers had unsuccessfully tried to abort them. Even more peculiar, the suicide method that was used (poisoning, stabbing with sharp instruments) corresponded to the device or procedure used by the mother.

From his studies, Feldmar was able to postulate that a person's memory could date from the time when the egg and sperm united – the moment of conception. Such research showed that the foetus may record memories even before the brain is formed at fourteen weeks.

Dr McAll continues: 'Medical studies also indicate that nicotine can cause hyperactivity in a child, and alcohol can cause mental retardation.' He finds it entirely plausible therefore to postulate that an unborn child could absorb prayer, and he relates the following story.

A woman who is at least five months pregnant can perform a test on herself to prove her baby's response to her love. When she places her right hand on the right side of her abdomen and her left hand on the left side, she can actually make the baby move under her right hand. To do this she simply imagines the baby under her right hand growing in strength and goodness, while being caressed by her touch. It will move to place its rounded back in the hollow of its mother's loving hand. If the mother then switches her loving concentration to her left hand, the child will move to do the same under that hand. If the mother does this little exercise daily, at a regular time, the child will kick if the 'love bath' is not forthcoming. Therefore, even the simple withdrawal of love can affect the foetus.

One of Dr McAll's most intriguing cases bears out Feldmar's findings.[5] Joan, a nine-year-old, was referred to Dr McAll by a general practitioner colleague. 'Before my first appointment with the child I studied the notes from her team of hospital doctors and the reports from her headmistress. At the age of five, Joan's sunny disposition changed suddenly. She became difficult to cope with and irrational, and she was finally diagnosed as an epileptic. Her mother was frightened and puzzled. She wrote to me, "When Joan goes into one of these states, her face becomes distorted and she will scream at me for minutes on end. She is so far from being her normal self that it makes me cold. The only way of dealing with the worst of these attacks is by prayer and then, after struggling and fighting even harder, she suddenly breaks down, comes willingly into my arms and sobs like a toddler. I feel completely inadequate to deal with her, and that is why we were wondering if we could come and see you." '

The child's headmistress shared this concern. She wrote, 'Joan easily loses her self-control and is given to outbursts of emotion. Her presentation of work leaves much to be desired and, even when copying, she makes innumerable mistakes, probably due to her inability to concentrate for more than a little while.'

Dr McAll continues, 'As I talked with Joan's parents, I searched for a pattern to her behaviour, but could not find one. They told me how the "attacks" had started suddenly when Joan was five and had fallen unconscious for no apparent reason. Many times since then she had injured herself and once she had split her chin open. Recently she had begun running out in front of cars, so her parents had to restrain her with reins for her own safety. Her father described how she would fight with the strength of an ox and would scream at him, "I hate you. You're not my daddy. Why was I ever born?" He also feared for his family's safety since, in one of her moods, Joan threatened her brother with a knife, demanding, "Tell me who you are." With just as much insistence she shouted, "I am not Joan."

'From the medical records it seemed to me that the doctors were doing all they could to help Joan, in terms of diet, drugs and other therapy. When we began to draw up the family tree, I explained that I was especially interested in discovering any one of the ancestors who had died without being committed to Jesus Christ, such as suicides. I seemed to have no success. From Joan's family tree it was apparent that, for the past four generations at least, there had been no such omission. Then we called Joan into the room. She sat on my knee and I asked her how many brothers and sisters she had. Her reply surprised me. "I have three brothers and three sisters," she said. "But Joan," I queried, "your mother says you have three brothers and only two sisters." Joan became extremely angry, jumped from my knee and stamped about, shouting, "I have three sisters, not two!" Pointing at her mother, she screamed, "Do you see that woman sitting over there? She is a murderer. She flushed my sister away down the closet. My sister is a close friend of mine. I know her. She's called Melissa."

'Joan's accused mother burst into tears and shouted, "Look out! She is going to have a fit!" Joan's father became red in the face and began to remonstrate with his wife. As they argued, I held Joan tight and said, "Let's just you and I pray to Jesus and ask him to look after Melissa and take her into his kingdom."

'It was obvious that Joan had hit a sore spot with her parents. Some time later, her mother told me that she had an accidental abortion through a doctor's rough handling, before Joan was born. She had not mentioned it when we drew up the family tree because her husband, Graham, had always denied that his wife had been pregnant on that occasion. At the time of the miscarriage they had been on holiday to help him recover from a nervous breakdown, and Joan's mother felt that her husband was too fragile to be forced to face the situation with her. She had never mentioned the incident to Joan, and no one knew the name she had wanted for the baby: Melissa.

'Since our spirit can be attentive to those who have died without being lovingly committed to Jesus Christ, it was not at all surprising that Joan knew about Melissa. Indeed, I had about 1,400 similar cases in my files. It seemed obvious that this uncommitted baby was the cause of Joan's difficulties and, perhaps, of the troublesome migraines from which her mother had suffered for years. We held a Eucharist for Melissa and the results changed that family's life. Joan's emotional outbursts, irrational behaviour and even her inability to concentrate all disappeared, never to return. Tests proved that her epilepsy was cured, and shortly afterwards she was taken off all drugs. Her mother's migraines were a thing of the past.'

The healing power of prayer and the Eucharist is further illustrated in the following story.[6] 'The Lancasters were concerned about three of their five children: the eldest was a drug addict, her sister was grossly overweight and the youngest child had been a thief since the age of seven. During questioning it emerged that three of the mother's pregnancies had gone awry and Elizabeth, the eldest child, was born after an abortion. Evelyn was born after a miscarriage, while Charles, the youngest, was adopted to replace a stillborn child. Since these three babies had never been committed to God, a Eucharist was celebrated, after which the whole family felt released. Elizabeth never touched drugs, Charles stopped stealing and Evelyn's weight returned to normal within three months.'

Dr McAll adds, 'It is important to name the baby. At a service for a premature baby boy who lived for only four hours and never had a funeral service, the baby's mother was bravely trying to thank our Lord for taking her little son home. She clearly heard, "No, you must first give him a name and show him that he has a mother's love and then commit him to me. Can a mother forget her infant? Even should she forget, I will never forget you. See upon the palms of my hands I have written your name." ' The words from the verse in Isaiah seem to hold true.

90

It is clear that in today's society many people – especially the young – are suffering from some kind of emotional or psychological disorder. A range of statistics reflects increasing problems in our offspring: adolescent psychiatric patients have increased by 350 per cent in the last decade; 10–20 per cent of young people are problem drinkers; eating disorders are rampant among teenagers; 65 per cent of all those who use street drugs have a parent who was addicted to drugs or alcohol. Many families are suffering daily, and they cannot ignore the problems, because every member is affected.[7]

Divorce seems to run in families. In southern California the divorce rate is as high as 65 per cent. It is now more than likely that if you get married, you will also get divorced. In a study of 1,100 British couples it was discovered that 49 per cent of women and 66 per cent of men were unfaithful. The children of parents who had extramarital affairs – even if that indiscretion was secret – were twice as likely to cheat on their spouses. And so a pattern begins to form.

Divorce is so common that people do not recognise it as a problem, in spite of the way it is causing the breakdown of our society. They accept it, just as they do many other supposedly 'minor' personality problems, which are passed off as idiosyncrasies. There are, however, many families who cannot ignore what is happening in their homes: they are suffering terribly, because one member is afflicted with profound problems that impinge on all their lives. These can range from depression or extreme nervousness to critical or negative attitudes, such as anger, bitterness and excessive fears, and to a weakness for overspending, gambling, drugs, alcohol and sexual perversion. But the family is baffled when a person suffers from such a problem, wondering how or why it has struck them. However, to confine investigations to the current family is far too limiting.

Only when we look closely at the history of a family can we discover the reason for present behavioural problems. Once we study past generations, we may well see how patterns of bad habits (and good traits, too, such as the gifts of music and art) are carried down through the ages, passed from one generation to the next. Then the previously impenetrable reasons for a person's poor behaviour become all too clear. More than that, the family tree offers not only the chance to explain that which has been inexplicable, but also the chance to heal, to break the bonds of the past.

How does transmission occur?

We each have twenty-three pairs of chromosomes, which are the basis of our heredity. And making up that code are billions of sub-units, which provide each of us with our unique genetic blueprint. One error can create a dysfunction that may result in disease. Some diseases are recessive, requiring two genes – one each from the mother and father – to become active (as in cystic fibrosis). You can be a carrier for the gene, which is passed on to your children, and if one day the husband or wife of that child is also a carrier, this then triggers the disease. Other diseases are dominant genetic disorders, whereby it takes only one copy of the gene to activate the disease. But the reasons for error are still a mystery to scientists.

Fortunately, bad genes are often eliminated over time. The eggs are unlikely to be fertilised if they or the sperm are defective. If they are, you may have a spontaneous abortion or, in some cases, a stillbirth. One-quarter of all physical ailments are thought to be genetically inherited.

There is a certain gene, located in the mitochondria (threadlike bodies in each cell), which is given to us by only our mother. Therefore certain genetic information is passed on to us from the maternal side of the family. If both emotional and physical characteristics are transmitted genetically, then we would suspect that certain characteristics – either good or bad – could only be transmitted from our mother.

Our genetic make-up is then modified by our environment. The surroundings in which we grew up, and the opportunities that we did or did not have, largely determine whether we develop our natural gifts, talents or abilities. This is what makes us unique – 'the forming or the malforming of the personality,' says Revd Hampsch. Scientists, sociologists and anthropologists have long studied these two basic components. They have found that the environment influences our desire to succeed and work, our sense of physical hostility, our need for intimacy and the amount of control the individual must have over his own environment. But 50 per cent of all personality traits are genetically inherited.

For example, one scientific study has shown that if his *grandfather* was a heavy drinker, a man is three times more likely than an average person to become an alcoholic. Furthermore, this particular form of alcoholism is apparently not reflected in the genetic structure. Similarly, according to Revd Hampsch, it has been found that biological parents who are criminals tend to produce children (even if they are given up for adoption from their early years) who exhibit the same criminal tendencies. On the other hand, if criminal parents adopt children from birth-parents who do not possess criminal tendencies, these children demonstrate very little criminal behaviour. While one might argue that these factors are environmental, experts here agree that the defective family environment is the avenue that allows ancestral disorders to be transmitted.

'The inherited factors we call nature, and the environmental factors we call nurture. The third element is often overlooked, which is spiritual heredity,' says Revd Hampsch. But how does the transmission of disease occur? After many years as a theologian and psychologist with extensive experience in this field, Revd Hampsch believes that God uses the genetic pool – or what is commonly referred to as 'bad blood' – to transmit a defect, which is either latent or exists merely in the form of a predisposition. The element that then triggers it is sin.

'When you have spiritual contamination from ancestral sin, many times you will see disorders and diseases that are passed on, either sequentially or non-sequentially. For example, if race prejudice is evident in the father and also in the children; or the mother is a manic depressive and so is the son; or atheism, divorce or suicide is passed directly down the line. Type-C alcoholism, where people become violent, is passed by the father and not the mother. Spiritual diseases can follow the same pattern,' Revd Hampsch says, 'especially when there is strong hatred, prejudice, occultism or witchcraft – you will see evidence of disorders that are passed on in this manner.'

Revd Hampsch refers to healing of the family tree as similar to transplanting a tree from a toxic dump site to rich, productive soil.

Disorders can be transmitted, sequentially or non-sequentially, through your direct line – which comprises parents, grandparents, great-grandparents – or through your horizontal or what is referred to as the consanguinial line – which comprises brothers, sisters, aunts, uncles, etc. The transmitted effect is greatest through the direct line, but all family members have an impact on us. Social and professional associates also play a moderate role, through what has been referred to as the clustering effect.

'The most powerful influences in the family tree are in the physical family tree, which uses the genetic structure as the vehicle for spiritual transmission. Usually that works within the natural family and therefore within the vertical line. But you can never discount the influences of your extended family or community,' he says. The Lord, in making the rules and regulations for us to live out our lives, was serious, it appears, about the consequences. 'If you really listen to the voice of your God and do what is right in his eyes: if you heed his commandments and keep his precepts, I will not inflict you with the diseases with which I inflicted the Egyptians; for I, the Lord, am your healer' (Exodus 16, 22–6).

The way to break the pattern, the ancestral bondage, is to have faith in God, 'who listens to our cry'. We have access to supernatural power, which not only forgives but heals, restoring us in body, mind and soul. 'By His wounds we are healed' (Isaiah 53, 4–5).

According to Revd Hampsch, 'non-sequential transmission' is often evidenced by depression in one generation, anxiety in the next, migraine headaches in the third and arthritis in the fourth. He says, 'In some cases the transmitted effect might skip a generation. In the area of drug addiction, this appears to be true. The children of those who smoke marijuana can have sleep disorders, nightmares, night terrors or apnoea. They may get it sooner or later, or it may skip a generation and the spiritual effects will contaminate the grandchildren. It can happen even if the children are born before the parents become addicted. This is spiritual transmission. These may be non-sequential transmissions, but they are very predictable.'

The bondage, which has been created through human error, we now understand can be healed. But what about those family members at a distance who would not understand this healing concept?

Dr McAll gives a remarkable example of how bondage can be broken and felt by family members in other parts of the world, further validating the nature of the problem as spiritual. He tells the story of Esther, a 70-year-old woman whose son, Samuel, was schizophrenic and in a hospital on the other side of the world.[8] From his symptoms, it soon became obvious that his disease was not due to a medical abnormality but was caused by his mother's lifelong influence over him. 'I suggested to her that we present the problem to Jesus and ask him to take control of both her and her son,' he says. 'As she was Jewish, this wasn't an easy concept for her and she needed time to think about it. She left me and went out into the night, greatly distressed. Suddenly, in the darkness, she saw before her a large, glowing crucifix. This could have been the result of her own imagination, as she turned over in her mind what we had been discussing. But she could not have imagined the voice of Jesus, which she heard. He told her clearly that she must release Samuel and also give herself to Him. She was compelled to accept Jesus in her heart and she also felt able to release her son. At that moment, on the other side of the world, Samuel, who had no knowledge of his mother's conversion, began to recover from his schizoid state, getting steadily better. Esther now calls herself a fulfilled Jew.'

This story seems to indicate the importance of the heart as a channel of healing. It is those strong feelings of love which are the conductors of God's grace. Revd Hampsch says that God needs the heart of the husband to heal the wife, and vice versa. He wants to borrow the heart of the children to love the parents, and the heart of the parents to love the children. (Remember: Pastor Simeon, in Chapter 1, said the same thing about the healing of babies and animals.)

There are two types of faith: one that we learn through the education taught to us by our parents, which is often reinforced in school or in our environment; the other is the type of faith that knows prayers will be answered – it is a supernatural 'gift', which only comes about through desire, which is then brought to fruition by prayer. This is the faith that believes, with absolute certainty, that what you ask for you will receive, if it is according to the will of God. This is the faith that accomplishes miracles. It is always best to pray for the 'right' outcome, or the 'right' job, etc. As Jesus said, 'Believe me, if you trust and do not falter, and you say to this mountain be lifted up and thrown into the sea, even that will happen. You will receive all that you pray for, provided you have faith' (Matthew 21, 21–2). 'If we experience the fact that God is listening to us,' says Revd Hampsch, 'we infallibly get an answer. You can't grit your teeth and say, "I'm going to be cured of cancer." It doesn't work that way. You have to pray, "Give me faith to believe I will be cured or I am cured of cancer." The charisma of faith enables us to be certain that what we ask for is going to happen, and you don't get that through willpower alone or by saying, "I believe, I believe, I believe." '

Revd Hampsch details five types of healing: spontaneous, gradual, phased, delayed and recurrent.[9] Spontaneous healing – in which tumours or the symptoms of a particular disease disappear in a matter of moments or hours – is the most infrequent form.

'Gradual healing usually begins at the time of prayer and continues over a period, from days to weeks or months. Phased healing, or "spurt" healing, occurs when a person has a series of partial healings at irregular intervals, a kind of step-healing, such as Jesus' healing of the blind man in two phases' (Mark 8, 25).

'Delayed healing, where nothing seems to happen at the time of prayer, becomes evident when there is remarkable improvement, or total healing, after a time lapse. One can nevertheless see the connection between prayer for healing and the healing itself, analogous to the act of the fig tree and its withering from the roots, recognised a day later' (Mark 11, 20).

Finally, recurrent healing is when, after a remarkable healing takes place, the effects may linger for quite a time, even years, and then a rclapse may occur. 'This often causes discouragement, and the person then needs to focus on the faith he or she did have to receive the temporary healing, in order to get through the relapse into permanent healing.'

Prayer is rarely answered instantaneously. 'Those familiar with the book of Daniel [10, 12–13] will know that his prayer was heard the first day, but was not answered until twenty-one days later. After prayer, however, you may notice that a burden is lifted and your spirit is lightened. This usually means the answer is assured, even though it is not yet manifested. It is in this compassionate ambience where prayer of the heart, and not of the mind, operates that God hears most readily, and which gets the most significant results.'

Preventative healing is probably the most important kind of all. There are many people who have cancer right now and do not know it until they feel pain. 'Then they come crying to God, "Heal me, heal me." They never pray in the pre-cancerous stages, and 65 per cent of those who have cancer will die of it,' says Revd

Hampsch. 'You may have enough faith to prevent cancer through prayer and other treatment, but you may not have enough faith to cure it, once you've got it. We make the mistake of only praying for a therapeutic cure once we have developed the disease. We don't pray preventatively, before the symptoms are manifested.'

Revd Hampsch and Dr McAll urge people to learn to pray preventatively for themselves, for their loved ones and to prevent future problems for their children and grandchildren. 'Prayers today may prevent your children from becoming crippled, or developing a severe allergy or becoming suicidal. This is the most neglected aspect of prayer. Preventative healing prevents a disease from happening. Much of this is done through our complex immune system, such as the thymus gland, which produces thyroxine and many chemical actions that kill off viruses and bacteria. If our immune system becomes weak, we are subject to different types of illnesses and allergies,' says Revd Hampsch.

As it says in Hosea, 'And they did not know I was healing them.' So the healing is continual.

Evil – getting beyond the myths

The question of evil is very complicated. It is a belief that causes embarrassment to many who believe in the concept of supernatural forces. Debunked by scientists, evil has commonly become known as the negative aspects of one's personality. But incidents continue to occur for which the only plausible explanation appears to be the 'spirit' theory. There have been many studies on the effects of the occult, poltergeist activity and hauntings, and it is obvious that, on occasions, these incidents can be passed off as nothing more than a figment of people's overactive imaginations. But sometimes this is not the case, and that is the point we are making here.

From a number of case studies it appears that the same demonic 'entity' can be responsible for inflicting depression, or more severe psychological problems, on people who use occult practices and can also cause poltergeist activity – objects that move around on their own. According to the experts, it is also this same demonic entity that can cause possession, as seen in the film *The Exorcist*, in which full-blown possession resulted after playing with the Ouija board.

97

It is only the manifestations which vary in degree that still remain a question. This area is referred to as the study of demonology.

Dr Scott Peck, psychologist and best-selling author of *The Road Less Travelled*, relates in his book *People of the Lie* the story of two exorcisms that he witnessed. He now believes in the devil. 'I've met "it",' he says. Here is the probing intellect of a scientist who, despite not being predisposed to religious theory, is convinced not only that Satan is real, but that there are probably many instances right before us when we are unable to recognise demonic forces. He gives one simple but profound truth as a guideline in distinguishing evil for ourselves: where there is a lie around, there is evil. The nature of a lie is deception. And this, according to many, is the agenda of Satan, who has been called the 'father of all lies'. It can start with human evil, which we clearly understand, and progress to something that is currently beyond the parameters of the medical profession to understand or heal.

For those people like myself and Dr Peck who have seen the manifestations of evil, it remains unforgettable. Once you have seen it, it is more than likely you will recognise it again and again. It is this lie and other more deceptive and abusive behaviour, which Revd Hampsch refers to as sin, that can act as a magnet for evil, creating transgenerational bondage. Revd Hampsch believes that the principles of demonology and healing of the family tree have a very close relationship: 'There is a constant overlap. These transgenerational spirits hang on and transmit these effects with God's permission.' But it is wrongful behaviour that initiates the process.

'As a test, God permitted Satan to attack Job, who was a righteous and holy man. Through the gift of virtue and fortitude, Job was able to cope with this spiritual warfare or these evil spirits. But one has to pray for this – and you will come out much better in the end, even if you go through as terrible a torment as Job endured.' Sometimes God has a plan for us, which we are unable to understand. And that plan can only be fulfilled through the strength created from suffering. If we strive to live pure lives, God will never abandon us during our trials.

Revd Hampsch argues that there is consistent evidence that evil can reimplant itself into successive generations, lodging in the blood-line, producing physical, psychological and moral deformities. These demons can superimpose themselves on every aspect of the human personality, with harmful manifestations that are then passed on to our descendants. Sin opens the door for the demonic to affect us – and, of course, our children.

But demonic forces cannot intervene, except where sin is present, either by the person himself or by his ancestor. Once the avenue is open for demonic intervention, contamination will continue until it is excised,' he says.

Both Dr McAll and Revd Hampsch agree that problems resulting from dabbling in the occult create the most tenacious form of evil and the most difficult to get rid of. What people today do not understand is that all mediumship, channelling, spirit guides, astrology, shamanism, Tarot cards, the *I Ching* and all forms of divination are strictly off-limits in the Bible. This dictate was given in the Old Testament and done for good reason, to protect us from the deceptive and dangerous interface with evil. Today most people believe that this notion of evil is scientifically unfeasible – and therefore intellectually embarrassing – totally fraudulent or just a bit of fun. Whatever the case, the occult business has become close to a billion-dollar industry.

Until you understand the nature of evil, you cannot understand that these occult techniques invite spirit contact and, in some cases, possession. The popular belief that our intuitive capacity can be enhanced by occult practices is mistaken. Tarot cards or an astrological chart act as contact material, similar to a magnet, attracting evil spirits. The problem is that when you invite evil into your life through the occult, if you are persistent, sooner or later it will turn up. There are countless case studies in which spirits have taken over people's minds, enabling them to speak different languages or to reel off impressive scientific principles, which they clearly knew nothing about. In one case (see Chapter 5), the blood pressure, heartbeat and all the vital statistics of a woman indicated that a completely foreign entity was inhabiting her. This is a serious business.

The type of activity and the frequency with which it is practised will often indicate the level of interface with the demonic and the potential for resulting problems. Just because your symptoms are negligible or even seemingly unapparent, this does not mean that the bondage does not exist. You simply have not done enough self-examination. If you are dabbling in the occult consistently, you are a victim and there is no escape. It is like being exposed to the HIV virus. And unfortunately it can affect your children, your prosperity, your mental and sometimes even your physical health.

I have devoted a whole chapter to tracing the effects of evil (see Chapter 5). I advise anyone dabbling in the occult to read it carefully. I am quite passionate about broadcasting the truth, because I myself was a victim of the occult and I know how long it took me to extract myself from its web. Your intentions can be pure, but evil is subtle and the deception is shrewd.

Patricia (whose surname I will not reveal, because she is somewhat embarrassed by this story) had been suffering from three generations of occult activity. Yet for decades she did not realise it. She grew up a Catholic and her mother was from the old school, refusing to believe in supernatural forces. She used to see fortune tellers occasionally, but without taking it seriously. When Patricia was a child, her mother bought her a Ouija board, which Patricia played, along with her friends. Eventually Patricia married and had a family. One day her husband came home from a trade-show convention with trinkets, which he gave to their youngest daughter, Anne, who was around ten at the time. One was a set of Tarot cards, which she played with her friends. Within a short time members of the family noticed that Anne had become skilled at the game.

This sounds harmless enough and Patricia was a good, religious mother. But she was totally unaware that her mother had cultivated contact with the demonic and had then passed it on to Patricia with the Ouija board which was then passed to Anne in the Tarot. Later Patricia developed cancer, but fortunately she was miraculously healed, thanks to her strong faith and the mercy of God. But one wonders whether evil could have interfaced with her weakness. Later still she discovered the demonic overlap with occult activities, but by then it was too late for her daughter. Anne had started to hear voices and consequently diagnosed as a schizophrenic. In her late teens she had a breakdown. Anne felt compelled to take a colourful picture that hung in her bedroom off the wall. Her mother asked her why she was so insistent about removing the picture, since it went so well with the room? Anne did not know why – she just felt strongly that she had to get it out of there. Only later, when Patricia looked at it closely, did she realise that it was a picture of a deck of Tarot cards. Subconsciously, this young girl recognised the source of her downfall. Tarot cards are a strong conduit for evil. This seemingly harmless game can have devastating effects. It can cause a slow disintegration of your personality and your self-identity, or depression and suicidal tendencies. In my opinion the younger you begin, the firmer 'its' grip becomes. Patricia had several masses said for healing the family tree and Anne's 'voices' subsided for a few years. But she still has problems. It takes consistent and dedicated efforts to rid yourself of such a powerful and destructive force.

Patricia's mother has since died, never understanding the harm that she caused her family or acknowledging the offensive behaviour of occult activities. And maybe that lack of repentance on the part of her deceased grandmother is perpetuating the problems two generations later, in Anne. She just cannot seem to get free of it. The pattern was subtle, and the demonic had successfully woven itself into an unsuspecting middle-class family. But the realm of the demonic needed an entrée and that door opened with the apparently harmless fun of fortune-tellers and the Tarot.

Revd Hampsch relates another story, of a man who had a problem with alcohol. George wanted to overcome this problem and had tried everything: proper nutrition; taking certain vitamins in which alcoholics are said to be deficient; he went to Alcoholics Anonymous, which is known to be the most effective treatment and has helped many. He also underwent therapy. George was very determined and he exhausted every possible idea or suggestion for help, but the urge just would not stop.

Then someone told him about a theory that alcoholism could be a spiritual problem. An evil spirit might be responsible for taking advantage of George's weakness or predisposition, and that was why he could not kick the habit – which, incidentally, AA refers to as a 'predator'. His friend told him to imagine it as a bacteria, which takes advantage of an open wound to create an infection. Sceptical, but willing to try anything, George accepted the idea of being prayed for by Revd Hampsch. Neither knew for certain that an evil spirit might be bothering George, but Revd Hampsch took a chance and said, 'In case there are any demonic forces . . . any addiction . . . any alcoholism . . . I command it to leave, in the Name of Jesus.' Afterwards he asked George how he felt. George answered, 'The same.' Revd Hampsch replied, 'Well, I hope it works for you.' And they went their separate ways.

A year later George ran into Revd Hampsch and told him, 'You know, Father, since that day I haven't touched a drop of alcohol. Once I even took a swig of whisky, just to see how I would respond. I had to spit it out, it tasted so horrible. I guess I am cured.'

Evil is a subject that, for the most part, has been totally discarded by society. People have for so long been educated in disbelief, but it is time for this subject to be evaluated in the light of day, so that people are aware of all the facts. We do not need to continue suffering from being left in the dark. In 1 Corinthians, 10, 21, Paul says, 'You can't drink from the cup of the Lord and the cup of demons too. You cannot have a part in both the Lord's table and the table of demons.' Which means that you cannot dabble in the occult and receive God's blessing, or even expect to remain problem-free.

Release of the 'unquiet dead'

Another area about which many people are curious, but do not fully understand the available theories, is ghosts. Both of our experts agree that ghosts are disembodied spirits, who often hound more spiritually sensitive people. Dr McAll has become rather infamous for his knowledge in the field. He has sixty-five recorded cases of hauntings that have ceased through prayer. These are not the common occurrences seen only by one person, but happenings observed by various stable people, in which they have witnessed objects being moved without human volition. He says, 'Having considered all possible explanations – mass hallucination by psychic contagion, occult involvement or psychiatric imbalance – it seems clear that there is a simple explanation. The ghost which is haunting a place may be a dead person needing prayer. If it is treated as such, I have never found an objective haunting to continue.'

Dr McAll tells of a remarkable incident that occurred in the Bermuda Triangle (an area of the Atlantic Ocean between Bermuda, Florida and Puerto Rico), which was reputed to swallow up ships and aircraft, often without trace. Most sailors, and many passengers, prefer to avoid the place. But in 1972 Dr McAll and his wife found themselves sailing through the triangle. 'We were on a banana boat when we were caught in a force-nine storm. We headed away from it, south, into the infamous Sargasso Sea. There one of the ship's boilers burst, leaving us silently drifting.

'In the quietness, my wife and I both distinctly heard a strange sound, like a steady, droning dirge, which continued throughout the day and night. At first we thought it was the Jamaican crew, but after checking we realised that they couldn't have been responsible. Then I found a magazine containing diagrams of the old slave ships which used this run, with details of how almost two million slaves were thrown overboard. The number of these undesirable or unsaleable slaves in the West Indies or America increased rapidly as they neared their destination, for conditions on board the slave ships deteriorated even further as the voyage progressed. The merchants often collected more money through their insurance for "lost" slaves than by selling them in Virginia.

'After returning home to England, it occurred to us that maybe we had heard that mournful dirge for a purpose. Perhaps we had a responsibility to pray for those wretched slaves who died uncommitted to the Lord, and to repent of the cruelty of those who were the cause of it.'

In July 1977, by certain interested bishops, a Jubilee Eucharist was celebrated at various places throughout England for the specific release of all those who had met their untimely deaths in the Bermuda Triangle. Some months later, in Bermuda itself, two Anglican bishops offered the same prayers. The curse of the dreaded place was lifted. 'From the time of the celebrated Eucharist until now, as far as I know, no new inexplicable accidents have occurred in the Bermuda Triangle. Perhaps evil forces are building up again even now in that place, and an accident or disappearance may occur, but we are certain that prayer is the weapon to destroy such evil and break such a force.

'Many authorities are convinced of the possibility of releasing places haunted by the unquiet dead. Prayers have been said where there have been a number of inexplicable or unusual accidents and, invariably, the evil curse is broken. At a particular site in Dorset, on which there were neither dangerous nor hidden intersections, it was found that there had been seventeen accidents on that part of the road. After prayer, in the subsequent six months, there was not one single accident,' says Dr McAll.

Notes

1. *Healing the Family Tree*, Dr Kenneth McAll, Sheldon Press, London, 1982.

Dr Kenneth McAll was raised in a family of congregational missionaries, educated as a surgeon at Edinburgh University and then chose the perilous fields of north China, during the Sino-Japanese war, as his first practice. It was there that he had an experience that was to change his life and he believes that his life was saved by the direct intervention of Jesus. In spite of his advanced years he travels extensively throughout the world to give lectures.

2.   *Healing Your Family Tree*, Revd John J. Hampsch CMF, Our Sunday Visitor, Huntington, Indiana, 1986. Audio tapes available through Claretian Tape Ministry, PO Box 19100, Los Angeles CA 90019.

Revd John Hampsch was ordained a Catholic priest in 1952 and is now a member of the Claretian Missionaries. He has served as a parish priest, seminary professor, college professor, lecturer, editor and newspaper columnist. He earned degrees in philosophy from Loyola Marymount University in Los Angeles and from Notre Dame University, with post-graduate work at the University of California. He taught psychology for twelve years in three universities and is a psychological consultant for NBC television network.

3.   Op. cit., note 1, pp. 41–3.
4.   'Embryos can remember, therapists say,' by Andrew Feldmar, *Chicago Tribune*, 1 November 1978.
5.   Op. cit., note 1, pp. 50–52.
6.   Ibid., p. 57.
7.   Op. cit., note 2.
8.   Op. cit., note 1, p. 16.
9.   Op. cit., note 2.

4

Apparitions and Prophecy

Throughout the twentieth century there has been a global upsurge of interest in the Virgin Mary, with countless thousands claiming to have seen visions of her. Apparitions of this beautiful woman, usually holding a child, and variously called Our Lady, the Blessed Mother and Madonna, have been recorded at more than 300 places in 200 countries. People have responded to these events in unprecedented numbers. Young and old, fit and failing, believers and even sceptical non-believers have flocked to the apparition sites in search of inner peace or a miraculous experience. They have rarely been disappointed, because the apparitions have frequently been associated with inexplicable healing or supernatural events: cures for the sick, statues that weep tears of oil or blood, solar phenomena and numerous other manifestations. Most importantly, they invariably involve prophecy, in which the Virgin is seeking to pass on to mankind messages that may affect the future of the world.

While many argue that these apparitions are nothing more than hysteria among the needy, or due to the vivid imaginations of the hopeful, the totality of the evidence is compelling. But it is right to be cautious when confronted by supernatural experiences. Even the most intelligent of believers may be open to deception – whether out of a desperate desire to believe something has happened, when it has not, or because of deliberate fakery by someone with a hostile agenda. With as many as 70 per cent of us claiming to have had a spiritual experience, it is not good enough simply to go with the flow: we must evaluate what is genuine from what is either delusion or deception. We have to realise how errors in reporting can lead to difficulties in interpretation.

Problems have developed in the past when visionaries have reported their experiences. The intensity of the inevitable interrogation, which is part of the evaluation process, has often resembled brainwashing and has proved severe enough to confuse anyone. It is also obvious that many people who experience visions inject their own opinions (often unconsciously), so tainting the divine message. For this reason, obtaining the facts is crucial.

Some of the greatest figures in history, like Joan of Arc, did not get it all right. She became confused during her interrogators' continual intimidation and claimed that she would be saved from death. Yet she was executed as a witch in a court ruling by the Church, which was then upheld by the University of Paris. It was not until twenty years later that she was exonerated and eventually canonised. In the twentieth century, some 500 years after her death, one of the world's greatest statesmen, Winston Churchill, called her the purest figure in European history. He recognised that the strength of Joan's supernatural experience had changed Europe for ever.

Veneration of the Virgin Mary as the mother of Jesus, the son of God, stretches back to the earliest days of the Christian Church. However, the Virgin's role has long been the subject of controversy. The Roman Catholic view, much disputed by most of the Protestant Churches, is that Mary, due to her special position, may well have been given extraordinary intercessory powers on behalf of the sick and needy before both God and her Son. While not having power in her own right, she is said to be a mediatrix of heavenly blessings, the impetus of healing of both body and soul.

It is the growing belief in these powers that has caused the devout, as well as the curious, to flock to the sites of her appearances. Many pilgrims then return home with a passionate desire to do something good for the world. Many have been healed of debilitating diseases or have witnessed strange solar phenomena, or have been profoundly moved by their visit. The majority report afterwards that their lives have changed for the better.

In Lourdes, France, the Virgin Mary appeared to Bernadette in

1858 and told the peasant girl the location of a spring where the waters would heal the sick. Now about 5.5 million people travel to Lourdes each year in search of the miraculous. The Virgin Mary's appearance in Fatima, Portugal, in 1917, which began the wave of prophecy during the twentieth century, now draws some 4.5 million visitors every year. An estimated 1.5 million a year turn up in the village of Knock, Ireland, where she appeared to fifteen people in 1879. And in Czestochowa, Poland, where she appeared as the Black Madonna, attendance has grown to 5 million annually. Yet, Medjugorje in Bosnia, a small village of just 500, has seen more activity than all the other apparition sites put together. Since 1981, when Mary appeared to six children, more than 20 million people have visited this remote village which, curiously, was never touched as the civil war raged around it.

Now it is possible to find a branch of the Marian movement in every major city in the Western world. Some 300 Medjugorje groups across America publish dozens of newsletters and its conferences are attended by up to 10,000 people at a time. She comes, Marianists insist, as a sign of God's mercy. They argue that she negotiates miracles in order to authenticate her consistent message that we on earth must change our lives. We should stop living for the moment, turn aside from gratifying the flesh and give up indulging in selfishness. Her messages warn that if we do not, then we are on a fast track towards destruction. If we choose to ignore her alarm, we could live to regret it.

Some people, without even visiting the Virgin's shrines, have responded to her forewarning by praying, fasting and examining their own consciences. They, in turn, have been rewarded by instances of miraculous healing. Fintan O'Neil, after thirty years as an alcoholic, heard the Medjugorje message and was so moved that he got down on his knees and asked God to forgive him and take away his thirst for alcohol. Without counselling, without help from Alcoholics Anonymous, he was cured. Similarly, once Rita Claus heard the message, she prayed to the Virgin alone at home in her bed and was able to walk, after spending twenty-six years in a wheelchair with multiple sclerosis.

Hundreds more, who have been moved by the Virgin's injunctions to pray for world peace, have reported their rosaries mysteriously turning to the colour of gold. Protestants who disapprove of Mary's veneration refer to this as necromancy – the calling up of the spirits of the dead, which is strictly off-limits in the Bible. Some denominations also object to the Catholic view that she is the Mother of God, which has influenced many Christians to ignore one of history's most significant and verifiable supernatural stories.

But even within the Catholic Church there is an undeniable reservation about the veracity of her apparitions. The hierarchy is assiduous in investigating all claims, often assigning bishops who are predisposed not to believe. They are stringent in their evaluations before authenticating visions, as in Medjugorje, which has not yet been officially approved, in spite of being, after seventeen years, the longest-running recorded apparition. The local bishop, right up to his death, remained adamantly opposed. Many of the clergy cannot come to terms with the fact that the Virgin Mary appears to the most unlikely of people, rather than to those dedicated to God's service. But Marianists point out that it is perfectly logical for her to choose to communicate directly with those who are the purest among us: children.

Unfortunately, the unique Marian story remains largely hidden in present society, mainly due to the media's distorted news values. So the vast majority of the population is unaware of the truth and unable to determine whether this heavenly visitor is God's messenger. Here, then, is an opportunity for you to examine the facts. Beginning with Lourdes, we will make a brief tour of the main apparition sites, and the extraordinary phenomena associated with each, before examining in some detail the most recent and most significant site, Medjugorje, which has created a spiritual fervour now spanning the globe. In the barrage of claims of apparitions, it is crucial to delineate fact from fiction in order to determine the truth. For every real apparition there are probably dozens of fakes, but that should not imply that the whole concept is a hoax. The genuine article, after enduring sufficient scrutiny, may have profound significance for us. Finally, we will consider the importance of Mary's prophecy and how it has recently been shown to overlap with what scientists are saying about the vulnerability of our planet.

Lourdes: The beginning with Bernadette

The story of Bernadette Soubirous is familiar to many. Yet the surrounding evidence of supernatural manifestations is still largely unknown. As a 14-year-old illiterate girl from a peasant background, Bernadette was so poor that the family once lived in an empty prison cell. But from the events in her life it becomes obvious that heaven is not concerned with material success or education, but rather with the heart.

As she was gathering wood by the River Gave, Bernadette heard a 'sound like a breeze' and saw in the mouth of the grotto something white, almost her own size, surrounded with light. The Virgin Mary appeared eighteen times between February and July 1858, and referred to herself as the Immaculate Conception.

Reports of the experience provoked widespread controversy in the area, even though Bernadette was just a young girl. But she reacted bravely to the intimidation tactics of the police. After the local mayor questioned her, he decided to shut the grotto, because he felt it was creating too much disturbance among the people. The prefect of Tarbes accused Bernadette of being mad. Her parish priest decided that a little authority and a few smacks would help her rethink her embarrassing and most unlikely tale. But Bernadette remained unyielding in her convictions. The little peasant girl could not be persuaded or manipulated to change her story. During this time, there were some 200 reports of visions of the Virgin Mary (all later proved to be fake), and it was not until four years after the fact that Bishop Laurence of Tarbes pronounced officially, 'We believe that Mary Immaculate, Mother of God, really appeared to Bernadette.'

Bernadette spent the last twelve years of her life in a convent. Her humility was summed up when she said, 'I served the Virgin Mary as a simple broom. When she no longer had any use for me, she put me back in my place behind the door.'

After continuing to review the evidence and her testimony, the Church slowly came to view Bernadette's vision with respect and consequently exhumed her body for investigation ten years after her death. Much to their amazement, they found that the body had not decayed and did not have the characteristic odour of death. Again in 1909, thirty years after her death, Bernadette's body was exhumed for canonisation and was found to be without decay. Church officials observed the same effect yet again in 1925, some forty-six years after her death.

On that occasion, Bernadette's body was examined by Church officials, police officials and two surgeons. The most striking detail was the lack of decomposition in her liver, a delicate organ that should have calcified rapidly after her death. Science, to this day, has no answer to account for these unusual circumstances. Remarkably, this is not an isolated incident. According to the Vatican, there have been other occurrences in history of those canonised who maintained full composition after death. But the Catholic Church, in its prudence, denies the miraculous. Will it wait until the day science has the answer?

Lourdes: A history of miracles

Even sceptics admit that remarkable things happen in Lourdes. After one visit, the Nobel Laureate Alexis Carrel (1873–1944) – the surgeon and scientist whose work on blood vessels paved the way for organ transplantation – was converted from militant atheism. Many less famous people have had similar experiences. More than 6,000 people have claimed miraculous cures after visiting the shrine or being immersed in the spring waters. Of these cures, 3,500 are considered inexplicable by scientists and doctors at the Lourdes Medical Bureau, but only sixty-five have officially been declared miracles by the Vatican.

To satisfy the Medical Bureau's panel of doctors (comprising both believers and non-believers), a cure must be sudden and, usually, five years must pass before it is reviewed. The illness must have been serious and organic, and it must be documented by methods such as X-ray or a biopsy. Under the bureau's rules, illnesses stemming from an injury caused by an accident are rejected. For instance, speech loss following a cerebral lesion cannot be taken into account. Similarly, any illnesses that might have a psychosomatic origin, such as ulcers, allergies or nervous disorders, have no chance of recognition.

These hurdles of proof are difficult to surmount. 'Out of the fifteen or so declarations that I come across every year, I have opened only five files,' says Dr Roger Pilon, head of the Lourdes Medical Bureau. These five cures have been subjected to several years of examination, counter-examination and re-examination by experts. The bureau calls on all the resources of science to discover whether a claimed miracle might have a natural explanation. Was the illness really incurable? Has it been completely cured? Could the cure be due to an emotional shock? Only when he is sure of having exhausted all possible objections does Dr Pilon submit the case to an international committee of around forty doctors, who meet once a year in Paris under the chairmanship of the Bishop of Lourdes. Further objections are presented and further examinations demanded. Cures that stand up to such testing are rare. Once cases are ruled to be medically inexplicable they then go on to the next stage: submission to the diocesan bishop in the home district of the 'miraculously cured' person. The bishop then orders a canonical inquiry, causing yet another delay, which can last several years.

Over the past twenty years, only nine cases of verified cures have been passed on to the bishops by the international medical committee. Of these, just three have been proclaimed miraculous. Ten cases are presently being studied by the international committee, which is withholding comment until, and if, they conclude that these are really 'Lourdes cures'. Sometimes the doctors reserve their judgement. Dr Pilon explains, 'Who knows? Science may one day be able to explain phenomena that are still mysterious today. There are so many new remedies continuously appearing to cure diseases that had been deemed incurable.'

The last miracle to be recognised was that of a Sicilian girl, Delizia Cirolli, who had suffered from a malignant tumour of the tibia (shinbone) since the age of twelve. Although cured in 1976, the miracle was not officially declared until 1989, by which time she had been examined on six occasions by doctors in Lourdes. In 1988 Joseph Charpentier, an electrician from the Moselle region of France, suddenly regained the use of his legs after nineteen years in a wheelchair. His cure, while visiting Lourdes for the sixteenth time, is still undergoing medical and ecclesiastical checks. He did not register his case with the Medical Bureau until prompted by the Social Security authorities, who removed his invalid pension without waiting for the medical verdict.

But many believe that Jacques Salaun's cure could well become the sixty-sixth 'official miracle'. For sixteen years M. Salaun had been suffering from a progressive form of multiple sclerosis, which gradually paralysed his forearms and stiffened his legs. He could do nothing for himself. His work as a wood-turner was out of the question. His son had to carry him from his wheelchair to his bed. Lourdes, he felt, was his only hope, and he made two visits there from his village near Chartres, south-west of Paris.

The 58-year-old man bathed in the pools along the Gave River and was immersed in ice water, one of several thousand hopefuls to do so each year.

He explained, 'I felt I needed to be plunged twice in the Lourdes swimming pool. Usually it is only once, but I felt it had to be twice. A woman let me go before her. In the water I didn't feel anything special.' So M. Salaun took the train back home. 'The following morning I prayed before getting up,' he said. 'Then I saw a dark-haired woman, the Virgin, barefoot with a little smile. She said to me, "Get up." I felt something strange running from the base of my spine to the nape of my neck, as if I was being crushed. I could feel heat from top to toe. I was burning and I felt ill. I looked at my hands. Before they were paralysed and without any strength and the left one was curved, but now they were both straight and normal. I said, "It's not possible." Then I got up and walked without a stick to the living room. I was shaking, my hands like a puppet, lifting my legs in the air without any pain. Everything was working, I walked normally without any pain. The first thing I did, I don't know why, was to cut slices of bread and make breakfast for my wife.'

His wife, Jacqueline, was overwhelmed. Their son, awakened by their shouts of excitement, walked in to see his father shaking his arms. He rushed to embrace him, weeping. It was the first time in his life he had seen his father filled with so much life. In the afternoon Jacques Salaun set off on his bicycle with his daughter, passing neighbours, who could not believe their eyes. 'It's not for us to say whether this is a case of divine intervention but, for the moment, this healing cannot be explained,' stated the village curate.

So will Jacques Salaun's cure be validated? It is not a question that preoccupies him. He sees his healing as a personal sign. If it is recognised, it will be even more of a rarity than those in the past. And what does Dr Pilon, head of the Lourdes Medical Bureau, think about miracles? 'It is not faith that produces miracles, but faith that recognises them.'[1]

The dangers of apparitions

It is a reasonable rule of thumb never to accept all that we are told at face value, even if we are the kind of people who like to think the best of others. Needless to say, this is even more true when considering supernatural experiences. How then do we decide what is true and what is false? Leading theologian and author, Father Benedict Groeschel, has grappled with this thorny subject and come up with a sensible set of criteria in order to separate the fakes and fraudulent claims from those that are genuine.[2]

We should keep this advice in mind when evaluating all reports of the supernatural. This is important in a wider context because sceptics are reinforced in their negative and antagonistic views whenever deceptions are revealed. These fakes enable the media to poke fun, so diverting people's attention from God's real works.

Groeschel is at pains to point out the central difficulty in obtaining a completely unbiased report from a person who sees an apparition. He explains, 'No divine revelation is immediately received by a visionary. It is filtered through the perceptive faculties of the human being who receives it.' An old Latin proverb illustrates the point perfectly: 'That which is received is received in the manner of the receiver.' Or, to quote one excellent analogy, when light passes through a glass prism, pure white light is distorted into a rainbow of colours. This may well be beautiful, but our perception is changed.[3]

Groeschel continues, 'What we see and hear is filtered through our individual make-up, taking into account our previous experience, our own expectations and the quality of our education (and consequent limitations of knowledge and, most importantly, language). Every individual's frame of reference is therefore slightly different.'[4]

To illustrate his point, he offers the example of Catherine Laboure, who had little formal education yet was able to predict the bloody disturbances of the French Commune forty years before they occurred and with their precise date. But she also made several other predictions that did not occur as she pronounced. When confronted with these errors, she simply apologised for getting the facts of the revelation wrong. She obviously did not know what to say since, as far as she was concerned, she thought she had got the message right. 'This admission of simply "getting it wrong" on the part of this simple visionary is something one should never forget,' says Groeschel.[5]

Before we continue, let us make an important distinction here:

113

a 'false revelation' is one that the visionary genuinely believes to be supernatural, but this turns out not to be the case. A 'fake revelation' is a lie, knowingly made up by someone. It is grossly unfair to label the tendency of visionaries to confuse or inflate their subjective expectations and preconceived ideas with the action of divine grace as fraudulent. Even if misguided, they remain sincere.

So what are the possible causes of false revelations? Severe mental illness, especially a certain kind of paranoid schizophrenia, is certainly a common one. According to Groeschel, any person suffering such problems is highly likely to conceive 'a grandiose need to make some monumental contribution to history'.[6] It is also possible that they might suffer from hallucinatory experiences. They are, in other words, deluding themselves. That is not a problem for the rest of us unless they get into a position to manipulate other people, assuming a messianic status based on the shaky foundations of their delusions.

Witness television preachers. As Groeschel points out, many of these unbalanced individuals influence millions of weak-minded people. Their 'needs for notoriety and power, combined with a charismatic personality, are capable of gaining great attention and support'.[7] They are different from religious charlatans, who know all too well that they are engaged in fraudulent activity. Preachers sincerely, but misguidedly, believe that they have been specially selected by God to spread the word.

False revelations may also arise from sincerely devout people, says Groeschel. 'Combined with a suggestive type of personality, they are clinically called borderline histrionic.'[8]

Now let us consider the perils of religious frauds, men and women who set out to deceive other people who, for one reason or another, are predisposed to believe them. Frauds have as long a history as Christianity. One of the most notorious frauds, the sixteenth-century Franciscan nun, Magdalena of the Cross, enjoyed an unrivalled reputation for holiness. She fooled people into believing that she suffered the stigmata, could levitate, went into ecstasies and had the gift of prophecy. She even convinced people that she lived without food. The high and mighty – along with disbelieving inquisitors – flocked to meet her. She deluded them all. It was not until she was facing death that she confessed, admitting that she had inflicted the stigmata on

114

herself. She had sold her soul to Satan, she said, and later underwent an exorcism.[9]

Frauds still flourish in modern times. About twenty-five years ago an Irish man gained a lot of attention when he claimed that, on entering a church, the crucifix and occasionally a statue would bleed. Medical tests proved that it was real blood mixed with saliva. But he eventually confessed that it was all a trick. He would bite the vein under his lips and surreptitiously spit at the statue while people were looking at it. As Groeschel bitterly points out, perhaps we should not be surprised that, having lost his position as a pseudo-mystic, this man was later reported to have become an evangelist in America.

Frauds aside, devout people can all too often deceive themselves. They convince themselves that God is giving them extraordinary signs. This mistaken belief is often fed by their own insecurity due, perhaps, to uncertain times (such as war) or their own domestic problems. Many have a profound need to find God and this understandable hunger for a religious experience may, given the wrong conditions, give rise to vivid experiences that seem to the individual to have their origin completely outside their being. Groeschel warns that one has only to scan the biographies of the founders of great religions of the world to realise that they were all motivated by, and usually engulfed by, what we are calling private revelation.

Groeschel concludes, 'I believe that the loving, divine Being does use private revelation for the purpose of encouragement . . . I also believe that the Lord can send warnings to an age that certainly could use plenty of warning. I think it is the height of incredible opacity to reject a reported revelation simply because one does not agree with its content, so long as it is not doctrinally erroneous or, clearly, mentally unbalanced. God has never consulted men, nor is there any evidence that Christ fitted his teaching to what people wanted to hear.'[10]

Fatima: The dance of the sun

In Fatima, Portugal, the Virgin Mary appeared to three young children: Lucia (ten), Francisco (nine) and Jacinta (seven), on 13 May 1917. She appeared numerous times to the children, always preceded by angels, who were visible only to the children.

Rumours of the apparitions spread quickly and some people ridiculed the children, treating their claims with the same kind of scepticism that Bernadette had faced. The fearful children begged the Virgin to give them proof, to persuade the sceptics, and so she promised to send them a sign.

Then, as predicted, at twelve noon on 13 October 1917, 70,000 people drenched by a downpour witnessed a solar miracle. A dancing sun began to make its way closer to the earth, looking like a ball of fire about to plunge from the sky. People began to panic, in fear for their lives. The phenomenon lasted for twelve minutes and instantly dried the soaked clothing of all those present, turning the mud to dust. This was indeed proof for everyone of the authenticity of the apparitions, and news of it spread quickly throughout Europe. People felt they now had to listen to what this beautiful lady had to say, and so began the wave of prophecy that has continued to this day.

The Virgin told the visionaries about the coming of Communism to Russia, which would then spread throughout the world. Identifying herself as Our Lady of the Rosary, she said that prayer was crucial to head off the wrath of God, his patience for the errors of an unbelieving people was growing thin. As our prayer goes up, God's mercy is poured upon us. She told them that fasting could suspend the laws of nature. And the prayer of the rosary was a vital weapon against the tactics of Satan, who was perpetrating destruction in the world.

It appears that the Virgin made it very clear to Lucia, who has since become a nun, that she herself is in a decisive, final battle with Satan. She had come to the world to plead with people to turn back to Jesus, who is known to Christians as the way, the truth and the life. Mary had been sent by God as His last warning before He chastises us for having lost our way.

In her predictions, the Virgin told of a second world war and the destruction of various nations if her message was not heeded. Marianists point out the significance of the nuclear arms threat created at the hands of the Soviet Union and the glaring potential for destruction, which was inconceivable at the time of the prediction. The Virgin went on to tell of God's punishment of the world through war, hunger and persecution of the Pope and the faithful. She told of a great sign that would usher in a new period – one that would bring a great war.

116

According to Sister Lucia, that sign was the light that lit up the sky on 27 June 1938. It was explained away as the aurora borealis (the northern lights), but Europe was on the brink of war and it was not long before Hitler's troops marched into Poland. Michael Brown, author of *The Final Hour* and many other excellent Marian books, says, 'This is how God works, not with Hollywood-style miracles, but with signs that are an inch above natural phenomena and all the more wondrous for their naturalness and subtlety.'[11]

But never was the power of Mary's message more obvious than on 6 August 1945, during the nuclear explosion at Hiroshima. A German Jesuit and seven of his colleagues were living only eight streets away from the epicentre, yet they escaped the death that claimed everyone around them. Over 200 scientists have examined these survivors, trying without success to determine a rational explanation as to why they lived. The survivors claim that it was the prayer which the Virgin requested at Fatima that saved them.

The importance of the rosary

By referring to herself at Fatima as Our Lady of the Rosary, the Virgin was stressing the importance of that prayer, which has figured in almost all the apparitions during the last century. In one sense, the rosary is merely a simple form of prayer used by Roman Catholics, but Marianists believe it is invested with a special significance. One of its first and most controversial supporters was St Louis de Montfort. He was accused of provoking innocent people by those who thought devotion to Mary was idol worship. De Montfort argued that it was easier to become a saint by imitating the life of Mary, because she was the most perfect example of saying yes to the will of God.

Even Catholics at the time doubted him when he said, 'The rosary gives marvellous spiritual fertility, so one can grow in all virtues.' The more the soul is watered with this prayer, he said, the more enlightened one's intellect becomes, the more zealous one's heart and the stronger one's armour against spiritual enemies. St Augustine was also emphatic about his feeling for the rosary: 'There is no spiritual exercise more fruitful or more useful to our salvation than continually turning our thoughts to the

117

suffering of our Lord.' The rosary is a prayer of meditation on those intriguing mysteries.

One of the most famous historical examples of the power of the rosary is that of Blanche of Castile, Queen of France. Before her husband Louis VIII inherited the throne in 1223, she was deeply upset because, after twelve years of marriage, she was still childless. When Friar Dominic (later St Dominic) came to see her, he advised her to say the rosary and ask God for the grace of motherhood. She faithfully carried out his advice and in 1213 gave birth to a son, Philip, but unfortunately the child died in infancy.

The Queen's enthusiasm was not dulled by this disappointment. She sought Our Lady's help more than ever before. She distributed a large number of rosaries to courtiers and to people in several cities of the kingdom, asking them to join her in entreating God for another blessing. In 1215 Louis was born, the prince who was to become the glory of France, the model of all Christian kings, who was canonised soon after his death.[12]

St Dominic and the rosary also played a pivotal role in the fortunes of Alphonsus VIII, King of Aragon and Castile. He had been leading a disorderly life and is thought to have suffered punishment from above for this. One manifestation was losing a key battle and being forced to take refuge in a city belonging to one of his allies. By chance, Dominic happened to be there on Christmas Day and was, as usual, preaching about the merits of the rosary. He mentioned that those who said the rosary devoutly would overcome their enemies and regain all that they had lost in warfare. The King sent for Dominic to ask if what he had said about the rosary was really true. Dominic assured him that nothing was more true, and that, if only the King would practise this devotion, he would see for himself.

The King resolved to say the rosary every day and persevered for a year. The following Christmas the Virgin Mary appeared to him at the end of his rosary and said, 'Alphonsus, you have served me for a year by saying my rosary devoutly every day, so I have come to reward you. I have obtained the forgiveness of your sins from my Son. And I am going to give you this rosary. Wear it and I promise you that none of your enemies will ever be able to harm you again.'

The Virgin vanished and the joyous King went off to find his Queen to tell her about the gift and the promise that went with it.

My niece Hilary Jackowiak with Pastor Simeon Kayiwa, after she was healed from facial hives and a milk allergy.

Robinah Serunkuuma (left), who was healed of full-blown Aids, and nurse Juliet Mugab Nakamanga, her superior at the Red Cross office where she is employed, who verified her healing.

MAKERERE UNIVERSITY

UNIVERSITY HOSPITAL

P.O. Box 7062, Kampala, Uganda

Tel: 42922 – Telegrams "MAKUNIKA"

Your Ref: ....

Our Ref: ....

Date   7 October 1994

Ms. Rochelle Gibler
MIRACLES Magazine
10 Bolton Gardens
London SW5 0AJ

Dear Ms. Gibler,

This letter is to confirm my interview with you in Kampala, Uganda,
September 30, 1994.

As I told you, most health facilities here are not computerized.
Laboratory or any type of test requests are hand written by the
patients' physician.   The doctor will write the request on one
side of the form and the results are hand written by the technician
on the back of the form.

In Uganda, this is standard procedure and these tests are accepted
by any hospital or physician.

The test results in question I can confirm are authentic:

1.   GRACE RUBANGA tested HIV positive on 22 June 1992 and was
      found HIV negative 15 December 1993.

2.   JULIET ███████████ tested HIV positive 20 March 1990 and then
      tested HIV negative on 21 January 1994.

3.   IRENE   NAJJA   was   diagnosed   with   hyperthyroidism
      (thyrotoxicosis) in 1985, more commonly known as a goiter.
      She was scheduled for an operation as per her medical records
      and recovered without requiring surgery in 1988.

I know Nurse Najja and can confirm one week the symptoms of her
case were extreme.   Surgery was mandatory and the next week the
symptoms had disappeared.

SIGNED:

DR. JANE BOSA
DIRECTOR

Dr Jane Bosa, head of Makerere University Hospital in Kampala, Uganda, verifies
Aids tests of those who were healed through Pastor Simeon Kayiwa.

Beautiful Pamela and her son at their home in Kampala. Simeon Kayiwa had seen that two of her children would be born with defects; one died but the little boy is now healthy.

From rags to riches: after a blessing from Pastor Kayiwa John Buyinza built his small empire from selling used clothing and he now owns his own home, several buildings and a taxi company in Kampala.

Maria Esperanza holding Ryan Hulick at her farm in Betania, in the mountains outside Caracas, Venezuela, after he was healed of spina bifida and water on the brain.

Maria Esperanza and her husband Geo Bianchini Gianni, with their family. Maria was told in a vision to leave her convent because her calling was to be a wife and mother. She was then given a date on which she and Geo would meet, the location – the Vatican – and the date of their wedding. Today she has seven children and fourteen grandchildren.

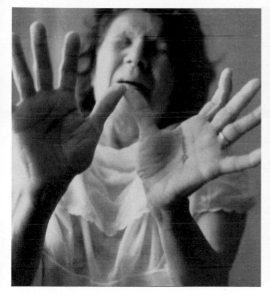

Maria Esperanza showing the wounds that appear on her hands every Good Friday before Easter, a phenomenon that has been witnessed by hundreds.

Military surgeon and hospital administrator, Dr Luis Gutierrez Burgos, who has attended Maria during the birth of the roses from between her breasts and while she suffers from the stigmata.
'I have heard stories about one saint or another experiencing unusual manifestations, but never before, to my knowledge, has this extraordinary experience been documented.'

People waiting to take the waters at Betania, where thousands of healings have been claimed through bathing in or drinking the water. In the background are plaques of thanksgiving posted by those grateful for their cures.

Statue of the Madonna at Betania, with a rare butterfly, which is associated with the presence of Our Lady.

Burning cross on Apparition Hill, the site of the first appearance of the Virgin Mary in Medjugorje, Bosnia.

Father Jozo Zovko, who went to prison for protecting the visionaries, is blessing a sick child.

Father Peter Rookey (second right) with Heather in Medjugorje, just after she had taken off her steel brace and stepped from her wheelchair.

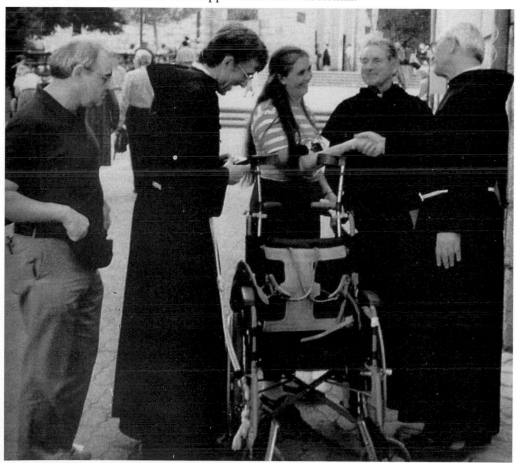

David Parkes (right), who nearly died of Crohn's disease, and Father Peter Rookey.

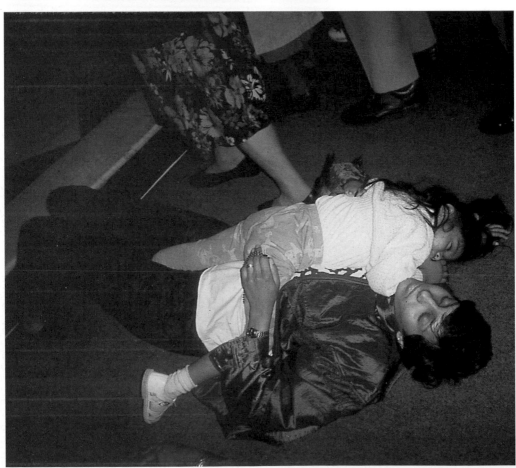

Mother and child 'resting in the spirit' after one of Father Peter Rookey's healing services in England.

She had been blind for some time, so he held the rosary to her eyes and her sight was instantly restored. Shortly afterwards, the King attacked his enemies, forcing them to return his territory. He became so lucky in war that soldiers rushed to fight under his standard, because it seemed that whenever he went into battle, victory was his. He never fought without first saying the rosary devoutly on his knees, ensuring that all members of his court joined in as well.[13]

Father Stephano Gobbi, a priest and renowned visionary in the current Marian movement, received the following message on 7 October 1992 from the Virgin Mary: 'My victory will be won when Satan, with his powerful army made up of all the infernal spirits, will be shut up within his kingdom of darkness, from which he will no longer be able to escape in order to do harm in the world. For this reason, there is to come down from heaven an angel to whom there is given the key of the abyss and a chain with which this angel will bind the great dragon, the ancient serpent, Satan with his followers. The chain with which the great dragon is to be bound is made up of prayers made with me and by means of me. This prayer is that of the Holy Rosary. The humble and fragile cord of the rosary forms the strong chain with which I will take as my prisoner the dark ruler of the world, the enemy of God and his faithful. Thus, the pride of Satan will once again be defeated by the power of the little, the humble and the poor.'[14]

The Virgin's pleas for prayers continue, as evidence of her predictions becomes more and more apparent. Many extraordinary miracles of healing have been witnessed, validating her veneration in the Bible, where it is said, 'All generations will call me blessed.' And indeed they do.

Garabandal: four little visionaries

Once again the Virgin Mary chose young children when she appeared in the mountain village of San Sebastian de Garabandal in north-west Spain. She appeared 2,000 times over four years, between 1961 and 1965, to four children, aged between ten and twelve. The apparitions were said to accompany several supernatural manifestations, witnessed by many, such as levitation and the appearance of a communion host on the tongue of the children, while in ecstasy. Before every vision, the children reported receiving an inward nudging from the Virgin and then ran to the place of her apparition, arriving at the same moment and together dropping to their knees in ecstasy.

Again, there was more prophecy. This time the Virgin indicated that everyone across the world would experience a supernatural warning before the predicted punishments. It is thought to be an interior reflection of how our soul looks before God. This sounds quite similar to the numerous reports of near-death experiences, in which one's life reappears, almost as a film. According to the visionaries, there will be a permanent sign in the mountains, in Garabandal, to signify to the world the divine origin of her apparitions. The sign will be foretold by one of the visionaries shortly before it happens, and, it is said, will accompany great healings and sudden belief by agnostics and atheists. As at Fatima, the Virgin stressed a punishment was to come, which was conditional upon the response to her continued messages for people to change their lives.

During the apparitions, the children were subjected to a variety of tests to determine the validity of the experiences: pinpricks, burns and a spotlight on the eyes. They did not show any of the usual reactions associated with a normal state of consciousness and therefore it was thought that the young children were in a state of trance. Author Robert François writes about the events: 'The two children, Mari-Lola and Jacinta, experienced the messages. They were heard screaming, the first time for an hour and a half. Between their awful screams they were heard beseeching, "Oh let it not come! Let it not come! May everybody have time to repent before . . . Forgive us . . . Let it not come." They called for help, wailed and thrust their arms forward, seeming to want to push something away.

'After the ecstasy they said, "We have seen the chastisement. It will be something horrible." They wept and wept, as did the spectators. Their cries impressed the villagers so much that they shared their fear, to the point that their knees shook and nearly all went to confess their sins.'[15]

Another author writing on the subject, F. Sanchez Pascual, quotes Conchita, one of the visionaries: 'Our Lady revealed to me what the punishment will consist of. But I can't say what it is, except this: it will be an effect of God's divine intervention, which makes it more fearful than anything imaginable. It will be less terrible for little children to die a natural death than to die of the punishment.' She warned that when it comes, it will be worse than being enveloped in fire.[16]

Mari-Loli, another of the visionaries, wrote to a Mexican priest, Father Gustaveo Morelos, 'At a certain time, not a single motor or machine will operate; a terrible heatwave will come down on earth and men will start experiencing a great thirst. They will search desperately for water, but due to the great heat, the water will evaporate. Most people will fall into despair and try to kill one another . . . but will not have the strength to do it. They will fall to the ground one after the other. That is when they will realise that it is God who justly permits all this.' Later she said, 'The chastisement cannot be avoided because we have lost even the meaning of sin.'[17]

Our Lady had warned us at Fatima, but apparently we were not listening. So she returned again. But the claims of these small children went largely unnoticed. The Church began to investigate, with all the scepticism characteristic of any scientific organisation. In the end, it gave its approval – Garabandal was the real thing.

But could the reports, even presented through the purity of small children, be taken as genuine, the devout wondered? Or should one ignore the details and just try to 'change your life'? This seemed more prudent and logical, given that the nature of the experiences was so severe and hard to believe. Most people continued to listen to the reports and went away, privately doubting what their church had recommended as a revelation, worthy of belief. And, as these things happen, the events at Garabandal were swept under the rug, and the urgency of heaven quickly became but a faint memory. Apparitions continued, but they were largely unpublicised, even among Catholics, until in 1981 the Virgin Mary turned up again with more warnings in Medjugorje, a village in Bosnia. People aware of past apparitions now became concerned – 'could we really be in danger of such magnitude?' The spotlight was now on all reports of appearances of the Virgin Mary . . .

Other reports surfaced, one of a nun in Akita, Japan, who saw a tremendous light around the tabernacle, a storage place of the consecrated communion hosts. A wound developed in her hand in the shape of a cross and began to bleed. Then a statue cried 'real human tears', which were chemically tested at a Japanese

121

university laboratory. The statue continued to cry, over 100 times. All those who witnessed the statue of the Virgin crying wondered anxiously what could such sorrow mean.

But Mary does not appear just to those who believe or even just to those who are Christian. She continues to emphasise, in her alleged appearances, that she is truly the Mother of us all.

Zeitun: Mary witnessed by the masses

And so in 1968, on top of St Mary's Orthodox Coptic Church in Zeitun, Egypt, a suburb of Cairo, more than 250,000 people saw the Virgin Mary. Moslems, Jews, atheists and Christians all witnessed her presence as a radiant light, moving around the church's dome, surrounded by luminous doves. Zeitun, it is thought, was a place that Mary had passed by when she, Joseph and Jesus fled from Herod.

The appearances lasted from a few minutes to eight hours and occurred two or three times a week for two years. One young girl, a maid whose employer stated that she knew this girl had no knowledge of Mary, said, 'I see a lady with a crown of light bulbs.' Many now believe that the woman mentioned in Revelations 'clothed with the sun, with twelve stars around her head' is Mary.

There were a number of healings at the time, which were later verified by a group of scientists and physicians. Dr Venice Khali, one of the witnesses, said, 'What I have seen, I believe. There were many miracles and healings, which you just cannot explain away in terms of medicine or science.'[18]

And so Mary makes her presence felt to everyone. Although she did not say anything on this particular occasion, could this not have been an indication that her messages were meant for all of us? Are her apparitions a divine wake-up call?

Medjugorje: The Virgin's message to the world

It was dusk on 24 June 1981 when four young girls and two boys were clambering across Mount Podbrdo above the tiny Bosnian village of Medjugorje. Vicka Ivankovic (seventeen), Mirjana Dragicevic, Marija Pavlovic and Ivan Dragicevic (all sixteen),

Ivanka Ivankovic (fifteen) and Jakov Colo (ten) were frightened by the appearance of a bright light in which they saw an incomparably beautiful woman, dark-haired and blue-eyed, wearing a grey dress with a white mantle and veil.

Above her head were twelve golden stars, similar to the way she was seen in Egypt, and she held an infant in her arms. She seemed to float above the ground and, when she beckoned them towards her, they fled in terror. Yet they all dared to return to the same spot the following day when the figure appeared again, identifying herself as the Madonna – the Queen of Peace – and telling the children that this was to be the last place she would appear on earth. But she would continue to visit them until her message was complete. She was to reveal ten secrets about the future of the world, but they were to keep this information secret from everyone. Because of the severity of the message, prayer was the only answer. The warnings at Fatima and Garabandal had been ignored and now the situation had become much more serious.

As you might expect, for children to keep a secret is close to impossible. Yet, for seventeen years, they have done just that. While they have described as far as they can the nature of the message, it appears that when they are about to reveal more than they should, they are affected by some unseen force, which stops them, sometimes in mid-sentence, from continuing.

We do know that of the ten secrets mentioned to the children by Our Lady, some have to do with the world, some with Medjugorje and others with the Church as a whole. One of the secrets partially revealed by the children is the Virgin's promise to leave a visible sign on the mountain where she first appeared, so that the world will believe. The sign, similar to the one mentioned in Garabandal, will be irrefutable proof of her presence and will be a cause for conversions. It will be given after the apparitions have ended. Most of the children claim to know what the sign will be and the exact date of its appearance.

The scientific proof of Medjugorje

The six visionaries agreed to undergo hundreds of scientific tests by researchers and technicians from around the world, some of which – such as pricking with needles – have been positively medieval. But the children (now, of course, grown into adults) have remained united in their beliefs and none of the research has contradicted them.

One man who has studied them, Father René Laurentin, acknowledged as a leading authority on apparitions, wrote, 'This was the first time that I saw an ecstasy in reality and it stood up to examination very well. There was nothing cataleptic about it, nothing tense or twisted. The visionaries remain quite normal, with practically no change in their bodily functions. I was able to have Professor Henri Joyeux carry out an encephalogram. It proved that during ecstasy the children were not in a dream state. So there is no question of dreams, and still less of epilepsy. All the young people fall on their knees simultaneously without any signal. At the same moment their voices become completely inaudible. They have no idea how or why. One just sees their lips moving as they speak to the Virgin, evidently very clearly and distinctly. When their voices come back, suddenly, one hears them reciting, 'Who art in Heaven.'[19]

Other researchers have been similarly impressed. They found that the seers react to the apparition at exactly the same time, to within one-tenth to four-tenths of a second. Tests with electro-oculogrammes show that, at the beginning of the apparition, their eyes stop moving simultaneously, re-starting at the conclusion with a variation of only quarter of a second between them.

Italian researchers, Dr Farina and Professor Santini, measured the sensitivity of the seers to pain with an algometer, an electronic instrument that calibrates the reaction of subjects to being touched with a piece of hot metal. When the apparition was not present, three of the seers reacted to the heat, just as anyone would, very quickly indeed (somewhere between three- and four-tenths of a second). During the apparition, pain no longer registered for them and researchers had to stop the test after seven seconds for fear of burning the seers.[20]

Dr Santini also used an estesiometer, a device that tests corneal reaction by touching it with a thin piece of nylon. He found that during the apparition the seers registered no corneal reflex whatsoever: touching their eyes did not cause them to blink or tear. Nor did their eyes perform as normal when a 100-watt bulb was shone straight at them. Sensations certainly travel, in a normal manner, to their brains, but a rupture occurs somewhere in the cortex. It is as if a telephone rings, but no one answers.

Their consciousness is somewhere else and does not respond. In short, the seers do not see or hear what is going on around them during the apparition.[21]

Professor Joyeux had the opportunity to film Vicka, one of the visionaries, plus a false visionary also in ecstasy. 'The difference is astounding between the false seer's exalted, agitated, little coherent gestures and the equilibrium, the alert communication, the transparent beauty that one can see with Vicka and the other seers,' says Father Laurentin.

'The test also gives credence to the difference between the supernatural which accomplishes nature, and the pathological which disfigures it; between the spiritual and the programmed which finds pleasure (by miming) the appearance of these spiritual gifts,' he concludes.[22]

They see the apparition in three dimensions. They can touch her; their conversations are coherent; the convergence of their eyes places the apparition about two feet above the horizon, and they all raise their eyes simultaneously as the vision disappears. Placing a screen between the seers and the point at which they suppose the Virgin to be does not interrupt their vision.

Among the dozens of psychological and psychiatric tests, those by Professor Cadilhac along with Professor Joyeux show the seers to be of mid-range – 'normal'.[23] Professor Emmanuel More, a nuclear physicist, and Paul Ameze, an electro-chemist, have determined that there is no radioactivity at Medjugorje and ionisation is five to ten times greater than the norm.[24] Given the results of all such tests, it is not at all surprising that the six visionaries have been taken much more seriously than many others who have previously seen apparitions of the Virgin Mary.

Father Jozo: jailed for his beliefs

Father Jozo Zovko, pastor at St James Church, Medjugorje, had arrived in the village only eight months before the six children witnessed the first apparition. He knew none of the seers, nor even many parishioners. He told me, 'When I first heard the news I was shocked. I couldn't believe what the children were saying and I was scared they weren't telling the truth. Perhaps they were convinced by non-believers, by those who could manipulate them, or maybe they were sick. When I spoke to them, I felt they were happy, but I was afraid to share in their happiness.' Despite his fears, he took the trouble to record every word they said and, he says, played the tapes over and over to himself.

One of his first visitors was the local bishop, Pavao Zanic, who initially advised Father Jozo to believe the children. 'He tried to persuade me that it was true. But how could I say I believed, when I did not? I couldn't accept these visions were real. Only later did I understand why Jesus asks all adults to be like children, to be simple and small. The six children believed it immediately and I envied them. An arrogant man can't accept such a simple, magnificent, divine truth. Yet Our Lady was following the path chosen by Jesus, to speak to the humble.'

Father Jozo is a handsome man, not just in his appearance, but in his aura. After being in his presence for more than a few moments, I felt him radiating a kind of piety, which was unlike that of any other person I have interviewed for this book. Conversely, he is analytical, distrustful of supernatural occurrences and he did not take anything at face value. He questioned the children closely, trying to decide if it were a hoax or if they were imagining things.

Then, on 1 July, just seven days after the first vision, Father Jozo was alone in the church praying when he heard a voice saying, 'Go out now and protect the children.' As he opened the door, all six children appeared, breathless and begging him to save them from the chasing police. He had scarcely hidden them when the militia arrived to ask whether he had seen the children. 'I did,' he answered. The militia ran off in pursuit.

Once news of the apparitions spread, people flooded to Medjugorje. 'My entire parish became a chapel in which all the people prayed,' said Father Jozo. 'Children waiting outside in the street for the bus were praying. Shepherds were praying. People going to the fields were praying. Children would spend the breaks between classes praying in the school yard.'

But just as Father Jozo became convinced of the authenticity of the children's visions, so Bishop Zanic grew to distrust them. There was also fierce antagonism from the Communist regime, which viewed it as some sort of Croat-Catholic uprising. When Father Jozo defended the children's visions of the Virgin, the authorities moved in. On 17 August he was arrested and two months later sentenced to three years in prison for 'fomenting

126

political violence'. He was released after eighteen months.

He said later, 'My going to prison was no accident, but it had nothing to do with my being stubborn or provoking the authorities. It was the logical result of the choices we all have to make at some stage of our lives. Every good priest should see the inside of a jail.'

Father Jozo does not comment on his imprisonment, but stories about it are told in the village. His cell door opened every night, say some; others say it was his shackles. Both stories point out that he stayed in his cell. After his release, he was not allowed to remain at St James, or even in Medjugorje, which was by then attracting millions of visitors. Bishop Zanic, who had become Father Jozo's prime adversary, transferred the charismatic priest to St Elijah Church in Tihaljin, some twenty miles from Medjugorje. But Father Jozo has not remained obscure: he preaches there to tens of thousands of visitors.

He says, 'Though its history is marked by the blood of martyrs, I don't really know why Our Lady chose this poor place, a desert without anything to admire, as a new Jerusalem.' But he does not regard that as the most important fact to emerge from the Virgin's appearances. It is her plan of prayer and fasting that interests him more. He continues, 'Our Lady said, "Please be converted." I thought she was calling on those who had left the Church, or those who didn't pray, or the unbelievers. I thought she wanted sinners to convert. But she surprised us. When she saw I couldn't understand, she said, "I am calling you, my son. Why do you look to them?" She didn't want to address those who were lost but awaken those who were close.[25]

'She said, "Pray the rosary every day. When you pray, do not only say just the words. Pray with the heart." I imagined this could come through deep meditation or concentration. But all my thinking didn't help. I was mistaken. "Look with your heart, find your enemies, forgive them, wish them a great blessing with great love." '

One afternoon Father Jozo repeated this message in his church. 'I asked them whether it was clear what Our Lady wanted and they said, "Yes." But when I asked them if they were going to do it, everyone was silent. This was a shock. Finally, I broke the silence. "Now we are going to pray for that 'gift' of forgiveness. Pray with your heart. Go deep down into your hearts. Close your eyes and ask God to grant us the gift to

127

forgive." And the painful silence started again as they struggled inside themselves.'

Father Jozo was uncertain what he should do, but after twenty minutes, in the middle of the church, a man's voice broke the silence with a prayer, 'Jesus, I forgive them, please forgive me.' Then he began to cry in a powerful voice. Father Jozo's eyes begin to fill with tears at the memory of this moment, which moved him so deeply. 'Then we all cried together. Everybody in their heart felt: I must pray these same words.'

He now says, 'Our Lady sent us her gift of a prayer to break the barrier of silence that had been gripping us. Among so many signs and wonderful moments, among so many changes in people and in nature here in Medjugorje, that afternoon was the biggest miracle of all. That evening we felt that all of the universe – all people everywhere – were praying with us in our hearts.

'The next day my parish was completely different. Some parishioners had not spoken to each other in generations. Like peasants all over the world, they didn't like each other, often because of minor differences, irrelevant things. They were envious of one another. In one night, all that had completely vanished. They began to work and eat together. They began to love each other.'

The same day, says Father Jozo, 'We saw a vision, a banner in the sky, from the cross on the mountain to the church tower [a distance of two to three miles], saying MIR, which is Croatian for peace, with big burning letters. This peace is the immense gift of Our Lady. I am sad when people don't understand what peace means. I am disappointed when a family doesn't know their peace can be through the heart of a child. This is peace that can't be given by man. It is a gift from God.'

Father Jozo concludes, 'Our Lady brought peace to our hearts and brings peace to everyone who comes to Medjugorje. She has opened our eyes, showing us that we're all the children of God, and that faith isn't what we think it is, but what God sees and thinks it is.'[26]

As with other apparition sites, there are numerous healings in Medjugorje, probably more than anywhere else in the world today. It is where I was healed, as you will see shortly.

On an evening in April 1985 Heather Duncan was going about her routine duties as a nurse in an Aberdeen hospital when she suffered a freak injury. While lifting a heavy patient who panicked, she crushed two levels of her spine. 'There was a sound like hands clapping twice,' she explained later. It was months before she discovered what had happened, unaware that she was making her injuries worse; unaware also that she had trapped the nerves to her legs and bladder. She knew only of the excruciating pain she suffered when walking. At the time she was not a Christian, nor had she ever heard of the small Bosnian village of Medjugorje, known for its miracles of healing.[27]

It was originally presumed by her doctor that she had merely strained her back or displaced a disc. But weeks went by in which she was unable to work, and in July she was referred to a physiotherapist. 'I could only walk awkwardly,' she recalled. 'The horrendous sciatica in my legs was the worst and there was a dull ache in my back.'

Then Heather's husband, Brian, had a brain haemorrhage and after surgery would only allow her to nurse him. Her son, Scott, was only ten and needed looking after. Her mother was also seriously ill. Finances were stretched. 'I was on adrenalin,' she said, 'having to do things for my husband and my son. It masked the damage I was doing to myself. I shouldn't have been carrying the shopping, walking up hills.'

Once Brian recovered, Heather deteriorated rapidly. By February 1986 she was in hospital, returning five times until June 1988. Doctors tried traction; it did not work. They tried Kaiaypaian injections (which are used in the US to tenderise meat), hoping it would release the trapped nerves. It did, but for just six hours. Heather had an operation to move the discs; that worked for only two days.

Heather explained, 'There was no huge deflation when treatments failed. I never had a terrible "why me?" reaction. After all, I had stopped practising as a Christian around the age of nineteen. But as I became progressively disabled, I wanted God again and I began to read my granny's Bible. I had a child out of wedlock – my son's father was a married man – and I always believed that this had happened for a good reason. All I had to do was wait and I'd find out what it was. This was no airy-fairy belief. I had a deep knowledge in my soul.'

In February 1988 Heather had a major operation called a spinal fusion, in which the patient is placed over a semicircular mould, to ensure the spine is as open as possible. Bone from the pelvic girdle is then wedged between the discs. During surgery her heart stopped beating and she had to be turned over for resuscitation.

The operation failed: her bones grew into the nerves they were supposed to protect. So she had another operation in May, using artificial bone. It also failed. By now Heather was bedridden. 'I still knew there was a good reason,' she said. 'I desperately wanted the sacraments. I wanted the mass, with a huge, gaping longing.'

Heather knew she was deteriorating. 'I was told I would never walk again. I would always be in a wheelchair and there was nothing they could do about the pain.' For some relief she was prescribed high doses of substitute opium.

It was in November 1989, four a half years after her accident, that Heather had reason to smile. 'I read an article on Padre Pio, the great mystic and stigmatic. I'd never heard of him. When I finished, I'd found the reason I'd been waiting for. I had an instantaneous revelation about pilgrimage and thanksgiving for pain (as a form of sacrifice for the wrongs we do in our lives). I can't even begin to describe the joy it gave me.' She told her priest, Father Christopher Brannon, that she wanted to make a pilgrimage and he suggested Lourdes. But she rejected any such idea. 'I said it would be misunderstood as seeking healing.' Father Brannon next suggested Medjugorje.

Then an extraordinary set of events occurred in succession. In December, Brian's only living relative died. In January 1990, Heather's mother died. At the end of February, Brian had a second brain haemorrhage. In April, Heather's uncle died. She said, 'When Brian had his haemorrhage, I decided God didn't need me to go on a pilgrimage, that the intent had been enough, and I forgot it.'

In September a friend's sister, Florence Loo, arrived from Singapore for a visit and said she too wanted to go on a pilgrimage to Medjugorje. She could act as Heather's helper. And so, 30 September 1990, they set off. Heather said, 'The trip wasn't easy. I could only drag myself on crutches twenty yards, on a good day. My right leg was totally gone and there wasn't much going on in my left leg. My right leg wouldn't bend because of the pain.'

At Dubrovnik she was carried into an ambulance, pleading with them in sign language to let her lie down, but she couldn't get through. She was carried on to the bus for a three-and-a-half hour journey. 'When we got to Medjugorje, I was wheeled straight to the church. There was a cross and candles outdoors, with young people singing, it was a beautiful soft evening,' she said.

'The next morning I had an overwhelming desire to walk the 400 yards to the church, but I only made it ten yards. Flo asked me if I wanted to take confession, but I refused. After mass I had to lie down for the rest of the afternoon, because later I wanted to go to church for the rosary in Croatian, where the alleged visions of Our Lady occur. I managed to get right in front of the Shrine of Our Lady. When I say the rosary, normally my head is bowed and my eyes closed, but I found it impossible to do that. I kept being drawn to look at the statue of Our Lady. As I looked at the statue, the expression looked sad. That seemed unusual, because the statues usually have a serene expression or a slight smile. The more I looked, the more unhappy the statue looked.

'I began to realise that I had been offered the chance of going to confession and ran away. I had to see if God was giving me a message, so I interrupted Florence's rosary and asked her what the expression looked like. She said, "Serene. Neither happy nor unhappy."

'I said to Our Lady, "You're not going to make me go. Nobody will make me go." Then I saw tears filling up her eyes. I shouted at the top of my voice, "Take me to confession now" and thumped the arms of the wheelchair. Half the church laughed. Florence was embarrassed. The wheelchair was too wide to fit the confessional, so two strangers lifted me in. It was the most complete confession I've ever done. Total reconciliation. I believe that it was essential so I could be healed. I didn't know that then, I just had the joy.'

'The next day I knew I couldn't take painkillers. I also knew I had to walk the 400 yards to the church as penance. I began walking at eight o'clock and barely got there in time for mass at eleven, having completed my rosary as I went. After mass, Father Miles Lovell told about a healing service conducted in the grave-yard by Father Peter Mary Rookey and recommended we go.'

Heather was adamant that she did not want to go to the healing service, but her friends had other plans for her. In defiance of her request, they carried her to the service. 'Everyone had their hands up in the air, and then I heard clapping and cheering. The crowd parted and a girl walked through, pushing a wheelchair. She was radiant. I knew she'd just come out of it. It didn't dawn on me to say: What about me? Then I heard, "Where's Heather?"

'I tried to get lower in my chair, praying, "Don't let them see me." Then the people who had carried me up saw me. I tried to hold onto the wheels. They said, "Let go, or we'll break your fingers." I held on till it began to hurt. They brought me forward. I was mortified. Someone called Father Rookey leaned over and he asked my name and what was wrong with me. I pointed to my name badge and told him about my back. He asked how far I could walk, and I told him about that morning and showed him the huge blister almost covering my hand. Oddly, it didn't hurt. He asked if he could put his hands on the damage. I said he couldn't, because I was wearing my Goldweith brace, which is surgical steel from my shoulder to hips. He put his hands on my head, arms and legs, praying quietly. I couldn't hear. He put one hand on the top of my head and the other on the top of my spine, the closest he could get to the injury.

'I can only tell you what others say happened for the next fifteen minutes. All I was aware of was Jesus giving me a crucifix to hold. I don't know whether my eyes were open or closed. I couldn't see my hands, body or wheelchair. There was no physical sensation. My body was gone. I'm told I went pure white, with my whole body shaking. Father Rookey asked everyone who was close enough to touch me. I didn't feel their hands or his. I'm also told they constantly repeated the Hail Mary. Then Father Rookey asked, "Do you believe Jesus can heal you?" I replied, "Yes. There's no doubt He could if He wanted to." But I didn't think He wanted to. "Are you willing to take a step in faith?" "Yes." "Silver and gold I have not, but what I have I give you. Arise and walk." It was what Peter said to a crippled man in Acts 3. I bounded to my feet; stood up and started walking. I was standing absolutely straight, which I couldn't do since I was hurt. People rushed up to me. Father Rookey shooed them away, saying, "Let her walk." First he was holding one hand. Then I was on my own. There was a step, which I went down. No problem. They were singing. I kept being asked how I felt. I didn't know. I asked God for words and I got, "How does the desert feel when it rains?" '

The whole place erupted. Everyone wanted to touch Heather. She had felt a burning when she was first brought to Father Rookey, then nothing. Then stifling heat again. Heat is one of the signs of healing. 'It was a hot day, but I was under the shade of a tree. I asked Florence to check my back to see if there were burns on it. By one o'clock I said, "I want to take my brace off." It was a torture chamber, utterly hideous. Florence answered, "Well, take it off. You can always put it back on if you need to." But that was the last time I wore it.'

When Heather returned home, her friends did not recognise her. Then she went to see her doctor, who did not recognise her, either. 'I told her the whole story and she examined my back. I bent forward and side to side. The X-rays showed no change from the ones done in June by the consultant radiologist.' After her doctor had seen the medical report, she told Heather that her X-rays showed that she should not be able to walk. 'Even now,' says Heather, 'they won't let me back to work with those X-rays.'

Heather's life is remarkably different now. She believes there has been a profound change, as well as the healing. 'I had been drawing close to God, but in comparison to now, I was millions of miles away.' For Heather, as far as prayer is concerned, 'It is as necessary as food.'

James: 'The twist in my life was uncanny. I am rejuvenated.'

At forty-two, James Linder (not his real name) had everything going for him: a beautiful wife, three young children and a successful career as a senior executive at a large European bank. As a £70,000-a-year operations manager in stock-market settlements, James was responsible for executing share transfers. It was a stressful job and, from his vantage point, he had a view of the bank's entire operation, so he was in a position to know where any skeletons might be hidden.

In 1984 internal inspectors asked James to cooperate with their investigations into alleged corruption at the bank but he also received a visit from head office representatives, who advised him to keep quiet. James was scared and went for help to an MP. He was told to go to the police, but James did not believe that they would investigate such a scandal.

Suspicions at the bank added to James's stress, which proved so disabling that after three months he checked himself into what he thought was an asylum for the 'psychologically troubled', which turned out to be a posh club for the corporate élite crippled by stress. The bank tried to prevent him from going, believing that he might reveal to psychiatrists the real reason for his near-collapse. After four months in hospital, he was dismissed from his job and the bank refused to cover his hospital bill, until psychiatrists threatened to go public with James's story.

For two years James tried, and failed, to find work, finally realising that he had been blacklisted. His world had turned into a downward spiral. He was depressed and bitter. 'I couldn't trust anyone after that,' he said. 'I refused to forgive and forget. It was a cancer that ate deep within me.' His life was spinning out of control. His marriage fell apart and his wife obtained a divorce. His will to live was dwindling and he decided to drown himself in a lake near his home. His children blurted out insulting comments as he was leaving the house. As he stood there on the banks of the lake, he thought about them. 'I just couldn't bear the thought of my children living with the memory of their last words to me as being so harsh. So I abandoned the idea.'

'Things were so bad for me,' says James, 'I even lost my lodgings, and my landlady had stolen part of the deposit.' But he did find solace in prayer, attending a weekly group run by a nun, Sister Josephine. She told him all about Medjugorje and, out of the blue one day, she said that someone had offered to pay for him to go to Bosnia.

'It was a week of tears,' he said. 'I couldn't stop them. Every service I attended, I was awash with tears. I was told this was a sign of healing, but I didn't fully understand. I ran into an African priest and he told me, "Don't stop crying. You will be healed. When you go home, watch what happens to you. When Jesus starts to work on you, he doesn't do things halfway." '

'I now realise that when people go to Medjugorje, they are selected to have a set of experiences that are individual to them, to alter the pattern of their lives.'

James heard Father Slavko speaking to a group of pilgrims before they departed. 'A woman sitting next to me was sucked right out of her chair and flung violently about twenty feet. She hit the ground and passed out, but was unharmed. Then another man's chair collapsed, the legs crunching like matchsticks. I froze and the crowd was stunned. As the man got up, people clapped and it broke the tension. Father Slavko said to the crowd, "If you think this is a coincidence, think again." In other words,' said James, 'there was spiritual power at work there.'

James did not know what to conclude from that experience. Why was that lady next to him? What was the significance for him? 'In the end, I thought I had always been a [doubting] Thomas. I always had weak faith. Until you see something like that, you aren't aware that all things are possible with God.'

But perhaps James was unaware of the power of evil and how, sometimes, it can lurk even in the holiest of places. Perhaps he was suffering from more than just depression, but God in His infinite mercy healed this man after thirteen years of psychological torture. Doctors today are baffled by his recovery. The depression has vanished. 'I feel like a twelve-year-old boy, with the mental depth of those past experiences. I never expected it. I didn't think I could get a break. The elation I now have is indescribable.'

James's experiences in Medjugorje coincided with the death of the owner of the bank. As he lost his life, James regained his. Now James does evening volunteer work at a hospice which overlooks the lake where he almost took his life. 'I am mesmerised by its beauty and it never ceases to amaze me,' he says. 'The twist in my life was uncanny. I am rejuvenated.'

My own introduction to miracles

The Medjugorje experience is not a remote subject for me. It changed my own life in so many ways, opening my eyes to a truth I had, for years, foolishly rejected. It is the reason this book has been written. It all began in 1986 when my mother, aware of my interest in all things spiritual, gave me a book about the Medjugorje visions. After I finished reading it, I suggested to her that it might be interesting for her to visit the village. So, the following summer, she and my father did so.

When they returned, my mother called to tell me about the extraordinary chain of events that began while they were walking up the hill where the Medjugorje apparitions first occurred. She had been suffering for some years from a heart murmur, which was not life-threatening but was a little worrisome. Suddenly she felt her heart turn around in her chest. Instinctively she pulled from her pocket the rosary beads she had purchased at the Vatican several years before. She could hardly believe her eyes. The silver links between the midnight-blue beads had turned the colour of gold, and the body of Jesus on the small cross had turned to a rose colour, as had the nails of the flip-side of the cross.

Even my solid, no-nonsense father (now deceased, may his soul rest in peace) recognised that something supernatural had taken place. I flew home immediately. This had really grabbed my attention. My mother showed me the rosary, and told me about all that was happening in Medjugorje. She told me about the messages given to the visionaries. She described it as an urgent call to prayer for mankind, which, according to the visionaries, is on slippery ground before God. We were being warned of what was on the horizon, if we did not change our lives and quit sinning. While the notion of sin was not very popular with me at the time, it was not exactly an alien concept, so I continued to listen.

I was enthralled by her story. Prayer was explained to me as incense before God, its aroma sweet. And it took heartfelt incense for Him to release His mercy on a sinful mankind. The prayers went up, and his grace came down. I thought it was a rather noble pursuit to pray for world peace and found myself asking her for another set of rosary beads. To put that in perspective, I cannot recall ever having said a rosary in my life before that moment. I also had a remarkable dream that week, in which a light three times encircled a white rosary on a black background. Then the beads rose up into a gold disc, dropping as gold dust while white doves flew out. It was certainly not my usual kind of dream.

Some three weeks later, I was saying a rosary in my New York apartment when, for no apparent reason, I remembered my mother telling me that sacrifice was the most powerful form of prayer. In Medjugorje, she said, people were encouraged to give up their favourite activity as a sacrifice. On the spur of the moment, I decided to give up my Tarot cards and threw two packs in the rubbish bin. I returned to the sofa to finish the rosary and when I looked down at the beads I saw that both the links and the clear beads had turned to the colour of gold. I was so unnerved that I began to cry. I called my father and told him what had happened. Like me, he could not understand it.

I thought for a very long time about this strange event, my mind turning over with scores of questions. What did it mean? Why me? Why now? What should I do now? I knew I was not imagining things. The beads were gold. Had I been visited by some heavenly being – an angel or a saint perhaps? In the end I concluded it must have something to do with the Tarot cards, they must be bad news, but I did not get much further than that.

In subsequent days and weeks I continued to pray and was encouraged by receiving many signs from God and the Virgin Mary. My prayers were being answered. (I now realise that such rapid responses are common at the beginning, to keep you on the right path. Once you have matured, it takes more effort to see your prayers come to fruition, unless you are Simeon Kayiwa or Maria Esperanza – or so I thought.) I was still puzzled by the rosary's change of colour and tried to find an explanation that was not supernatural. Maybe it had something to do with the rosary having been bought in Bosnia. Could the metal be changeable? Maybe it was a fluke?

So I prayed on another rosary and, amazingly, a similar phenomenon occurred. This time the links turned to gold and the body of Jesus turned pink, just like my mother's rosary.

I decided to test it for a third time on Christmas Eve with a beautiful pearl rosary. I prayed, 'Lord, for a Christmas present, if You are really with me, please turn the links next to the pearl beads pink, and the other links gold.' I woke up on Christmas morning to find the rosary changed in exactly the way I had asked. I knew then that it was an answer from a personal God, who had listened to the prayer of my heart. God was not some obscure force out there in the universe, like gravity. And it definitely was not due to the power of the mind. That experience was a turning point for me.

My brush with evil

The following summer my parents returned to Medjugorje and this time I went along with them. I soon discovered that there is a tangible power in that village, which prevents you from focusing on anything other than God. I had business problems but I could not concentrate on them, and when I told my father about it, he said he was affected in the same way.

The visit proved to be uplifting, not at all the kind of chore some people might imagine a religious pilgrimage to be. But I did have a dramatic and strange experience during the trip. On my flight over from Chicago I talked to Theresa, a nurse – a pleasant, normal woman, aged about forty, not a religious fanatic – who, like me, was merely curious. About three days into the visit I found myself sitting near her at a lecture in St James's Church. Just before the talk was about to end I was surprised when her mother, who was sitting between us, whispered nervously to me, 'Would you please help me with my daughter. Please, I need help.' Then I realised that Theresa was heading towards the altar. I motioned to my father and a photographer friend to grab her.

This was a different woman from the one I had met on the plane. Her eyes were glazed, her face was visibly different and her personality had changed, as if some force had taken her over. It made me nervous. She was a big, strong woman and the next day I heard that she had to be restrained by our two tour guides, who were at least six foot two inches tall, while begging incessantly and compulsively for a priest. She said she felt a great need to confess. Various priests turned up and whenever she managed to break free, she would try to escape in a crazed attempt to get to the church. I was told she began speaking in an unknown language, saying all sorts of diabolical things.

Later her mother explained that they had tried to travel to Medjugorje six months earlier but, two hours after take-off, Theresa made a scene on board, announcing to everyone that she had had an abortion and wanted to be forgiven. The plane landed in New York and she was checked into hospital for psychiatric evaluation. Doctors found nothing wrong with her and she returned to work as a nurse, carrying on a normal life. Now, finally in Medjugorje, the holiness of the place was drawing from her something that appeared at the very least to be abnormal.

During the two-hour bus ride to Dubrovnik airport for our flight back to the States, Theresa was again in an anguished state. I felt so sorry for her, but the sight of her made me very uneasy. Her eyelids were heavy, almost half-shut, and her eyes were hazy. I just could not imagine what had happened in her life that was having such a dramatic impact. At the airport, when her escorting guides took their eyes off her for a moment, she approached me while I was looking in a shop window.

She hugged me and asked me to pray for her. She still seemed to be covered with an intense fog, and within minutes of her touching me I was overwhelmed by a horrifying sensation. It is difficult to describe. The best I can do is to say that it felt as if my consciousness was being ripped from my body. I tried to keep my composure, but I could not walk and leaned back against the wall, gradually sliding down to the floor, sitting with my head on my knees.

I struggled to keep my sanity and to remain conscious. Somehow, I knew this was evil. Thank God I was not alone. I had bought a little book of prayers and my mother turned to one that was specifically marked 'to defeat the power of Satan'. Oddly, though I had never read it, I knew exactly which page it was on. I repeated it over and over. Although I was not certain what to do, I thought that, if I relaxed, it might mean relinquishing my life.

Several hours into this lengthy course in hell, I recalled watching a television programme about a priest who was an exorcist. A mother had brought her little girl to see him, saying that she had been dedicated upon birth as a daughter of Satan. He described the girl as a beautiful little creature and, without thinking, he hugged her. A seasoned exorcist should never have made such a mistake because, as he gripped the girl, the 'thing' jumped into him. It was, he said, the worst feeling of his life. His parish had to pray for him for three months before the evil left him.

During the entire eight-hour flight delay I continued to fight this thing that had hold of me. I poured holy water over myself; I even drank it. Nothing seemed to work and then, just as quickly as it had arrived, it left. When we boarded the plane I was so exhausted that I could barely walk. I got on the plane and did not open my eyes again until we reached Chicago. Even after nine hours of sleep I was still exhausted. By this time everyone around me knew that something had happened. I was so embarrassed, but this was not the end of my embarrassing moments.

After I got home I tried to analyse what had happened. What could have brought on such a ferocious experience? Once you have had a brush with true evil, you do not forget it. But this was blatant and aggressive, something no psychiatrist would understand. At the time I remember being so grateful for the strength of mind to endure this experience, without my psyche being fragmented.

Deliverance

I had decided to return to Medjugorje the following summer but, a couple of days after making my travel plans, I slipped on a New York street and fractured my knee. I was soon encased in a plaster cast, thigh to ankle, and it appeared there was no hope of making the trip. As the time neared to leave, I persuaded my doctor to replace the cast with a brace. The pain was so excruciating on the plane that I believed I had made a serious mistake. So I prayed and, as I landed in London, the pain disappeared permanently. A few days later I joined my parents in Medjugorje.

I had heard strange reports of people having unusual experiences after receiving a blessing from Father Jozo, the priest who first shielded the visionaries. So we travelled twenty miles into the country to hear him speak; we arrived late and the church was full. As I hobbled in with my mother, Father Jozo stopped speaking in mid-sentence and looked straight at me. All eyes followed his. Then he began talking again and the church radiated with his presence. He had, after all, been the fount of the stream of peace that flowed from this obscure mountain oasis across the world. It was he who translated into reality Our Lady's message of conversion of the heart.

After his talk he invited people to receive his blessing and, when they did, the reaction was extraordinary. Nine out of ten people he touched collapsed, as if they were fainting. When my turn came, his finger barely touched my forehead as he made the sign of the cross. Yet it happened to me too. There was an odd, woozy feeling and then I lost the ability to stand. It was similar to fainting, but I did not lose consciousness. After a minute or so I began to feel an electric current pulling something out of the back of my neck and I started to shake. Then I felt it in my forearms, from elbow to fingertips, a strong current moving back and forth continually, like I had plugged my fingers into a light socket. My arms were paralysed and the sensation forced me out of the 'resting' state I was in.

There I was, lying on the floor in the front of the church, unable to move. I thought: if this is healing me, why isn't the sensation in my leg? I was feeling increasingly uncomfortable when Father Jozo's interpreter came over to offer comfort. She said, 'Everything that happens here is from God, so do not be afraid. Tell the Lord you love Him.' In fact, what I did say to the Lord was: whatever is happening here is okay with me, but could you please hurry up, because I can't take it much longer. As the current continued to flow, the paralysis made me think that whatever I had done with my hands was so sinful that I had lost the use of them for good.

Once again, I was feeling a sense of tremendous embarrassment, with people crowded around me. After twenty or so minutes I recognised among them a young priest to whom I had talked the year before. He knelt down on the floor beside me and I said, 'Father, I have an electric current going through my forearms. Could you please pray for me until it goes away?' I'm sure he wondered about my comment.

He put his hands on my cheeks and said, 'These are the hands of Jesus.' For a brief moment I really thought they were. I experienced that walk-on-water kind of faith, and after a few minutes the current stopped. I could move my arms. As I got up, Father Jozo came over to see if I was alright, he blessed me again and told me (through his interpreter) that I would dance again. One common trait among all the people I have interviewed with this kind of extraordinary gift is a sense of humour. Since they all work through His authority, I am guessing that Jesus had a sense of humour as well.

The only way I can describe how I felt after coming round was that it was as if I had been through a washing machine. I hobbled outside for some air and saw a young man whom I had met days earlier. I asked him if he had received the priest's blessing and he replied, 'No, I don't think I want to. Some strange things are happening in there.' Without telling him of my dramatic encounter, I suggested that it might be something he might not want to miss. He came back fifteen minutes later and I asked if anything unusual had happened. After the blessing, he said, he was unable to get his hands apart, as he had clasped them in prayer. I said, 'Do you think someone is trying to tell you something?' He just looked at me oddly and wandered away.

I was euphoric for the following ten days. I was so high that you had to peel me off the ceiling. From that moment, I knew God and feared Him. I realised that He was the greatest power of all heaven and earth, just as He had told Simeon in a vision. I was certain now that the God that had been spoken about in my childhood was no myth. I had believed in the power of prayer and had received numerous experiences which had confirmed that heaven intervened on earth. But, after having been exposed to even a drop of this incredible power, everything looked deficient by comparison. A man who relies on science alone to explain Creation, man and the universe is sadly overlooking the key to the mysteries of life.

The pressure on my chest had lifted, along with the constant depressed feeling from which I had suffered for at least a decade, although I did not really understand what the electric current was and what it meant. I went back to the priest who had tended me on the floor. He did not understand it, either. No priest in the village could give me an explanation. They had not heard of anyone who had experienced anything similar. I thought that perhaps I had been given the gift of healing or something rather grand.

About six months later I met a woman named Martha, who had experienced visions of the Virgin Mary for sixteen years. I told her of my experience and she said, 'It sounds like deliverance to me.' I had no idea what this could mean, so I quizzed her. She asked me if I had ever dabbled in the occult and, being terribly naïve at the time, I asked her what she meant. She replied, 'You know, fortune tellers, astrologers or psychics.' I said, 'Oh yes, when I lived in Arizona I saw a psychic once a week, just as entertainment.' The information she gave me made so much sense that I became more and more intrigued with this unusual phenomenon, which she called deliverance. Martha then asked if I was aware that all occult methods were prohibited in the Bible. Of course I was not aware of this.

Martha had a gift that is called interpretation of tongues – it was a true gift from God, unlike the gifts many spiritualists claim (see Chapter 5). She prayed over me, and as she neared the end of the prayer she gasped, which made me rather nervous, and then she made me even more concerned by saying, 'I see all your income past and present bound in chains.' I still did not understand how seeing psychics could lead to that, but I took her advice and renounced all those activities, asking God for forgiveness.

142

Finally, as I read the Bible and researched what others thought about the occult, I realised that Martha was not alone in her convictions. I now understood how offensive all occult activity is before God. I concluded that the electric current travelled only in the infected areas, the hands and forearms, which I used for the Tarot cards. I remember the day that realisation dawned on me; I was shaken by the ramifications of what the totality of this experience meant.

Spending money on this activity can prevent the flow of prosperity. Not only do we interface with demonic spirits but, by turning away from God and seeking answers from other supernatural means that stand in opposition to spiritual law, we are guilty of sin and breaking the First Commandment. Unfortunately it is sin that creates an opening for demonic intervention. We may receive temporary healing or information that appears to be true, which can seduce us into 'its' web of mystery. But, in the end, we may have sown the seeds of our own misfortune.

We continue to see extraordinary evidence of healing from this small Bosnian village and now it is time to turn our attention to the actual messages. What is the significance behind the messages of the Virgin Mary that continue throughout the world?

What should we believe?

Prophecy must always be treated with caution, but we ignore it at our peril. As with the warnings of Benedict Groeschel about apparitions, it is important to separate fact from fiction.[28] But what is prophetic truth? Visionaries find themselves in a difficult position, trying to recall faithfully not only what was said during an apparition, but how it was said. Under close and repeated questioning, they often get confused (just as Joan of Arc did) about the content or form of the messages. The problem deepens if they are lured by interrogators into saying what the messages might mean. And it worsens if they are influenced by the interpretations offered by others – no matter how well-meaning these might be. Soon, the purity of the heavenly message recedes. Our own human faults have prevented us from grasping God's word.

That is quite apart from discerning true visionaries from false. As we have seen with the bogus apparition claims at Lourdes, people often tell lies. Then there are the sincere, but also false, claims by those who lead saintly lives and imagine that they are receiving messages. Such delusions – and fake apparitions in general – could well be the enemy's work to discredit the real thing. In these circumstances it is probably wise (if sometimes frustrating) to leave the process of authentication to the Catholic Church. It sets such high standards of evidence that it has certainly ruled out many cases of true divine prophecy. But we can feel confident that it has weeded out all the false ones in its scrutiny.

Perhaps there is no greater test of authenticity than whether prophesied events come to pass. Examples are the alleged chastisements that may have resulted from ignoring warnings of God's wrath, such as the Black Death, or bubonic plague, which destroyed one third of Europe's population in the fourteenth century. It was preceded by phenomena similar to that which occurred at Fatima: fireballs and lights in the sky.

Historians have long concealed the frequency of the Virgin Mary's appearances on earth. In fact, Mary has been seen since AD 40, appearing to numerous knights and priests. Even Constantine the Great saw a vision of her in the sky. Christopher Columbus also experienced mystical phenomena. Before sailing on the *Santa Maria* to discover America, he prayed at a Marian shrine in a place called Guadaloupe. His crew sang the Hail Mary nightly on the voyage, and the first prayer said on American soil was the Salve Regina.[29]

The Virgin has constantly urged us to look at the signs of the times, the strange weather patterns across the globe, the growing number of disasters declared each year. While it is never good to become too fearful of prophecy, we should never downplay the intervention of heaven through Mary.

Many analysts of apparitions believe that underlying almost all of the Virgin's messages is a central theme, a warning about one event that is relevant to the unfolding of all the others. This is the Apostasy. One dictionary defines it as 'desertion of one's faith, religion, party or principles'. Another calls it the 'abandoning or falling away from one's allegiance'. It underlies all her messages in which she is asking us to examine our consciences and re-evaluate our lives. She warns that we have come frighteningly close to provoking God's wrath by turning our backs on Him with blatant disrespect. Our senses have been polluted by an atheistic media, desensitising us to the voice of our conscience, submerging ourselves in self-gratification. She says that we have lost the meaning of sin and the consequences of evil, so our world has become a spiritual desert.

In one key message given to another noted visionary in the Marian movement, Father Stefano Gobbi, on 31 December 1984 the Virgin said, 'Every day you [the people] are being fed with the poisoned bread of evil and given to drink at the polluted spring of impurity. Evil is being proposed to you as something good, sin as a value, and transgression of the law of God as a way of exercising your autonomy and your personal freedom.'[30]

There are many places in the Old Testament where people were held to be collectively responsible for their actions. The Virgin Mary says that it is the blanket darkness created through sin which allows evil to run rampant, confusing people, disabling their vision and their ability to be objective in regard to the needs of their soul and of humanity. Unless we are able to come to grips with her warnings and heed her advice, she will not be able to hold back the hand of God. She says that if the number and gravity of our sins increase, there will no longer be a pardon.

Father René Laurentin, widely regarded as the world's foremost Marian expert, writes, 'Chastisement is a word that needs interpreting in the messages, as in the Bible. The language is anthropomorphic, based on the image of rearing a child or even training an animal. Today these words are looked on with horror, often excessively so. Some bishops have said of Aids that it is not a punishment, but a medical and technical problem. What is true in this rather one-sided conclusion is that God does not punish from the outside, as it were, out of a sense of vengeance. He created a good world and submitted it to humanity. "And God said to them, Be fruitful and multiply, and fill the earth and subdue it; and have dominion over the fish of the sea and over the birds of the air . . ." (Genesis 1, 28). To this end, "he left man in the power of his own inclination" (Sirach 15, 14); he gave him freedom so that he could rule over the kingdom.

'Our sin destroys the order and the ecology of divine creation. We develop and degrade the world over which we rule. Ecologists are aware of this at the level of the natural rhythms of the world. But there is not sufficient awareness at the level of moral and religious balance, through which creation has an essential relationship with the Creator. We are like a woodcutter who saws off the branch on which he is sitting. This moral and divine balance, in the final analysis, is the most important aspect . . . By destroying the relationship of the creature with the Creator, sin destroys the creature itself. Through sin we are wounded, physically, bodily and spiritually, and the world is destroyed. The evidence is as clear as day. None of this is vengeance poured out from above but is the intrinsic consequence of human error. Self-destruction is a form of imminent justice.'[31]

Many people therefore believe that it is necessary for our world to be purified. This is expected to come about in a variety of ways, both natural and man-made. No one will escape the punishment – not the young, the innocent or the devout. It is comparable to the Angel of Death striking down the first-born in every home in Egypt.[32]

For several centuries the Virgin Mary has spoken of forthcoming problems, but modern apparitions, beginning with those in the nineteenth century, are marked by Our Lady's specific forecasts of a great trial for humanity. In 1846, in what is generally recognised as the most complete and detailed message Mary has ever given on the tribulation, the Virgin reportedly disclosed to 14-year-old visionary Melanie Mathieu in LaSalette, France, what the world could face from the errors that would come from mankind's way of thinking.

'God will strike in an unprecedented way. The seasons will be altered. The earth will produce nothing but bad fruit, the stars will lose their regular motion, the moon will only reflect a faint reddish glow. Water and fire will give the earth's globe convulsions and terrible earthquakes will shake cities and swallow up countries . . . fire from heaven will fall and consume three cities . . . Woe to the inhabitants of the earth! There will be bloody wars and famines, plagues and infectious disease. Voices will be heard in the air. Men will beat their heads against walls, call for their death, and on the other side death will be their torment. Blood will flow on all sides. Who will be the victor if God does not shorten the test?'[33]

In many of her apparitions, Mary has sought to help us understand such harsh words. She has often stated that much of what lies ahead is conditional. The purification, its occurrence, the extent and consequences depend upon the prayers and conversion of people. Likewise, while some of these events may come from the malice of men, the devil and natural causes, Mary is telling us that a divine, miraculous intervention, which could limit or prevent many of these occurrences, depends greatly on us. According to the Medjugorje visionaries, these events cannot be prevented, only mitigated, through prayer. They may come directly, or will be permitted by God.

As it says in Matthew 24, 29–33, 'After the tribulation of those days, the sun will be darkened and the moon will cease to shed its light, the stars will fall from the sky and the hosts will be shaken loose . . . He [Jesus] will dispatch His angels with a loud trumpet call and then gather His chosen . . .'

Punishment by fire is mentioned continually in the apparitions of the last hundred years, most often described as balls of fire coming from the sky. It is also mentioned over 400 times in scripture, but if any of this strikes anyone as far-fetched, then the predictions of modern scientists are just as sobering. Until four years ago, no one ever really thought that it was possible for a comet or an asteroid to hit the earth. Over the years scientists had led us to believe that such a cataclysmic event happened perhaps once in 100,000 years. But in 1997 a CNN documentary, 'Fire in the Sky', revealed that during a ten-year classified study there were some 250 so-called high-altitude detonations just above the earth's surface, which equates to one every two weeks. In 1994, when comet-hunters Shoemaker and Levy discovered a comet that was going to hit Jupiter, suddenly government agencies were forced to take seriously the alarms of scientists. The documentary went on to describe the threat posed by these heavenly bodies.

Comets, the left-over debris from the formation of planets, are often huge, with atmospheres a few thousand miles wide and tails stretching millions of miles. To get some idea of their terrible effects, the first fragment that hit Jupiter struck it at a speed of 140,000 miles per hour. The explosion rose 2,000 miles above the planet's cloud cover and, in its turn, created a cloud larger than earth, which lasted almost a year.

Now scientists know that over 2,000 objects of over a kilometre in diameter are in the earth's orbit. Many think it is no longer a question of *if* a comet could hit, but *when*. Mars, many believe, used to be a green planet, but due to the impact of planetary objects it is now a dead planet. Venus is littered with craters the size of small planets. It is also thought that a comet was responsible for the annihilation of the dinosaurs.[34]

But comets are small compared to asteroids – massive rocks that are pieces of unformed planets. The impact of one the size of a basketball would cause a nuclear-type explosion, levelling a major metropolitan city. Most asteroids are one mile across and travel at speeds up to fifteen times faster than space shuttles. If one hit earth it would explode with the combined force of all the world's nuclear arsenal. It would obliterate everything. If it landed in an ocean, it would create tidal waves that would travel miles inland, wiping out whole cities. The initial impact would cause the whole planet to shake. Fires would break out across the entire planet. Then a dark black cloud would form around the globe, cutting off all sunlight for as long as a year. The temperature would drop and nuclear winter would set in. Very few, if any, humans would survive.

British astronomer Mark Bailey tells of a mysterious light over London in 1908 which lit up the sky so brightly that even at night people could play cricket or read without artificial light. The newspapers were full of speculation, but had no answers to the cause of this most unusual phenomenon.

Soon afterwards, seismographs recorded shock waves emanating from a remote region in Siberia. Leon Kulick, a Russian meteorologist, organised an expedition to recover the valuable minerals from the meteor. When he approached the recorded area, he passed mile after mile of forest laid flat like matchsticks. After two further expeditions he decided he would never find the impact crater or the meteor. Dr Jasper Woll of the Royal Greenwich Observatory believed it was a meteor that had caused the effect but one which exploded over the earth's surface, sending shock waves down and devastating the forest floor with an energy yield of 30,000 mega tonnes. If it had exploded three hours later it would have destroyed Moscow, killing ten million people.[35]

The second most destructive example of meteor activity happened in the mid-1930s in a Brazilian jungle. The sun darkened so that it looked blood-red (similar to descriptions in prophecy today). Balls of fire ignited the forests, destroying 800 square miles. The Indians must have thought the world was coming to an end, but fortunately the area was not populated.

At the time of the great Chicago fire of 8 October 1871, scientists were tracking a comet that was dangerously close to earth. Some suggest that fragments from the comet fell to earth and ignited the fire in Chicago which was said to have been caused by Mrs O'Leary's cow. But there were a dozen separate fires on the same night that covered a four-state area, which were even more destructive than the Chicago fire. A small town in Ohio called Peshtigo saw the worst fire in American history. Between 7 and 8pm, there was a glow in the western sky, with a thunder that never ceased. 'A fire storm blasted them off their feet and everything was moving horizontally. The very air seemed to be on fire. Forests were uprooted and laid flat. People ran for the river but their hair and clothing burned spontaneously,' said one witness. Peshtigo was devoured, 1,200 people died. Survivors reported seeing meteorite phenomena, balls of fire falling from the sky, just prior to the conflagration.[36]

It is uncanny when we reflect on the similarities between the predictions of scientists and the prophecies of the Virgin Mary given to peasant visionaries. Both foretell of disasters for this planet and its peoples. Are we witnessing the greatest wake-up call of all time?

'This is what I want to tell you. Don't be delayed, therefore, by the predictions I give you in the effort to make you comprehend the times in which you are living. Like a mother, I am telling you the dangers through which you are going, the imminent threats, the extent of the evils that could happen to you, only because these evils can yet be avoided by you, the dangers can be evaded. The plan of God's justice always can be changed by the force of His merciful love. Also, when I predict chastisements, remember that everything, at any moment, may be changed by the force of your prayer and your reparative penance.

'Do not say therefore, "How much of what you predicted to us has not come true." Instead, give thanks with me to the Heavenly Father because, at the response of your prayer and consecration, your suffering – and on account of the immense suffering of so many of my poor children – again He alters the period of justice, to permit that of the great mercy to come to flower . . .' (the Virgin at Medjugorje).

Father Rookey: healing across the world

Peter Rookey is the priest who prayed over Heather and helped her step from her wheelchair at Medjugorje. The healing gift granted to him has stood both the test of time and the rigorous scrutiny of the Roman Catholic Church. For this reason, and because I have witnessed his services throughout the world, I can recommend his healing to you. He travels extensively, and it is more than likely that he will be holding a service near you soon.

Although he is a Catholic priest (and I know many of you may be discouraged by his religion and his office), you will see that the nature of healing can be deceptive (Chapter 5). Often there is more to it than meets the eye. Unfortunately because I have had a few dangerous experiences, I always remain sceptical of the supernatural arena. I regard it as vital for people to understand the potential dangers involved with spiritual healing. But what I can say with certainty is that, thus far in this book, the people and places I have mentioned are safe. If you need healing, I would recommend visiting any of them.

Healing came early into Father Rookey's life, and in the most dramatic fashion. At the age of eight, he picked up a firecracker discarded in the street and blew on the smouldering fuse. It exploded and blinded him. 'The doctors couldn't do anything with my eyes,' he recalls. 'I was healed gradually, only with prayer, from my mother especially. She was a great pray-er. I was blind for a comparatively short time, perhaps less than a year, but when you can't see, it seems like eternity. I think the seeds of my becoming a priest were sown at that time. When you're down, you promise the moon. You know, "Lord, anything but this. Please. I'll even be a priest", that sort of thing.'

Father Rookey's own healing came little by little, as is the case with many of the thousands of people who now attend his services around the world. But other people are healed instantly. There is no way of telling which – if any – outcome will happen.

Energy and charisma are the words best used to describe Father Rookey, and the bounce in his step is the same as if he were thirty. Now in his eighties, he continues to travel the world for healing services, with great enthusiasm. He has enormous warmth and is someone whom you like instantly, no matter what your religion or background.

So I decided to visit the healing priest in his own surroundings. He invited me to what he called a 'gala dinner' at a Chicago country club. Apparently he frequents some of the smarter spots in town, as his friends try and coax him away from the demands of countless thousands who need his attention. As we walked into the luxurious setting, everyone greeted him as if it were an everyday haunt. After dinner he went into the main room and sat down to play the piano, as if he owned the place. It quickly became obvious, as everyone gathered around, that Father Rookey is a man who is surrounded with great love and affection.

It was out of the ordinary for him to have dinner so early in the evening. Usually he has only one meal a day, after midnight, as he is convinced that fasting, along with prayer, sharpens his ability to transmit God's healing power and gives him greater spiritual strength to fight the devil, as you will see later. After three hours' sleep, he starts praying at 5 a.m. for two hours before mass, leaving him another hour's prayer to fit in during the day.

Peter Rookey was born in 1916, a First World War baby, and whenever he is asked about his birth, he says it reminds him of his brother's joke: 'Where was the war when you broke out?' It is a typical Rookey remark. His conversation is peppered with jokes, puns and anecdotes. He was only thirteen when he left his family of twelve brothers and sisters for a seminary in Chicago. He was ordained in 1941, but his real work as a Roman Catholic priest started in 1948, when he went with seven priests to set up the Holy Founders of the Servites in Benburb, County Tyrone, Ireland. He says, 'From the first days we were there, people came to be blessed and some of them came back and reported they had been cured. So the first thing you know, busloads of people are arriving and we had to have the services outdoors, and that's how I started.'

But healing ministries traditionally arouse apprehension in some parts of the Roman Catholic Church. This seemed to be the case with Father Rookey, despite his success. 'I did this work for five years in Ireland, and then one day I got a telegram from Rome saying that I had been elected Assistant General of the Servite Order. So I spent six years in Rome.' Along with the move came a request to stop his healing services.

This was also the beginning of years of moving around the globe. 'After I left Ireland they asked me to do every other kind of job but healing,' he says, without rancour. 'I ran an international college at the University of Lausanne. Then I was almost five years in Germany, working in Bavaria and around Düsseldorf, followed by Sweden and the Middle East. After that, I spent more than sixteen years in the Ozark mountains.'

151

Rookey was quite controversial for a conservative Church, considered too hot to handle, by those who know his story well. It appears that it was easier to keep the healing priest out of sight than deal with the overwhelming public reaction to his unsuppressible healing gift. During this time Father Rookey consulted Padre Pio, the great mystic whose own work was kept from public view by the Church for decades. Padre Pio's only advice was obedience. One of the greatest moments of Father Rookey's life came when he was freed in 1991: he was asked to leave the Ozarks and take up his healing ministry again in Chicago. Nowadays, he travels the world, holding healing services attended by thousands, work made more effective by the seven languages he has learned over the years. Here are just a couple of examples of his amazing gift that I felt you would find interesting.

David Parkes: 'I saw the whole thing as hysteria on a grand scale.'

David Parkes started out as an athlete. But music soon pushed sports aside. After winning Ireland's National Talent Contest, he formed a band in his native Dublin, in which he performed as the lead singer. But in 1977, at the age of twenty-seven, Parkes developed Crohn's disease, a condition that attacks the bowel. He lost a lot of weight and suffered constant diarrhoea and vomiting. Ten operations in as many years to remove the ulcerated parts of his colon did not help.

Just before Christmas 1988 David's condition worsened. By New Year doctors told him nothing else could be done. He faced death. To help pay his huge medical bills, David's band performed a charity concert. They advertised and tickets sold well, many people coming especially because they thought it would be the last chance they had to hear Parkes sing. In the audience was Heather Parsons, a local travel agent who booked trips to Medjugorje and knew Father Rookey well. That night she had a premonition that, if David Parkes would see Father Rookey, he would be healed.

The following April, David and his wife Anne were given tickets to visit Medjugorje in a party escorted by Father Rookey. David had no interest in anything religious, but the trip appealed to him because he and Anne had spent their honeymoon in Yugoslavia.

Parkes met Father Rookey at the airport and gave him a hard time. 'I don't wish to speak to you,' he told the priest adamantly. 'I am very ill and I want to be left alone.' He explains, 'I was totally disenchanted with Medjugorje. There was one restaurant, two bars, the house we stayed in wasn't even fully built. It was a backward place and I had no interest in it whatsoever. I saw the whole thing as hysteria on a grand scale. They were religious freaks. Everyone kept falling over backward when they were blessed in church. In the end I wasn't sure if it was genuine. I thought they felt that, if they kept standing, they would be the odd one out, feeling rather self-conscious. My wife kept urging me to go up and be blessed, but I resisted. Finally I decided it was better just to go up and get it out of the way, to make her happy.

'The next thing I knew I was looking up into people's faces. I asked who hit me. Apparently I was out for twenty minutes. I felt so foolish. And I could feel burning heat in my head and from my fingertips to my toes.'

That same day David ate a rather greasy meal and normally would have been ill. Three days after he returned home, he visited the doctor. His physician was amazed at what he saw. There was no sign of disease in David's body. He no longer needed his medication. He was healed! And he has been well ever since.

The gift given to Father Rookey is powerful. Often you will see that this gift is operable at a distance, showing us that our prayers are heard by an intimate personal God. If your husband or wife or family members desperately need help, but rejects even the mere suggestion of healing by a priest, you can go to the healing service yourself and stand in for them, by proxy. Often this will yield surprising results, as it did with Bernard Ellis.

Bernard Ellis: healing at a distance

Outsiders would have been convinced that Bernard and Sue Ellis had it all. They were the epitome of the high-living 1980s couple. They lived with their five children in a palatial house with swimming pool and stables, set in fifteen acres of rural Surrey. Staff looked after the house, grounds and horses, so the family had time to ride with the Old Surrey and Burstow Hunt. 'Sue and I thought we were happy because we were earning lots of money and living in a big house,' Bernard says.

Bernard, a Jew, married Sue, a Roman Catholic, in 1967. 'I never changed my religion, because we were in love and it didn't seem to matter that we were different religions.' He had been in the import-export business since he was sixteen. 'Our company, Anglo-World Steel Exports Ltd, had great success buying and selling stainless steel. But the more money we earned, the more I relied on "things". I used to take Atavan, an anti-depressant, and washed it down with large quantities of brandy. After a while the Atavan didn't work, so I took more and more. I was gulping pills and swigging more brandy straight from the bottle. So I was drug-dependent, alcohol-dependent and in a terrible mess. Then my business started to fail and none of the psychiatrists I saw was able to help me. The doctors tried to treat me by suppressing my anxiety and I used to suffer from panic syndromes.

'Panic syndrome is a terrible thing. You can't escape from it. And then we were practically bankrupt and my beautiful wife said, "It doesn't matter. You should only be well", and she was desperate. I was spiritually sick and physically sick. So Sue started to pray and started to ask other people to pray. She wanted to bombard heaven with prayers for this poor fellow she loved.

'By this time I had been ill for about seven years and I was getting worse. I remember about this time I was standing on New Street Station in Birmingham. I'd gone to try to trade my way out of my problems, but I had no confidence. People who had been friends for fifteen years had placed a really good transaction for my company on a plate and, because of my lack of confidence, I turned it down. I was in such a bad way I talked myself out of it.

'When I got to the station I realised I'd turned down the contract that could have saved us. As the train was coming into the station, I heard a voice whisper in my ear, "You're useless. You're no good. Throw yourself under the train." After that happened, Sue got me to carry a cross because she was worried that I was being attacked by the devil. I didn't know what she was talking about, but I knew her intention was good, and when you're at the bottom of the barrel you'll do anything. A doctor even suggested to Sue that she have me hospitalised.'

Around this time Sue spoke to a woman called Mary Paynton, the housekeeper of a friend of Father Rookey's. Unknown to the Ellises, Mary met Father Rookey soon after in Belfast and stood in by proxy in one of his healing services. She asked him to pray

154

for Bernard Ellis. At that moment, on 24 August 1981, Bernard was on the other side of the world, on a last desperate business trip to Malaysia. Suddenly that day Bernard felt startlingly better. 'It was like a great weight lifted off me,' he says. 'I called Sue and told her, "I'm feeling good today. It must be the climate." ' But when he returned home his depression didn't return. 'Then Sue got me to stop taking the Atavan, which I'd been on for ten years. I had no problem in stopping and doctors have since told me it was impossible, that people sometimes have to be hospitalised because of the side-effects.' He also stopped his excessive drinking.

It was another year, when he finally met Father Rookey, before Bernard discovered what had happened. He knew vaguely that he had been prayed for, but he did not really appreciate the life-changing connection until they bumped into each other in Medjugorje.

Now Bernard is convinced that Father Rookey's prayers made all the difference. 'The day he prayed over me in Belfast when I was in Malaysia I got better after eight years. That's after eight years of being really bad. I'd been a depressive for twenty-five years. Yet all that changed. Coincidence or supernatural, it's whatever we believe in – faith.'

Bernard told me this story as we travelled through the London traffic taking Father Rookey to a healing service. These days Bernard spends six weeks a year as a volunteer, booking Father Rookey's appointments in the UK and sometimes telling his own story at the healing services. Bernard is now an ardent Christian. He also raises money for refugees and relief supplies in Bosnia and has collected millions.

As for his business, Bernard says, 'Every year since that day in Malaysia my profits have been higher. It seems that the more time I give to helping others, the better the business goes.'

Forgiveness

Lack of forgiveness can often be an obstacle to receiving healing. Often God will direct someone gifted like Father Rookey straight to the root of the problem and healing will ensue, as in the following story.

'When we were in England in May of 1992, we were asked to

pray over a young man who had six days to live. He had bone-marrow cancer. As we began to pray over him, the Lord directed me to ask him a question. I asked the young man, "Is there anyone in your life you must forgive?" He nodded and said, "Yes, Father."

'We began to pray that this unforgiveness would be healed. His tears began to flow, and he wept profusely. The crying this man was experiencing was an outward sign of the inner healing that was taking place. We invoked the powerful intercession of Our Blessed Mother, and my brother Servite, St Peregrine, who is known as the patron saint of those suffering from cancer.

'The lady who requested the prayers for this young man attended one of our healing services a year later. She witnessed that the young man had recently returned to Australia. He told his friend that, at the moment he forgave that person in his life, he was healed. He is now working on a crocodile farm in Australia.[37]

Exorcism and the devil

According to Father Rookey, he has met the devil. He has seen the 'old boy', as he calls him, manifest himself on more than one occasion. And it is always a struggle to free the person who is being held captive, so to speak. For most people, it begins with dabbling in the occult (see Chapter 5). Even worse, once the person is relieved from the grip of evil, the 'old boy' can return with even more force, if he or she does not stay away from occult practices and keep their life shiny clean. Here is a letter written by Don Meehan who witnessed an exorcism at one of Father Rookey's healing services.

'I had never been to a healing mass, much less an exorcism. As I stood watching this beautiful outpouring of unselfish and generous love coming from the priest and the forty witnesses to this poor helpless soul, I realised I was witnessing an event few people on this planet had ever seen or ever will see. There wasn't a camera or a recorder. I couldn't sleep that night, thinking I must do everything possible to remember what happened and write it down to the best of my ability.

'Over 1,400 people attended Father Rookey's mass at Our Lady of Mount Carmel Church in Doylestown, Pennsylvania, on the night of 20 January 1992. Most of them had received from him the special blessing known as "the laying on of hands". After the service, a young man began yelling and screaming violently and acting strange, and had to be held down on the altar by at least four strong men. The paramedics were called, but soon realised that they really couldn't help: the man was apparently "possessed" by an evil spirit.

'While about forty people watched, Father Rookey put a cross to the young man's face, which set him screaming, growling, snarling and spitting. Father Rookey then began to perform an exorcism over this young man, as prescribed by the Catholic Church. The alleged demonic activity was similar to what was shown in the movie *The Exorcist*, only now it was really unfolding right before our eyes. Not one of the forty witnesses left this man's side, staying until the end, repeating every prayer they knew over him.

'The man stuck his tongue out. He continued to snarl and spit. He couldn't bear to look at the cross, screaming things like, "Get that man away from me. Get that cross away from me. I hate him."

'He spat again and again on the priest, and growled and twisted his face and body into terrible contortions. He rolled his eyes and crossed them repeatedly. The face, especially around the eyes and mouth, was the picture of hatred. Then there were moments when the young man appeared to be in control and would say in his normal soft and gentle voice, "What's happening to me? I'm sorry for this. Am I going to die?" And he would burst into tears. Then the tongue would go out again, the eyes would roll, the voice would change and the demon apparently would regain control.

'It all began when at least 150 people of the 1,400 who had received the "laying on of hands" enjoyed the gift that Catholics call "resting in the spirit". To describe it briefly, after the blessing or laying on of the healing hands, some recipients will just collapse into the arms of a "catcher", who is positioned behind the recipient to gently let the person go down flat on his back. It is similar to fainting, except that the person retains consciousness and is aware of what is going on around him. Catholics believe that the Holy Spirit actually takes over the person's faculties at that time. It generally lasts from a few seconds to over a half-hour or longer. This particular young man was among those who "rested in the spirit", but failed to come out of it and became violent.

'The exorcism went on for at least two hours, with the forty witnesses continuing to pray. The demon seemed to suffer most when Father Rookey poured the holy water into the man's mouth and on him, and put his cross in front of his face (which is part of the prescribed rite of exorcism of the Church). Christian literature claims that the cross or crucifix, and the name of Jesus spoken, are most threatening to an evil spirit. There appeared to be a turning point when Father Rookey took a rosary from Medjugorje and touched it to the man's head, throat and lips, and called on the "Lady of Medjugorje" to [help] expel the demon. (It is also taught by Catholics that the rosary is the most powerful and destructive weapon against evil.) All forty joined him in chorus.

'After about two hours the demon apparently gave up and left the man's body. The young man, totally exhausted, was finally able to stand up and leave the altar. Father Rookey said later that "possession" can often manifest again after a healing service and recommended that this person attend another healing mass the next evening and attempt to locate an exorcist in the Archdiocese to continue the prescribed prayers. He told us about a case where a lady was infected with five demons and he was able to identify only one, who said he was Lucifer, and it took a year for exorcists to expel the remaining demons.

'The same man did return the next evening, surrounded by his entire family, and received a special blessing from Father Rookey. He was cheered by the 550 people, as he told of his story of being "possessed" from the previous evening. He had "beat the devil" and apparently had been healed.'[38]

The exorcist is a highly specialised office, requiring extreme mental and physical strength to endure the fight and win. It has been restricted to highly trained priests. Technically, there is supposed to be one exorcist in each diocese, but they maintain such a low profile that you may never reach one and end up taking the problem to a mental hospital or psychiatrist, who in the end accomplish very little. When it is a problem with the spirit, unfortunately orthodox medicine is of absolutely no value.

Father Rookey says, 'I have seen many cases of possession. Sometimes, as soon as I hold my hand over them, the old boy can throw them down on the ground violently and they begin to growl and yell and writhe around, all the usual signs of possession.

'Just as a mother or father are the hands of the Lord in their families, the Holy Spirit can use even the greatest of sinners to do his work. We are all sinners before God, but we are made in his image and likeness. And the greater the sinner we are, the uglier we become in our image.

'I see this very visibly when I am called to carry out an exorcism, when the demon makes the countenance of the person concerned so grotesque. Oh, it's like something right out of hell. And then in contrast, after the person has been delivered, he has such a beautiful countenance and bearing.

'Padre Pio, who had the stigmata for fifty years – longer than anyone in history – said that there are more demons attacking us now than there are people who have been born since the beginning of our world. But the good news is that there are more angels protecting us, so if we call on this protection we have nothing to fear. But my greatest fear is the constant one we all [should] have, of offending God, who has given us everything, including life.'

Notes

1. 'Lourdes: What Makes a Miracle', Claire Lesegretain, *Miracles and the Extraordinary* magazine, London, Issue 1, 1994.
2. *A Still Small Voice*, Father Benedict Groeschel, CFR, Ignatius Press, San Francisco, 1993. As Groeschel points out, he has drawn extensively on the standard work in this field, *The Graces of Interior Prayer* by Father Augustin Poulain, SJ, Routledge and Kegan Paul, London, 1950.
3. Ibid., p. 29.
4. Ibid., p. 29.
5. Ibid., p. 34.
6. Ibid., p. 43.
7. Ibid., p. 43.
8. Ibid., p. 43.
9. Ibid., pp. 36–7.
10. Ibid., p. 87.

11. Michael Brown, Marian Conference, Notre Dame, Indiana, 1997.
12. *The Secret of the Rosary*, St Louis de Montfort, Montfort Publications, Bay Shore, New York, 1954, p. 74.
13. Ibid., p. 75.
14. Father Stephano Gobbi, Internet address: http://www.mmp-usa.net/lastpm.htm?
15. *Call of the Ages*, Thomas Petrisko, Queenship Publishing, Santa Barbara, California, 1995 (for an overall view of the apparitions and messages). Quoting from *O Children Listen to Me*, The Workers of Lady of Mount Carmel, Inc., Lindenhurst, New York, 1980, pp. 369–70.
16. Ibid. Quoting from *The Apparitions of Garabandal*, F. Sanchez Pascual, St Michael's Garabandal Center, Pasadena, California, 1966.
17. Ibid., p. 372.
18. 'Marian Apparitions of the Twentieth Century', video by Marian Communications, Lima, Pennsylvania, 1991.
19. *The Apparitions at Medjugorje Prolonged*, Father René Laurentin, The Riehle Foundation, Milford, Ohio, 1987, p. 44.
20. Ibid., pp. 46–7.
21. Ibid., pp. 47–8.
22. Ibid., p. 54.
23. Ibid., p. 45.
24. Ibid., p. 45.
25. Father Jozo Zovko interview 'A Call to Holiness', video by Marian Communications, Lima, Pennsylvania, 1988.
26. Ibid.
27. 'A Walking Miracle', Patricia Miller, interview in *Miracles and the Extraordinary* magazine, London, Issue 1, 1994.
28. Op. cit., note 2.
29. Op. cit., note 11.
30. Op. cit., note 14.
31. Op. cit., note 15. Quoting from *Apparitions of the Blessed Virgin Mary Today*, Veritas Publications, Paris, 1991, pp. 377–8.
32. Ibid., p. 416.
33. Ibid., p. 360.
34. 'Fire in the Sky', CNN documentary, 1997.
35. Ibid.
36. Ibid.

37. *Do You Believe That Jesus Can Heal You?*, Margaret M. Trosclair, Mary's Helpers Publishing Company, Marrero, Louisiana, 1996, p. 56.
38. Ibid., pp. 102–7.

5

The Occult and the Demonic

We like to think we know what evil is. We use the word to describe horrific acts, sometimes by individuals who perpetrate brutality on a relatively small scale, usually by groups of people who set in motion unspeakable genocidal violence. So child murderers and serial killers are described as evil, as are tyrannical dictators such as Adolf Hitler and Idi Amin. And, of course, our description is correct. The Holocaust was evil. The bloodthirsty reign of Amin in Uganda was evil. The paedophiliac murders in Belgium were evil. The genocides in Rwanda and Bosnia were evil. Some of these cases happened recently, so we cannot view evil as an historic subject, though I suspect that many of us would like to, because we think of it as little more than primitive behaviour from barbaric times. Nevertheless, that kind of mind-set influences the prevailing view, which persists in seeing evil as an extraordinary event; a thing apart from our 'advanced' society, a manifestation of unusual events in special circumstances involving peculiar people; an oddity that has no resonance in the 'normal' world.

In other words, we think of evil as nothing more than extremely bad behaviour, a human condition brought about by some kind of personality dysfunction, maybe due to genetic or environmental factors. We explain away human evil in the language of psychiatry, talking of people acquiring manipulative, sadistic or psychotic tendencies, which lead them to commit violence, murder or terrorism. We even cloak the evil of tyrants by referring to it as megalomania, a psychiatric condition. In a sense, we are comfortable with this assumption because it suggests that we – human beings – retain ultimate control. A sickness, however bad, is understandable, if not treatable. This is the widely held viewpoint of politicians, scientists, psychiatrists and even the majority of the clergy, who all believe that evil is not a concept but a description.

The problem with evil having been denuded of its essence is that to speak of it in its original terms, as a manifestation of the work of the devil, is to invite incredulity. Evil in that form has been relegated by modern society to superstition. People do not believe in the existence of Satan and evil spirits, regarding all such claims as illogical or irrational. They cannot conceive of a diabolical intelligence, endowed with subtle persuasive powers to influence or target weaknesses in individuals, families, society, countries and the wider world. People reject the idea of an organised evil, an independent and deceptive agent whose existence is directed continuously towards defying God's will.

Through this act of denial, people have been blinded to the devil's infinitely more subtle intrusions into our lives. His work is obvious in the bloodier examples I have already mentioned, but I want to explore his exploitation of powers that he disguises as being good for us. The effects of this form of evil can be just as devastating as the violation of rape and just as long-term, and lethal, as cancer. It is an evil that paralyses the spirit and therefore affects every aspect of one's life. I am referring to the widespread use of occult practices across the world, practices that people adopt in the mistaken belief that they can improve their lives by knowing the unknowable, by learning of the future and making contact with the dead.

By definition, 'occult' means knowledge of secret or mysterious supernatural agencies that are not commonly revealed. I believe that these supernatural agencies are not a mystery and that the truth is as plain as day: these practices interface with a destructive and diabolical force, which is as old as mankind. Channelling, astrology, fortune-telling, et cetera have been around for centuries, but age does not necessarily correlate with wisdom or truth.

Among so-called 'thinking society', demonic or occult activity is considered fraudulent and totally without merit. It has therefore been derided by those in authority, from politicians to doctors. Even so, both Boris Yeltsin and Ronald Reagan were reported to have flirted with astrology. We also know that Hitler used the black arts to access occult powers in order to advance his convictions on an Aryan race. His quest to achieve transcendent consciousness was pivotal in his motivation, according to Dr Walter Johannes Stein, a Vienna-born scientist who acted as a confidential adviser to Winston Churchill during the Second World War.[1] We also know that Idi Amin – a man who killed his wife in front of his children – was a practitioner of the dark arts. He often sacrificed his victims and drank their blood.

These are but two examples among centuries of recorded testimony, illustrating both the power and the danger of the forces of darkness. In spite of warnings that stretch back to the Old Testament, modern society rejects any such evidence, blinding us to the malignant influences that continue to shape our destiny. But is it prudent to dismiss centuries of documentation?

It is odd that we take such a stance when, according to Gallup polls, some 70 per cent of us have had a spiritual experience. Perhaps it was an uncanny coincidence or a premonition. Maybe it was a sense of being guided to safety. Several million people have reported near-death experiences, many with disturbing visions of hell. So, by implication, we recognise that belief in the supernatural does not compromise our intellectual integrity. But we just cannot bring ourselves to take the next logical step: belief in the supernatural force of evil.

There has been plenty of information about the dangers of dabbling in occult practices. But more and more people are lured into it, not least because they see it as 'just a bit of fun'. So common is it now that the psychic world of the occult – with its assorted healers, channellers, astrologers, fortune-tellers and card-readers – has turned into a billion-dollar industry. It is far from fun, however. The spiritual domain is neither wholesome nor helpful, as advertising leads people to believe, nor neutral. See it instead as a raging battlefield, with players far more intelligent than people. Once you cross the line into that occult arena, you are immediately susceptible to the wiles of the devil. Though the symptoms may vary in degree, there is no escape.

That raises the other central problem. There are few chances of rescue, because most health-care professionals and clergy are unable to recognise and treat the symptoms. The few who do, such as Revd John Hampsch, are inundated with requests for help. He said recently, 'Fifteen years ago I rarely got a call regarding people who were suffering due to occult problems. Now I spend six hours a day on the phone dealing with these problems.'[2]

Today, I would estimate, millions are suffering needlessly from occult damage due to ignorance. Compare it to being exposed to the HIV virus. Once infected, it may be some time before the symptoms will appear, but they inevitably do. Depression, anxiety, physical, emotional and even financial problems may be related to experiences people have had after channelling, visiting psychic healers, doing Tarot cards, even consulting astrologers.

I urge you to read this chapter with an open mind. Put your scientific rationale to one side for a moment, take a step back and look at the big picture. Scientists readily acknowledge that they do not have all the answers. So get beyond the myths. While some of the information provided here may sound extreme, there are not enough words in this world, or time on this earth, to underscore the importance of educating yourself in the truth about spirituality. An error in judgement could result in you suffering from evil – evil that could ruin your entire life.

I did not believe in the devil until a decade ago, even though I grew up as a Christian. It is this lack of recognition of the demonic in the Western world which C.S. Lewis addressed so well: 'There are two equal and opposite errors into which our race can fall about the devils. One is to disbelieve in their existence. The other is to believe, and to feel an excessive and an unhealthy interest in them. They themselves are equally pleased by both errors, and hail a materialist or a magician with the same delight.'[3]

The media does not help. It is big news when a body is dug up from someone's kitchen floor, but the newspapers would be embarrassed to run a piece on supernatural evil. In their view, it is illogical and therefore not newsworthy. The media are consumed with interest in murder but totally uninterested in the most sophisticated crime that plagues our society: murder of the spirit. This iron curtain of scepticism remains, in spite of science never conclusively disproving the existence of a supernatural realm. Is this not suspect? Could a perverse artifice be at work behind the scenes?

Unfortunately, the Church is not of much value here, either. The clergy may be more conscious than most about the devil, but few address evil or teach the dangers of the occult. This error of omission perpetuates the problem, making people uncertain whether occult techniques are right or wrong. Theologians may prefer to address people's needs by promoting an experience with the divine as a more palatable and optimistic subject for a Sunday sermon. Perhaps lack of experience also leaves them at a loss for words.

Whatever the cause, it was this black hole in understanding that led to my misfortune with the occult. And, unfortunately, I hold the Church responsible. The only way to resolve this problem is through education and awareness, reinforced by the Church and helped by a new breed of psychologist. Not one who thinks that love is going to heal all the world's ills, or one who believes that we are all part of the same cosmic whole, where good and evil are part of the same and truth is therefore a matter of opinion. No, this new breed of psychologist has to understand the penetrating, deceptive powers of darkness.

With the variety of spiritual options on offer, it is no wonder that even the devout can become confused, let alone the earnest student searching for answers. The choices range from *The Course in Miracles* to Scientology; from a variety of meditation techniques to all sorts of health-care alternatives. The link between them is that they integrate a mixed bag of philosophies, confusing the basic Judaeo-Christian and Moslem concept of God. People are no longer sure who God is or whether He exists at all. If you listen to popular spirituality, God is not personal, God is realised within us: the potential and the power rest with man. God is the force that binds all things together, like nature and the universe, with man ultimately in control.

But how is it possible for us mere mortals to command or initiate changes in nature? We hear threats about our planet being struck by comets or asteroids, we see the number of natural disasters escalating to incomparable heights, and we note how the weather pattern is shifting around the globe. Is it not obvious that man can never be in control of such volatility?

The immediate danger of dispensing with God and with Christian ethics is the undermining of the central notion of morality: determining right from wrong. By allowing subjective, less restrictive criteria to guide our behaviour, we may feel we are being liberal or, to use modern parlance, more politically correct. But this has led us astray. It has allowed us to justify all sorts of bad conduct. We choose to ignore the Ten Commandments because we like to think times have changed and that those ancient rules of behaviour need not apply any longer. In so doing, of course, we also discount the punishments for breaking the commandments. Threats of devastating retribution, of disease and destruction for worshipping other gods or for indulging in forbidden practices are not taken seriously. We do not even consider them to be a risk. We do not believe.

It is a common belief among those who promote the concept of relative values (what is right for you may not be necessarily right for me) that all spirituality is a path to God. To validate their position, advocates often quote the Bible, but always out of context, emptying it of its true meaning. If you have been brought up to respect the Bible as the recorded word of God, you might want to review all the places where it condemns the practices of astrology, channelling, spirit guides, shamanism, psychics and mediums. It also outlaws the darker arts, such as witchcraft, necromancy: conjuring the spirits of the dead to foretell the future (as in a seance) and all divination techniques: Tarot cards, the *I Ching*, the Runes, numerology, palmistry, dowsing, and so on.

The history of the occult

As far back as the Egyptians, scripture reveals the evil of false prophets, who obtained their powers to foretell the future from 'demonic gods'. The practices of magic, sorcery and necromancy were common among the priests of such gods, even down to duplicating the miracles of Moses. The punishment for this activity was death. As it says in Leviticus 21, 27, 'A man or woman who acts as a medium or fortune-teller shall be put to death; they shall have no one but themselves to blame for their death.' For those who practised these occult techniques, as well as for those who liaised with 'familiar spirits' or spirit guides and 'wizards' (which today we call mediums and channellers), scripture is specific about the consequences. Leviticus again (19, 31)

168

says, 'Do not go to mediums or consult fortune-tellers, for you will be defiled by them. I am the Lord your God . . . I will turn against such a one and cut him off from his people.'

Nebuchadnezzar, the King of Babylon, summoned all the magicians, astrologers and soothsayers of the time to interpret his dreams. But he found none as skilful as Daniel and his three friends. Later, the King admitted that it was Daniel, and not the psychics, in whom the spirit of the holy God dwelt: 'and for you no mystery is too difficult and no vision or dream beyond your interpretation'. People do not realise that there are prophets and mystics today who have the power of the One True God, like Simeon Kayiwa and Maria Esperanza, which are pre-eminent over the menacing powers of evil spirits.

Channelling, psychics, astrologers and fortune-tellers, no matter how well-meaning they may be, are not endowed with divine gifts. God will never operate through practices that He has already ruled off-limits. Once you grasp the idea of supernatural power, it is not difficult to determine who has it and who hasn't. I admit that to comprehend exactly what kind of power all these psychics really have (the ones who are not frauds) can be disturbing, especially if you are one of them or have been seeing one regularly. But ignorance is not bliss. The goal posts just do not change from one millennium to the next, let alone from century to century.

In this chapter I will attempt to illustrate how people can meet evil through occult systems and how natural gifts can be polluted by the demonic, damaging the lives of the practitioners as well as their clients. The price you may pay to seek out the spiritual mysteries of the universe through these ancient techniques may be far greater than you realise. In reality, you may find yourself sowing the seeds of your own misfortune.

In the Old Testament laws were not meant to prevent us from attaining wisdom and knowledge, but to protect us from taking the wrong path, just as the natural boundaries in our mentality separate our consciousness, in order to prevent it from expanding, which happens under trance or with certain drugs. Scientists still do not possess a complete picture of the inner workings of the mind. They may understand the brain – the hardware – but the mind, or software, is still a mystery. Therefore to engage with an unseen and potentially dangerous domain is not logical, given the lack of scientific certainty. We know that the body has a complex immune system to fight off disease, so why should we not be equipped with a defence system within the brain to protect us against unknown factors in the spiritual realm?

This concept may not be widely understood, but it is really quite reasonable once you study the spiritual world. The guards which the mind possesses against transcendent or altered states of consciousness are barriers for our own protection, to keep out that which we are incapable of perceiving: the forces of darkness that lurk in the spiritual realm. We relinquish that control under mind-altering drugs, certain types of meditation, hypnosis and occult methods. For example, it is commonly known that when a person is hypnotised, the hypnotist is able to transfer thoughts into the subject's mind. A female psychologist from California went to a hypnotist to overcome her fear of public speaking and found herself months afterwards stealing small items from the stores, never having done this before, illustrating the susceptible nature of our mind.

God condemned the occult, labelling it as sin, but when the concept of sin has been all but erased from our frame of reference, it becomes even more important to analyse exactly how we put ourselves in danger with these methods, and exactly why God finds them offensive.

Let us quickly review the concept of the devil. Lucifer's name means the angel of light and he was, according to the Bible, God's most gifted lieutenant. Like all other angels, his gifts were superior to those of man. However, he began to feel his importance too great to be subjected to the authority of God. As it says in Isaiah 14, 12–19, 'You used to think to yourself, "I will climb up to the heavens, and higher than the stars of God, I will set my throne . . . I will climb to the top of the thunderclouds, I will rival the Most High." '

Scripture teaches that humans are created in the image of God, but as separate creatures and subordinate to God's power. The angels were created in the same light, and it appears that they too were given free will. In the end, it was the exercise of free will, along with pride, that caused Lucifer and his cohorts to be banned from God's presence for ever. Revelations 12, 7–11 gives the following account, 'And a war broke out, when Michael and his angels attacked the dragon. The dragon fought back with his angels and was defeated and driven out of heaven. The great dragon, the primaeval serpent, known as the devil or Satan, who

170

had deceived the world, was hurled down to earth and his angels were hurled down with him, out of heaven.' It is interesting to note that they were thrown to earth, which must therefore indicate that some of the devil's minions are still circling.

At that point Lucifer became known as Satan or the 'adversary'. And it is he who is truly the greatest enemy of man – apart from ourselves, of course, and our own lack of control over our free will. The words 'devil' and 'diabolic' come from a Greek word *diaballein*, meaning to oppose. In John 10, 10, it says that the thief (Satan) comes to kill, steal and destroy.

Best-selling author Dr Scott Peck tells of the time when his young son was asked to define evil. The boy replied, 'Daddy, it is live spelled backwards'.[4] I have always maintained that God made the profound mysteries of life simple enough to be understood even by children. The manifestation of evil is the slow death of the spirit, like being bound in a straitjacket, which eventually affects every aspect of life. It used to be referred to as a curse. The terminology may have changed, but the effects remain the same. Body, mind and soul are interlinked and, when one is out of sync, the other parts will suffer. Interface with the spiritual realm of evil destroys, creating a slow disintegration of the psyche, resulting in loss of identity, insecurity and often more severe psychological problems.

Demonic oppression and possession

Dr Scott Peck, author of *The Road Less Travelled* and *People of the Lie*, has made a close study of evil and, as a result, has acquired the necessary vision to understand the complexities of the interface with evil.[5] He has witnessed two exorcisms and, as a result, was convinced about the existence of Satan, and the devil's ability to penetrate the psyche and, to some degree, inhabit the body. These cases were extreme, but they illustrate evil's capacity to integrate with a human being. After his experience Dr Peck stated, 'I now know Satan is real. I've met it.' This is his account.

'When the demonic finally spoke in one case an expression appeared on the patient's face that could only be described as satanic. It was an incredibly contemptuous grin of utter hostile malevolence. I have spent many hours before a mirror trying to imitate it, without the slightest success. I have seen that expression only one other time in my life, for a few fleeting seconds on the face of the other patient, late in the evaluation period. Yet when the demonic finally revealed itself in the exorcism of this other patient, it was with a still more ghastly expression. The patient suddenly resembled a writhing snake of great strength, viciously attempting to bite the team members.

'More frightening than the writhing body, however, was the face. The eyes were hooded with lazy reptilian torpor, except when the reptile darted out in attack, at which moment the eyes would open wide with blazing hatred. Despite these frequent darting moments, what upset me the most was the extraordinary sense of a 50-million-year-old heaviness I received from this serpentine being. It caused me to despair the success of the exorcism. Almost all the team members at both exorcisms were convinced that they were at these times in the presence of something absolutely alien and inhuman. The end of each exorcism proper was signalled by the departure of this Presence from the patient and the room.'[6]

It is important to point out that this viewpoint did not come from the mind of a religious fanatic, but from a scientist with a discerning intellect. Dr Peck is a noted psychiatrist. There are many well-documented cases of possession, as we saw in the account of Father Rookcy's exorcism (see Chapter 4).

Revd Hampsch also relates an experience he had with a patient, a drug-addicted Vietnam war veteran, who was referred to him after eleven mental institutions and numerous psychiatrists had failed to help him. The man complained that an evil spirit arrived every night to throttle him, leaving marks on his throat. The psychiatrist, unsure whether this might be true and aware that she could not help, asked Revd Hampsch to meet the patient.[7]

The man's apartment, said the priest, was in 'a dingy building, with a naked light bulb hanging in a long dark corridor. I pushed aside cobwebs and knocked on his door.' He was confronted by 'a ferocious-looking man with glaring red eyes, a frightening experience'. When Revd Hampsch explained that he had come to pray with him, the man said offhandedly, 'Yah, yah, yah, come on in.'

The first thing the priest noticed on entering the room was that it was 'saturated with cigarette smoke. You had to cut your way through it. And I'm allergic to it, so it was a hardship for me.' Then he asked the man about the nightly visits by evil spirits. He confirmed what he had been told by the doctors: 'Yes, every night my bed goes up and down and they shake it around and grab me by the neck.' Then he revealed the marks where he claimed to have been attacked.

Revd Hampsch said, 'I didn't know whether I was dealing with something that was really demonic or whether it was psychotic.' But he decided to go ahead with his normal approach, saying, 'In case there is an evil spirit here, I rebuke it in Jesus's name.' He also told the man to repent of sin. As he did this, he noted that the man's face relaxed and his eyes calmed. 'The whole thing seemed to be over with, as far as I could see,' said Revd Hampsch. 'He looked very peaceful, very happy, even though there were no immediate dramatic signs, other than the change in his facial features.'

The priest was about to say goodbye when he had a sudden thought. 'As I had my hand on the door knob, I thought: Gee, I wonder if he might have a spirit of nicotine also. I didn't even know if there was such a thing, and I still don't know. But what did I have to lose? There was a big tray of cigarette butts piled high and the curtains and carpet stank of stale cigarette smoke. It was nauseating. So I prayed and said quietly, under my breath, "If there is a spirit, I bind it and I cast it out in Jesus's name." That's all. It took about five to ten seconds.'

Revd Hampsch did not see the man for a year or two, until he turned up at one of his masses and approached him afterwards to say, 'Reverend, I haven't had one attack from the demons since you prayed. I'm happy. I've got a good job with Meals on Wheels. I'm getting married next week and going to a prayer group.' As the priest started to leave, the man said, 'Wait a minute, Reverend, you know when you walked out of my apartment? Well, just after that, I totally lost the taste of cigarettes and haven't smoked one since.'

Revd Hampsch says, 'I still don't know if there is such a thing as a spirit of nicotine. But I have a suspicion of it sometimes, when I see things like that. At least it shows God wants to answer prayer. This guy was open and wanted to be helped, and here he is free of drugs, free of nicotine and free of the demonic attacks. He got a complete cleansing in a matter of minutes.'[8]

The overlap of mental illness with the demonic is a tricky one, because it is necessary to discover whether an evil spirit might have superimposed itself on a weakness. Dr Peck says that possession differs from multiple-personality disorder, in that with the latter the 'core personality' is virtually always unaware of the other personalities. In the two cases of possession about which he wrote, that was not so. In one, the person was aware of the destructive and alien nature of this entity. In the other, the personality showed itself as blatantly evil.

In demonic oppression, initially one is unaware of the interface with evil and, because its symptoms are subtle, the diagnosis is very difficult. Here are some general guidelines. First, one must try to determine the nature and degree of the violation. Was it a childhood rape, psychological damage or occult activities? Of course, sexual, psychological or physical assaults are less likely to result in problems of a demonic nature. If the occult was involved, you need to know whether these activities were self-imposed or directed by other members of the family.

Then it is important to know the age of the person at the time of the violation: the younger and more innocent they were, the more vulnerable they are to diabolical intervention. If the violation was the direct result of occult activities on the part of the parents, then some degree of the demonic will undoubtedly manifest itself. It is only when you see some lingering aspect that psychiatric treatment or medicine cannot clear up that you need to examine possible demonic interface. The symptoms can be physical, psychological – such as addictions, phobias or depression, possibly eating disorders or an inability to maintain relationships – or even financial, such as continuing failures, which do not seem to diminish, regardless of remedial action.

Sandra: a lifetime fighting against evil

At thirteen Sandra Solares was given a Ouija board, which she and her friends played with during the evenings. It seemed like harmless, girlish fun. In later years, though, she began to consult it continually when alone, asking it morbid questions, such as when she was going to die. It always gave her answers, and even accurately predicted her marriage and the divorce of her parents. From this experience she became interested in all types of spiritualism, reading everything she could get her hands on. Slowly her personality began to change, turning from a

174

responsible and kind person into one who was selfish and aggressive, given to provoking fights.

She heard voices and held conversations with entities that no one else could hear, which reinforced her bad behaviour. 'Later,' she explained, 'I learned that these incarnate or evil spirits disguise their voices, using vocal patterns which seem familiar, such as those of dead relatives. They are therefore able to put thoughts into our heads.' Her health deteriorated and she began to bleed heavily from her bladder. Doctors, baffled by the cause, told her husband to prepare for the worst.

In the past her grandmother, an avid Christian, had often tried to persuade Sandra to go with her to church, but she always refused. Now, with her life at stake, she was so desperate that she was willing to try anything. Having become wise to the trouble she had created in her life by dabbling in spiritualism and occult activities, she attended healing services and prayed for deliverance (which amounts to a minor exorcism). At one of them she was surprised by the wise words of a ten-year-old giving a Bible lecture. Sandra told me, 'He was trying to explain who God is and why it is that I didn't feel his love. Being tainted by so much sin, I couldn't feel it. Sin is a barrier, preventing people from loving themselves. Instead, they are just gratifying themselves, physically or materially.'

After the group held prayers of forgiveness, which apply to what is called inner healing, they moved on to physical healing. Sandra said, 'I had such pain in my kidneys and urinary tract that I thought no one could heal me. When it was my turn, in my heart I said, "Lord, I'm not sure if this is all real, but if you are really there, please come into my heart. I need you. Please take over." All of a sudden I was hit by a surge of light, as if a small tornado was filling me with love. The pressure lifted from my chest and tears poured out, but not of joy or sadness.' (Many people who experience inner healing sob uncontrollably.)

Sandra continued, 'When I got home I took a shower, and the lights started to switch on and off by themselves. The shampoo bottle moved by itself. The door opened. The dining-room table moved back and forth. My husband was very nervous and upset, but I knew what was going on and explained to him. The Lord had opened my eyes, so I realised that I had made the spirits mad and that the devil wanted to scare me. Before, I had believed these spirits were good and bad, but now I knew they were all bad. After a while these happenings did subside.'

She went back for more deliverance prayer, knowing that one must continually do so, until all trace of 'it' has left one's life, because evil spirits do not give up easily. In fact, it proved to be a long and dangerous battle. 'Since I had been so involved in Satan's ways, he wouldn't leave me alone for quite a while,' Sandra told me. 'He attacked me seriously, mostly physically, and twice tried to kill me. I was able to see him and smell him on these occasions.' These attacks involved not only her, but her husband, her daughter, her unborn son and even the family's pet dog. They began a couple of months after Sandra began the programme of healing prayer.

One night, while staying at her aunt's house, she awoke to get a bottle for her youngest child. When she returned to her bedroom, she started to feel sick and noticed in the bathroom mirror that her face was very pale. 'I thought I was getting ill and decided to lie down on the floor before I fainted,' she said. 'Then I felt Satan on top of me, pushing me down against the floor. I felt as if he was laughing. There was also a smell like rotten eggs. I couldn't speak or scream, or anything. Although I opened my mouth, no noise came out.

'I couldn't call out for help to my mother or grandmother, who were in bedrooms close by. But I had learned from the Lord a wonderful way of protecting myself when I was going through the healing programme: the gift of tongues. During the attack, I started praying in tongues in my mind, repeating the name of Jesus until the attack subsided. Then everything disappeared and when I got up I looked perfectly normal.'

The second major attack came a few months later, when Sandra was in La Paz, Bolivia, during *Alacitas*, the day when people worship the god of abundance. This pagan festival had attracted to the market place many people who believed in its superstition and witchcraft. The tradition involves buying small items symbolic of what people want in real life, such as houses or cars. They then have it blessed at the church and take it to the witches, for special powers to be conjured up before the god of abundance supposedly rewards them. Sandra, unaware of the implications of this ritual and five months pregnant at the time, was there with her husband and his sister to buy some trinkets for her children. She did not realise she was walking into the enemy's camp.

She said, 'We were about to cross the road in the direction of a witch, who was selling small statues of gods and the devil, which are used as good luck charms in Bolivia. The woman suddenly turned towards me and stared with such hatred. I started to feel ill, almost fainting, while my husband immediately felt as if he had a terribly bad toothache. My sister-in-law and my husband carried me away and soon my husband's pain subsided, but mine continued. And I started getting a very high fever.'

Sandra ended up in hospital for a couple of weeks with a severe kidney infection, and none of the medicine that the doctors gave her worked. She went on, 'As soon as I was left alone, my bed moved up and down. I was too terrified to close my eyes because, when I did, I could "see" Satan pushing my bed against the wall.

'The doctors were very worried and feared for my life, as well as for my baby's. After a few days, my grandmother came to visit and put a rosary around my neck. She also brought a tape-recorder and put on some Christian music. I was immediately able to sleep and, from that moment on, I recuperated from the infection. The doctors were puzzled but very happy. Until then I didn't believe in the rosary. Now I know its power.'

Still the devil had not given up. Sandra's next attack came when she was having her baby. It was decided that she should have a Caesarean section and would therefore need an epidural. But it was improperly administered, delivering the drug to her upper rather than her lower spine. She temporarily lost her sight and began to scream. 'Finally,' she said, 'when I was able to see again, I looked up to witness two large red eyes against the wall, looking down as if mocking me. I knew it was Satan and thought for sure I was going to die.'

Meanwhile, unaware both of Sandra's terror and of the anaesthetist's mistake, the medical team went on with their work. 'A doctor started cutting and I started screaming,' recalled Sandra. 'I began praying, asking Jesus to protect me and my baby, and asking Mary to pray for me.' By this time the doctors decided to give Sandra a general anaesthetic, because she was moving around too much. 'The last thing I saw was Jesus and Mary beside me, both looking down at me with such love. Then I knew everything would be all right, and I woke up later on to find out that I had a baby boy and that everything was fine.'

There have been other bizarre encounters with Satan at times.

In one old house where Sandra's family lived, their dog was for ever trembling, howling and barking for no apparent reason. They also suffered two fires at that house that could never be explained. But the most troubling incidents involved her daughter, Natalia, when she was five years old.

'She was in the bathroom by herself and came out looking pale. She told me she heard a man's voice saying, "Natalia, you're going to be mine!" She was very scared and soon started having nightmares. We prayed a lot with her and, for quite a while, she slept with a rosary around her neck and an open Bible on her chest. The nightmares finally stopped and she was fine.'

According to Sandra, Natalia has the gift of discernment. 'She can feel when there is something evil in her presence. Once, when we held a prayer meeting in the basement of a member's home, we all began to feel uncomfortable and none of us could really get into the prayer. Natalia walked around the room afterwards and then pointed out to me the statue of a mythical god, which was standing in the corner. That's where the evil is coming from, she told me, and when I approached it I could feel it too. We told the woman about it and she spoke to a priest who does not believe in such things. He said that evil lies only in the hearts of man, not in objects. But we know that it can lurk in objects as well.'

The attacks still go on, but they happen less frequently and Sandra says that her faith gets stronger and stronger all the time. Now thirty-five, she has the kind of job that surprises sceptics, who think people claiming to be bedevilled are suffering from hysteria and therefore live at the margins of society. Sandra is an assistant at the International Monetary Fund.

Protection from possession

'Possession,' argues Dr Scott Peck, 'is no accident.'[9] It is also, in his opinion, very rare for genuine possession to take place. He prefers to see 'human evil', which is much more common than possession, as occurring without demonic influence. This is where he and I differ. Possibly, at the time he wrote his book *The People of the Lie* (1983), the degree of demonic oppression was not as visible as it is now, when the full impact of the 'psychic industry' has become apparent. He does, however, concede that in the cases which he believes can be called possession, the majority have had some link to the occult.

If a person has been baptised, this will provide a certain amount of spiritual protection against possession. But it does not guarantee prevention from lesser problems, such as oppression, depression and infestation. With the sacrament of baptism in place – as insignificant as some may believe it to be – one has a greater degree of power against the forces of evil. The second key defence against these forces is the family unit. And the third is prayer, which obviously means having a relationship with God (see Appendix I).

Looking back at one of the cases we have already considered, involving the Vietnam war veteran, it did not appear to be possession, though it may fit into one of the lesser categories of evil. Without knowing whether the man had any occult involvement, the problem of demonic infestation (such as the marks around the neck) and demonic oppression (the spirit of nicotine) most likely came from his involvement with drugs.

Drugs can leave the mind open for what I would call demonic invasion or intrusion. By experimenting with alternate states of reality, one drops one's psychic guard. Hallucinogens like peyote are particularly dangerous, and it is significant that this drug was often used by Native Americans to induce shamanistic trances. Excessive alcohol can have the same effect. In that sense, involvement with the occult and mind-altering drugs act as a similar vehicle for evil. The next story illustrates the nature of this intrusion of the mind and the power of its sweeping malignancy

The power of invasion

The paranormal has been rigorously investigated and there have undoubtedly been a lot of fraudulent claims over the years. But one should not dismiss the world of the supernatural simply because of a few widely publicised reports of trickery. Colin Wilson, a prolific author on paranormal subjects, after researching poltergeist activity similar to that experienced by Sandra Solares, concluded, 'The spirit theory is the most plausible, unfortunately.'[10] The interface of the mind with that of others is not really questioned today. Belief in extra-sensory perception (ESP) is commonplace. For believers in telepathy, even the relatively simple idea of receiving a phone call from someone you were just thinking about suggests that the mind could well be open to other influences as well, especially if such an experience is induced.

American author Dave Hunt writes about the disturbing example of Eileen Garrett, who was referred to before her death as 'the greatest living medium'.[11] The *New York Post* said of her, 'In the aristocracy of the psychic world, Mrs Garrett remains the most fascinating.' She had noteworthy friends and associates: H.G. Wells, Carl Jung, Aldous Huxley, William Butler Yeats and Sir Arthur Conan Doyle.

Garrett's paranormal powers were first exhibited in early childhood and for more than thirty years she had spirits who spoke *through* her, claiming to have 'passed to the other side'. These spirits of the dead were, she said, called Uvani and Abdul Latif.

Latif did not confine himself to Mrs Garrett, having supposedly communicated with many mediums across the centuries. But the Garrett experience was extraordinary. Hunt continues, 'While under his control, Eileen Garrett (like other mediums before her) was able to speak fluently and write in a scholarly and philosophical manner in Arabic, Hebrew, Hindi, Greek, Latin, Coptic, French, German and Italian on a wide number of subjects. These disciplines included medicine, history, theology, physics, music, mineralogy and anatomy.'

Conan Doyle, creator of Sherlock Holmes, arranged for stenographers to take down an entire book dictated by Latif when Garrett was in a trance, which was later published. Mrs Garrett was amazed but frightened by her first hypnotically induced trance, when she realised that a male voice – Uvani – had 'spoken through her mouth'. She convinced herself that Uvani and the other entities who followed him were 'psychological phenomena' rather than the beings they claimed to be. In such a way she protected her sanity. She also allowed herself to be medically tested. In one such investigation – conducted in New York by Dr Cornelium H. Traeger, a specialist in arthritis and heart disease – the doctor adopted the common psychological view that the entities were splits in Mrs Garrett's psyche. Again, Mrs Garrett wanted desperately to believe it. But Dr Traeger could not easily explain some of the phenomena he discovered while Mrs Garrett was in a trance. He tested her blood flow, respiration, pulse, heart pressure and cardiac reaction and, according to an associate, Dr Elmer Lindsay, 'The results were . . . so surprising that Dr Traeger hesitated to show them to his colleagues.'

Lindsay said, 'No human heart could show records so diametrically opposed and divergent . . . The tests were carried out with the full cooperation of Mrs Garrett's two chief guides, Uvani and Abdul Latif . . . When the bleeding time . . . blood counts [etc.] were checked, the results suggested an actual change in the physical composition of the medium's blood when she was entranced [and different for each control entity].'[12]

Other tests by Hereward Carrington, director of the American Psychical Institute, indicated that the various voices speaking through Mrs Garrett were independent personalities rather than splits in her psyche. And a polygraph lie-detector test confirmed that each entity differed fundamentally from the medium and from each other.[13]

Clearly, the knowledge which this woman possessed was not of her own learning. So the assessment Dr Peck provides of the differences between multiple-personality illness and possession would hold true in this case.[14] The induced hypnotic trance opened the door, dropping the conscious guard of the psyche, allowing other entities not only to invade her but to inhabit her as well. With even a remote possibility of that occurring, one wonders why mediums or psychics dare to take the risk. Often astrologers or psychics will admit that there are spirits behind the craft but, in their ignorance – even if acting in good faith – they want to believe the spirit world is friendly, a place where 'masters' exist who are willing to pass on secret knowledge that will reveal the mysteries of life. This naïvety means that they have no protection against the powers of darkness – no matter what they believe, no matter what they tell you. Their artifice is pathetic: surrounding themselves with imaginary white light for protection does not hold a candle to the cunning deceit of demons.

It is, of course, disturbing to imagine that one's mind can be penetrated by an alien force, which can then influence all that one says and does. No wonder this kind of activity was specifically banned by the scriptures.

181

The fashion for psychic discovery is not a new phenomenon and should not dupe us into believing that the powers of darkness have ever left us. Around the thirteenth century, as the Christian message took hold across Europe, pagan superstitions were by no means obliterated. Many converts still stuck to the old ways, continuing to practise heathen ceremonies alongside their new religion. If anything, witchcraft and the occult strengthened their grasp. Mistakenly believing that they now enjoyed God's protection, people fooled themselves into thinking that 'the black arts' offered cures as well as curses.

Sorcery and witchcraft were not considered a crime or even, outside church circles, thought morally suspect. It was mainly women who dabbled in witchcraft, and there were all sorts of innuendoes linking female sexuality with Satanism. But the tide turned dramatically in the period of insecurity after the Black Death, when people were unsure whether their own behaviour had been responsible for engendering the plague. A moral panic broke out, unleashing a savage reaction, in which the ill-informed and prejudiced held sway. By 1400, accusations against supposed witches – often with little genuine proof – led to widespread barbarism, with thousands dying horrible deaths. The problem was that the detection of supernatural crime had been left to the ignorant, and the witch-hunting process deteriorated into mass hysteria.

Two centuries later, the terror was still going on. Between 1609 and 1633, at least 900 women were tortured in iron-studded chairs heated over fires.[15] Unsurprisingly, confessions were easily extracted, regardless of the truth, and the victims were then burned at the stake. But the end result of this practice, seen from the viewpoint of more civilised modern times, was the conviction that witchcraft was a farce. One of the arguments widely accepted was that of anthropologist Margaret Murray. Writing in 1921, she claimed that witchcraft was merely an old relic of a pre-Christian fertility religion dating back centuries.[16] Others thought that the insanity grew from Christianity itself, because of the high standards imposed by the Church regarding sexuality.

Whatever the case, people have come to view the notion of witchcraft as hocus-pocus – a symptom of an age when the population lived in ignorance. There never were any witches, just silly old women pretending to be so, or simpletons who were easily led. Following the suspect logic of this line of thinking, people nowadays believe that there was no evil, either. Their judgement has been clouded by the undoubted hysteria of the Middle Ages. They are obviously right to point to the fact that many innocents, such as Joan of Arc, were put to death. But that does not mean that witchcraft did not occur on a wide scale. And it certainly does not mean that evil did not exist.

Sceptics also point to the fact that the last execution for witchcraft in Britain was in the 1750s (even though the Witchcraft Act was not finally repealed until 1951), as scientific reason was now thought to have swept away the notion of belief in unprovable phenomena.[17] But the passing of the witchcraft craze did not signal an end to interest in the dark forces. It resurfaced in a more sophisticated form, and among a largely different class, in the middle of the nineteenth century.

Spiritualism was born in rural New York in 1850 when two sisters, Margaret and Kate Fox, promoted their psychic experiences after a series of poltergeist activities occurred in their home. These became popularly known as 'the Rochester Rappings', after the Fox family reported that phantom footsteps and knocking on walls were regular happenings in their house. At times the vibrations were strong enough to literally shake the beds. The hair of Mrs Fox, the girls' mother, went white in a week.[18]

Most experts believe that this kind of activity – in which, typically, small objects move around, dishes break and lights flash without any apparent reason – is normally associated with teenagers. Others mistakenly believe it to be linked to stress. Indeed, nearly all writers who have studied these phenomena have reached similar conclusions. Colin Wilson writes, 'By the time I began to write *Poltergeist* there was not a shred of doubt in my mind. Poltergeists are exactly what they claim to be, disembodied spirits . . . Playfair [another researcher and writer about paranormal activity] learned that witchdoctors (or shamans) can summon poltergeists and direct them to cause trouble to certain people. Witches have, of course, claimed to make use of spirits.

'I must admit that all this left me feeling rather shaken. I had studied "the occult" for ten years [at the time, in 1987] and had never doubted for a moment that most of its mysteries can be explained in terms of unknown powers of the human mind – telepathy, clairvoyance, psychokinesis, and so on . . . It was startling to suddenly be confronted with evidence for the existence of spirits. I had never actually taken the position that there are no such things as spirits; but I had always assumed that, if they exist, they play only a small part in paranormal phenomena. Now I found myself obliged to recognise that they play a central part ... I found this conclusion thoroughly embarrassing. But honesty compelled me to admit that [the powers of the mind] simply fail to explain the facts as completely as the spirit theory.'[19]

Even in the earliest manifestation of spiritualism, there was evidence that evil lurked in the spirit realm. Within a short time, the Fox sisters began conversing with a spirit who called himself 'Mr Splitfoot'. They were told they had been chosen to develop a new religion, which would become well known. The spirit said, 'You must proclaim these truths to the world. This is the dawning of a new era. When you do your duty, God will protect you and good spirits will watch over you.' According to the Foxes, the basic tenet was that the human spirit survives death – and this has become the case in all forms of spiritualism in the 150 years since then. Mediums who enter into a trance, like Mrs Garrett or Uri Geller, have all reported that they are able to contact the spirits of the dead.

The Fox sisters, who did not question the source of their activity, followed orders from their spirit guide and saw spiritualism spread like wildfire throughout the United States and then Europe. But for Kate and Margaret, their promised protection did not materialise and eventually they became raving alcoholics. Nothing could satisfy their craving and they lost all sense of moral responsibility. One American newspaper described Margaret towards the end of her life as an 'object of charity, a mental and physical wreck, whose appetite is only for intoxicating liquors ... the lips that utter little else than profanity once promulgated a doctrine of a new religion.' Kate was reported to have said that spiritualism was 'the most wicked blasphemy the world has ever known ... I loathe the thing I have become.' And when asked for another seance, she replied, 'You are driving me to hell.'[20]

As early as 1852, spiritualism was introduced to England and Germany, and was established in both countries within seven years. Witchcraft and necromancy had gained a new hold under a new guise. Hundreds of thousands of people across the 'civilised'

Christian world were now attending seances.

Spiritualism's next great boost came from a young Russian woman, Helena Hahn, who married a Russian general called Blavatsky. Having been clairvoyant as a child, she studied the occult extensively and travelled throughout Europe with some of the popular mediums of the day. Among them was Daniel Dunglas Home, a talented Scottish-born medium who was said to make tables rise to the ceiling and to be able to stick his face in hot coals. By the time Madame Blavatsky moved to America in 1873 she had become a chain-smoker, weighed 16 stone 6 lb (230 lb) and was noted for her foul mouth.

In spite of these character defects, she was to have a great influence on the popularisation of spiritualism. She formed a study group called the Theosophical Society – from the Greek words *theos*, meaning god, and *sophia*, wisdom – and branches were soon set up in city after city in America and Europe. Her book, entitled *Isis Unveiled*, became an instant best-seller and was taken up as a sort of society 'bible'. She asserted, among many other things, that spiritualist phenomena had been recognised for centuries and that old magical texts contained truths, which were known to her. She claimed that she had been commissioned by discarnate entities to regenerate the doctrines of karma and reincarnation.[21]

Madame Blavatsky claimed that the book was revealed to her in Tibet by these secret masters. Many disciples later, and after some bad publicity, she went off to India and achieved further success which was lionised by A.P. Sinnett in a book based on the teachings of the secret masters, *Esoteric Buddhism*. Many people tried to debunk her, but her famous disciples stood by her, such as W.B. Yeats, who recorded that her cuckoo clock hooted at him when he was alone with it, though it was not working at the time.[22] After her death, the movement was taken over by Annie Besant in 1907. Shortly thereafter, Besant discovered the Brahmin child Jiddu Krishnamurti, declared him an avatar (god-realised being) and brought him to the West. But in 1929 Krishnamurti permanently rejected the god-business.

It was at about this time that Charles Darwin and his theory of evolution left the uncomfortable impression of a life without God, creating a spiritual gap in people as big as the Grand Canyon and a craving for something that would replace the hope that had been lost through scientific discovery. When Sinnett, a respected editor of India's most authoritative newspaper, revealed that secret masters were available to guide the vulnerable, it struck a chord with millions of people. A door had been opened and, even though the language has been modified, its effects continue today.

Jung's dark secret

Carl Jung is revered throughout the world as one of the most influential pioneers of psychology, and is known for his work on the 'collective unconscious'. Millions laud him in the belief that his theories are the answer to some of the most impenetrable problems of the human psyche. There are detractors, of course, especially those who deride the importance he placed on dreams. But what few of his critics – and still fewer of his fans – realise is that Jung had a dark secret: he was a lifelong participant in the arts of the occult.

At just three years of age Jung reported his first vision. Not that this was surprising in his family, where supernatural experiences appear to have been common for generations. Several of his family had been involved with seances. It was said that his mother's home was so full of spirit activity that she had to make an effort to keep 'it' (the mystical force) contained, so that her father, a Protestant minister no less, could write his Sunday sermons. Jung's grandmother once went into a trance for three days, during which she described with uncanny accuracy people unknown to her, whose existence was subsequently proved. Later, after her death, Jung's grandfather held seances to contact his wife and it is claimed that he had lengthy conversations with her.[23]

As we know from Chapter 3, this type of activity is passed on, as new members of each generation cultivate contact with the spirit world. The ties get stronger and the manifestations become more apparent. Given Jung's family history, it was therefore entirely natural that he should have been deeply attracted to the occult. Apparently, after his split with Freud in 1912, Jung's spirit manifestations increased, horrifying him and leading him to the brink of suicide. It was at about this time that a new mentor arrived on the scene: Philemon, a spirit guide. Jung, aware of the response that this was likely to attract from his colleagues and followers, felt it impossible to share such an experience with them. He knew it would have harmed his reputation irreparably. So it remained a secret. Even his doctoral thesis, entitled 'Psychology and Pathology of So-called Occult Phenomena', was hushed up to avoid controversy.

Until this time Jung had argued that all minds were a part of something he called the collective unconscious, which he described as the source of unknown powers. He repeatedly defined the impulses of the unconscious as 'exteriorisations', but he eventually rejected the theory in favour of the spirit world. He wrote, 'Philemon represented a force which was not myself . . . It was he who taught me psychic objectivity, the reality of the psyche . . . He was a mysterious figure to me. At times he seemed to me quite real, as if he were a living personality. I went walking up and down the garden with him, and to me he was what the Indians call a guru.'[24]

Eventually, Jung came to suspect that not only Philemon but the many other spirit entities that he and his family had cultivated for years were not part of his famous collective unconscious but, in reality, dangerous independent beings. He once wrote: 'Hardly had I been in bed for half an hour than everything was there as before: the torpor, the repulsive smell, the dripping . . . something brushed along the walls, the furniture creaked . . . there were rustlings in the corners . . . The phenomena grew still more intense during the following weekend . . . I cautiously suggested to my host that the house might be haunted, and that this might explain the surprisingly low rent . . . The fifth weekend was . . . unbearable . . . there were rustlings, creakings, and bangings; from outside, blows rained on the walls. I had the feeling there was something near me, and opened my eyes. There, beside me on the pillow, I saw the head of an old woman, and the right eye, wide open, glared at me . . . I leapt out of bed with one bound, lit the candle and spent the rest of the night in an armchair . . . my health had suffered under these experiences . . . I consider it out of the question that it was a delusion of the senses.'[25]

After a conversation with Professor James Hyslop of Columbia University about 'the proof of identity (of the spirits)', Jung said, 'He admitted that, all things considered, all these metaphysical phenomena could be explained better by the hypothesis of spirits than by the qualities and peculiarities of the unconscious. And here, on the basis of my own experience, I am bound to concede he is right. In each individual case I must out of necessity be sceptical, but in the long run I have to admit that the spirit hypothesis yields better results in practice than any other.'[26]

Towards the end of his life, Jung became a victim of the forces to which he submitted his unconscious, the very same forces that caused the slow disintegration of his psyche, which all those who court occult powers inevitably experience at some point. His struggle to remain in control was evident as he wrote, 'I needed a point of support in "this world", and I may say that my family and my professional work . . . remained the base to which I could always return . . . [or] the unconscious contents could have driven me out of my wits . . . I have a medical diploma from a Swiss university, I must help my patients, I have a wife and five children, I live at 228 Seestrasse in Kusnacht – these were actualities which made demands upon me and proved to me again and again that I really existed, that I was not a blank page whirling about in the winds of the spirit, like Nietzsche [who died insane].'[27]

Jung, like so many others before and after him, came to the same unfortunate conclusions about the source of mystical powers and poltergeist activity. Here was the man who gave scientific credibility to the consciousness movement eventually admitting that the entities he thought of as part of his collective unconscious were, after all, hostile beings existing outside the inner workings of the mind. He was forced to confess that the most sensible explanation for this activity was, in fact, the spirit world. As so many others have since discovered, it was the altered state of consciousness that he so avidly sought, and advocated for others, that nearly destroyed him in the end. Yet all of this remained hidden.

Channelling and spirit guides

Channelling is the popular modern term used today by those seeking guidance from a so-called higher source, just as Jung did. It is developed through meditation or visualisation, by opening up the consciousness to what is referred to as the 'universal mind'. It is often suggested to people lured into this activity that they visualise a 'guide' to facilitate the experience. Some practitioners claim that these spirit guides have an independent existence, while others believe it is merely an elevated or advanced aspect of the unconscious that becomes accessible through occult techniques.

From what you have already read, you will realise that once you enter this trance state, you open yourself to possible invasion from the spiritual world. Therefore, by issuing an invitation to a spirit entity – whether by visualisation, guided imagery or induced trance – you should appreciate that there is no certainty that what you are 'seeing' or receiving is really an aspect of your own consciousness. The evidence clearly points to the contrary.

Many people assume, incorrectly, that the spirit world is a friendly environment. As Jung conceded, 'Beware of naïvely assuming that the issue of spirits and ghosts has been settled.'[28] We have seen centuries of evidence describing encounters with the demonic and are therefore aware that Satan does not openly announce his presence. It is far more likely that his true form is rarely visible until the most advanced stages of possession, similar to what Dr Peck witnessed during the exorcisms. He, or 'it', can pose as an angel of light, supposedly dispensing truth and wisdom. But though the devil has been referred to for centuries as a liar, deceiver and murderer, people go on believing that it is an honour to achieve a spirit contact, mistaking the demon for insight into their 'higher self'.

Rarely has this been expressed as well as in C.S. Lewis's book *The Screwtape Letters*, where a senior devil, Screwtape, is instructing a junior devil, Wormwood, on the tricks of the trade. 'Our policy for the moment is to conceal ourselves. If once we can produce our perfect work – the Materialist Magician, the man not using, but veritably worshipping, what he vaguely calls "Forces", while denying the existence of "spirits" – then the end of the war will be in sight. But in the meantime we must obey our orders. I do not believe you will have much difficulty in keeping the patient in the dark. The fact that "devils" are predominantly comic figures in the modern imagination will help you. If any faint suspicion of your existence begins to arise in his mind, suggest to him a picture of something in red tights, and persuade him that since he cannot believe in that (it is an old textbook method of confusing them) he therefore cannot believe in you.'[29]

Of course, this is not to say that all guided imagery will have negative effects, or that it is not a useful technique to combat disease. Quite the contrary. If you are engaged in a battle with cancer, or any other terminal illness, clearly it is important to have a positive mental attitude. Sometimes, to overcome the fear, it becomes necessary to meditate on a positive picture, which may in effect help to strengthen the immune system. Many therapists use symbols, animals or guides to initiate the process.

The danger occurs when you solicit any type of guide and seek its advice. That is the point where you cross the line into an occult practice and enter the domain controlled by the powers of darkness. This technique becomes identical to channelling, or acting as a medium. In certain circles within the medical profession, this is becoming dangerously popular, while patients are oblivious of the vulnerable position in which they are being placed. Many therapists are well aware that the techniques they are using are shamanistic, part of an ancient art of healing which, in their view, should be revived for our well-being. Again, their intentions are good. But patients place their trust in therapists who, sadly, do not know all the facts.

Until recently, spirituality has not been the concern of orthodox medicine or psychology, so doctors are not equipped with the knowledge to give advice about what is dangerous and what is not. In a sense, they too are victims of the overlap between the scientific and spirituality which has been integrated into alternative health care. Spiritual practices are subtly woven into so many treatments that people are unaware of what may be genuinely therapeutic and what may be occult, and therefore dangerous to them.

Before we review how these practices have crept into the field of medicine, let us first take a look at what is currently being promulgated by organisations such as the National Spiritualist Union (NSU), an occult organisation that teaches people how to become psychic healers or mediums. Whatever their grandiose claims and the sincerity of many who take up such practices, please remember that this activity is strictly prohibited in the Bible. Therefore God does not sanction such practices, nor does He provide protection from what spiritualists call malign spirits (regardless of the persuasive arguments of the NSU and its followers). To follow them is to enter the realm of the demonic.

Occult training

In most American and European cities you will find an NSU branch advertising its claim to teach people the tricks of the

190

occult trade. Their courses promise to provide you with everything you need to know to become a fully fledged medium, ready to go out and set up shop. These schools will train you to develop what they affect to call latent psychic talents or abilities. This is accomplished, they say, through meditation, prayer and visualisation. But we can be sure, knowing that all occult techniques are off-limits before God, that 'prayer' is a misnomer: it cannot therefore involve God's participation.

One of the leading NSU trainers is Bob Coller, who runs courses for mediums at Stanstead Hall, Essex, the English NSU headquarters. He claims that a growing number of people are showing interest in developing their psychic abilities. But he does not encourage everyone to do so. He takes his job seriously and tries to assess the mental stability of potential trainees before agreeing to train them. He does this, he says, to avoid knowledge falling into the 'wrong' hands – those who might misuse their power, perhaps, or be unable to handle it. 'Being a medium is a great responsibility, so we make sure that our students are mature enough to handle the information they are getting,' says Coller.[30]

This misses the point, of course. No one is mature enough to 'handle' the effects of the occult. Indeed, whether he is conscious of it or not, Coller's weeding-out process is more likely to be aimed at eliminating those predisposed to psychological weakness. In other words, those unable, at least initially, to fight off the effects of occult techniques, which are bound to cause depression and/or a slow disintegration of the psyche.

Some of Coller's students want to become healers, while others prefer to be mediums, psychic writers or artists. In a magazine report lauding both the NSU's and Coller's achievements, writer and journalist Gillian Cribbs wrote, 'Meditation is the route to art and writing and potential healers get hands-on experience at the college.'[31]

Coller offers a rather simplistic way of checking whether a supposed psychic is a fake. He suggests that they should be asked whether they can contact a specific relative (or demon). 'If they agree, they are charlatans, because the spirit world decides who comes through, not the medium.' It is thought by most spiritualist advocates that, if a spirit wants to make contact, it will approach the medium's guide. But many dismiss the whole idea of guides, according to Cribbs, saying that they are simply aspects of higher consciousness or memories of past lives. 'A trainee works on strengthening contact with the spirit guide (or higher self) through meditation, prayer and visualisation,' says Cribbs. As the 'bond' [or bondage] develops, the begging medium is told to continue to practise furthering the spirit contact. These evil spirits will not always turn up on the first try. Although the classes insist that a trainee learn how to protect him- or herself from an experience with what they call a 'malign spirit', the method they use is absurd. They insist that lighting a candle alone and asking God or the heavenly light to shield the medium with love is enough to guarantee protection from the demonic.[32]

As I clearly pointed out before, it would be entirely contradictory for God to provide protection for those who dabble in the occult, which is in direct defiance of what He is willing to support in the spiritual realm. The consequence of such practices is the loss of God's protection. At the heart of the problem lies the fact that all these practitioners – psychics, mediums, channellers – are deluding themselves. They are either unaware that such practices are off-limits or they choose to ignore it, scorning the danger from the spirits whom they contact.

At the College of Psychic Studies, Cribbs says that in trance mediumship a person is completely taken over by a guide, 'who impress their voice, mannerisms and even physical features on the medium'.[33] (How, incidentally, could this be anything other than possession?) Consider the case of trance medium Mary Absolum, who claims that her guide is a Chinese philosopher, who came to her twenty-one years ago. 'I suddenly went into a trance,' she said. 'I thought I had fallen asleep, and had no recollection of what I said. But when I came around, I felt energised by the experience. People in the group said my voice had changed and I had adopted a masculine persona.'[34]

It is obvious that she views this experience as an achievement, as do many others. But surely it is frightening to think of so many people living in ignorance, powerless in the face of such deceptive powers of darkness? If a woman, through channelling, is suddenly taken over by a male persona and has no recollection of the incident, we can rule out imagination as a cause. Such practices at the NSU are monitored and well organised, so hysteria or hallucination are also ruled out. The only rational explanation is that they are indeed encountering the spirit world. What they cannot believe, or choose not to believe, is that it is the demonic spirit world. They cannot see through its disguise. People refuse to search further for the truth. Sometimes this may be due to the ego, as one becomes known as a healer or a medium, or to the potential money they can earn, or because they have made a career around it and feel they are locked in by a wrong choice. Given the complications these people will inevitably experience, it just might be preferable to change career. Cribbs states that Mary Absolum always says a prayer before working to fill the area with peace and then, wrongly, asserts that she has never encountered a malign spirit.

Cribbs also mentions another psychic who works in trance under a spirit guide: Edith Sampson, who runs Sylvan Trust, a healing centre in north London, with ten associate healers. Edith was raised as a Christian, and I am certain that she was as unaware as anyone of the forbidden nature of psychic practices and their interface with the demonic. She says her guide is a Welsh doctor who died more than 100 years ago, claiming to have verified information about him through local records. This does not prove by any means that this entity is a doctor, but suggests that the spirit world possesses vast knowledge of the past. If these spirits have been around since the beginning of time, as recorded testimony indicates, why would they not have access to history? And why would they not try to deceive us with carrots of the truth?

According to Cribbs, there is yet another world beyond the spirit world, which can be contacted through the School of Channelling. Tony Neate, a channelling expert and teacher, argues that it is a higher state of consciousness, 'the next step beyond trance mediumship' [35] He says, 'It can be through a discarnate entity or simply accessing a higher state of awareness and usually results in inspirational speaking or writing, rather than contact with loved ones.' Neate, like so many others, including Jung and Freud, grew up as the son of a strict Christian, a Methodist, and rejected his religion because he found the rules a bit stifling, and found spiritualism was more attractive.

While attending a spiritual group, he became aware of a tall presence with immense energy and power. This entity claimed to be 'a high priest of the sun'. Neate says that his guide has come through over the years with advice and inspiration, just as Philemon did for Jung.

Although it may sound ludicrous, you can see that channelling is actually more dangerous than all other occult techniques. From colleges on psychic healing to some of America's leading universities (Stanford and Boston College), occult concepts are now accepted and taught as part of human potential. It therefore becomes vitally important that people are aware of the facts, and the dangers, before they succumb to the fashion of dabbling in the spirit world.

Physicians and spirit guides

More and more orthodox doctors are being lured into occult practices, believing, in my view misguidedly, that what they are doing is good for their patients. One of the leading proponents of alternative therapy is Dr Bernie Siegel, oncologist, medical professor and best-selling author of *Love, Medicine and Miracles*. Like Jung, Dr Siegel has a spirit guide named George, whom he found during a directed meditation/trance technique, which he took up on advice from oncologist O. Carl Simonton and his wife, psychologist Stephanie Mathews.

They became well known through their use of visualisation techniques in helping cancer patients to fight the disease. The Simontons, says Siegel, convinced him to try a directed meditation. 'I approached this exercise with all the scepticism one expects from a mechanistic doctor. Still, I sat down, closed my eyes, and followed directions. I didn't believe it would work, but if it did, I expected to see Jesus or Moses. Who else would dare appear inside a surgeon's head? Instead I met George, a bearded, long-haired man wearing an immaculate flowing white gown and a skull-cap. It was an incredible awakening for me, because I hadn't expected anything to happen . . . George was spontaneous, aware of my feelings, and an excellent adviser.'[36]

When a spirit guide appears, as did Siegel's George, as a gentle loving figure, one is apt not to question its intent or its origin, especially when it comes from inside 'the head of a surgeon'. Moreover, if the entity's advice is wholesome, it is automatically thought to be some profound truth that should be heeded. Doctors and therapists who advocate getting in touch with the 'higher self' today will often tell you that this entity is actually part of oneself and the source of infinite knowledge. But there is

194

a very fine line between what is wholesome here and what will interface with the demonic.

George's influence on Dr Siegel was profound, affecting his work and, unsurprisingly, persuading him to perpetuate the practices. He says, 'I was still toying with the idea of a career change. When I told him [George], he explained that . . . I could do more by remaining a surgeon, but changing myself to help my patients to mobilise their mental powers against disease. I could combine the support and guidance of a minister or psychiatrist with the resources and expertise of a physician. I could practise clergery, a team my wife coined . . . George said, "You can go anywhere in the hospital. A clergyman or therapist can't. You are free to supplement medical treatment with love or death-and-dying counselling, in a way that non-physicians are not" . . . [George] has been an invaluable companion ever since his first appearance.'[37]

This sounds admirable: a doctor providing care above and beyond the call of duty. Very few doctors nowadays are willing to go that extra mile. Unfortunately, that unselfish attempt from a kind-hearted person could result in substantial risk. Cultivating a guide is a minor form of possession, and if doctors persist in this type of shamanistic therapy they should offer spiritual disclaimers.

But there are larger questions to answer here. How can anyone assume that these entities are a source of inner wisdom? How can the 'it' be wisdom and truth, when the origin cannot be verified? How can we simply absorb their wisdom, which is consistently in opposition to the God of the Jewish, Christian and Moslem faiths?

Let us consider what George's intent or agenda might have been. First, George was winning converts. By gently nudging Dr Siegel to help people use their mental powers to fight disease through the same occult or shamanistic method of seeking a guide for assistance, the doctor will have successfully introduced the spiritual world of the occult to the patient under acceptable terms. The patient would probably never have dabbled in the occult unless the technique was endorsed by a doctor. Second, George was assured of an enthusiastic and unquestioning reception. The patients, having then placed their faith in the spirit guide, might be deceived into believing all that they are told – so-called truth, along with more pejorative advice, which they are bound to follow. The demonic spirit world would have gained another conquest.

Another respected, and no doubt equally well intentioned, doctor who has been drawn into the occult is Dr Raymond Moody, the pioneer researcher into near-death experiences whose book *Life After Life* gave scientific credibility to an area that has fascinated millions down the ages. Dr Moody has designed an 'apparition chamber', in which clients are invited to gaze into the mirror, 'a crystal-clear pool of darkness', where they see their dead relatives.

It all began, the doctor has explained, with an accidental encounter with his late grandmother. Dr Moody had wanted to talk to his maternal grandmother, but his paternal grandmother popped up instead. 'I went into a place called the apparition booth, and in the room's dim light I gazed into the depth of the large mirror . . . I did this for at least an hour, but felt not even a twinge of her presence.' Later, however, sitting alone in a room, 'a woman simply walked in . . . I realised this person was my paternal grandmother, who had died some years before. I remember throwing my hands up toward my face, exclaiming, "Grandma".'[38]

This, Dr Moody says, was 'one of the most life-changing events I have ever experienced'. It may well have been but, unfortunately, he was unaware of what was really taking place and eventually was seduced by the manifestations. Apparently, the reason he did not see the grandmother he was seeking was because she was not the subject he 'needed' to see. Remember that at the school for psychics one of the ways to filter out charlatans is to ask potential 'seers' if they can guarantee who will turn up. If they say yes, they are a fraud. Dr Moody would pass such a test, indicating that he is definitely getting 'proper' results, but he remains unaware of what he is really entertaining in that mirror.

This singular 'spiritual experience' triggered Dr Moody's transition from orthodox doctor to a convinced – and convincing – mirror-gazing occult practitioner. But invoking spirits of the dead in a mirror is no different from doing so in a seance. In the Bible such activity would be defined as necromancy, which as we have said is strongly forbidden by God. And with good reason. Once again, we see no questions raised by this scientist about proof of the entity's identity. As far as he was concerned, 'it' looked like grandma and so 'it' was.

Dr Moody built his apparition room on top of his Alabama home, and in his book *Reunions: Visionary Encounters with Departed Loved Ones* he instructs readers on how to build their own. To enhance his arguments and validate his use of this questionable occult technique, he cites illustrious forebears. Among them are John Dee, a sixteenth-century scholar and favourite of Elizabeth I, who chatted with angels through his obsidian mirror, and Abraham Lincoln, who reportedly spotted a 'strange double image of himself' while gazing in the mirror.

Dr Moody is surprised that this technique is not more common, but suggests that 'one reason seems that practitioners have maintained secrecy about their techniques'. Not Dr Moody, however, who goes into inordinate detail about the way he creates his spiritual road to self-discovery. For him, the aim of mirror-gazing is to 'create a doorway to other dimensions of the mind'. He has definitely created a doorway, but to what? He is clearly unaware, as he takes hundreds of others through it.

To get clients into the right mood, Dr Moody advises eager subjects to rid themselves of caffeine and other stimulants. They spend some time chatting over a light lunch and take a country walk, before looking at photographs of their departed loved ones. Then they step into the chamber of darkness. Dr Moody promotes his new practice by insisting that scientists love the truth 'deeply' and are constantly conducting a systematic search for the truth. Contrary to Dr Moody's beliefs, this practice is in my view far from a search for the truth and doctors must educate themselves to realise how dangerous these practices are for both themselves and their patients.

The difference between what the psychics of today and Dr Moody are doing is that he does not invite 'it' within, into the realm of his own consciousness, as does Dr Siegel and the countless thousands who are learning occult visualisation and encountering the powers of darkness. It would take an entire book to detail the ramifications of the therapies that overlap with the occult. But I offer a simple guide to you in all such cases: before you accept any treatment that has a meditative aspect which solicits the higher self or a guide, think twice. Use your common sense; say no, regardless of who is prescribing it. This could save you years of trouble. Remember: many on this delusional road may experience benefits, but they will be short-lived and will result in psychological or emotional trouble. It is

197

better to be safe than sorry. One more thing: even if you mistakenly believe you can cope, think of the next generation – your children and their children – who may suffer because of your active participation in such matters.

Automatic writing

Another occult art that is learned at psychic schools is automatic writing. This is considered to be 'advanced' in the sense that, for an entity to dictate through a person, the person must be highly receptive to the spirit world and in reality the spirit must obviously 'possess' the body. Books that have been dictated by the spirit world through this process, such as Madame Blavatsky's *Isis Unveiled* and others written by Aleister Crowley, Alice Bailey, Napoleon Hill and Edgar Cayce, to name but a few, all seem to have a similar agenda: the advancement of man as a potential god, the divinity within, which can be developed through the wisdom given by those entities. This refutes every concept associated with the Christian, Moslem or Jewish monotheistic God. If there was an exception to the rule – in which just one of these entities actually promoted the God of the Bible – one might not suspect a definite agenda from the spiritual world of the occult, but the statistics alone associated with the transmission of this information can lead to no other conclusion.

Channelling expert Tony Neate claims that channelling is a more advanced technique, which often results in automatic writing. By far the most widely read book in this vein is *The Course in Miracles*, which has been popularised by author and lecturer Marianne Williamson in her book *A Return to Love*. *The Course* was conceived in the late 1960s by Dr Helen Schucman, a brilliant psychologist at the College of Physicians at Columbia University. At the time, she was an agnostic bordering on atheism who received revelations from an entity claiming to be the 'Son of God'.

Father Benedict Groeschel, the psychologist and author whose work on the dangers of apparitions we explored earlier (see Chapter 4), was a psychology student under Dr Schucman when she was about sixty years old. He tells how her revelations started with an 'experience of light' on a subway train.[39] She saw the light filling the car and shining on the faces of the people around her. Shortly afterwards, she felt compelled to write down what

198

this entity, claiming to be the Son of God, was saying to her. It turned into 1,100 pages, which became *The Course of Miracles*, and a book of poetry.

The Course is supposedly centred on the Son of God, but it depicts Christ as a rather anaemic figure, similar to every other spiritual or mystical figure in history. Father Groeschel argues that each sentence seems to contradict the preceding one, 'making it impossible to discover any real theological meaning from it'.[40] This is evident in every book that depicts the spirit world, because it is part of their agenda to confuse and delude the vulnerable. According to Father Groeschel, Dr Schucman's book has certain very puzzling characteristics. 'They do not represent Helen's own thought or convictions. When I met her, she still didn't know whether she believed in God at all. Years later I would still observe this separation in her thought and her conflict about the book. She would often be angry at the book. She once told me, "I hate that damned book".'[41]

Father Groeschel continues, 'Some passages are very strange, defining as real only what is everlasting – a Hindu frame of thought. Suffering is not real; neither is sin. She would say that she knew the meaning of the sentence she was writing, but did not know what was coming after it. She did not appear to hear words, but to know what they would be.' While Father Groeschel believes that what Dr Schucman experienced was not automatic writing but internal dictation, as he describes her state of mind towards the end of her life it becomes quite apparent that she had interfaced with the demonic. He writes, 'Two very disturbing but insightful facts gradually came into view for me and threw some light on this very strange chapter in my own life. One was the incredible darkness that descended upon Helen Schucman in the last years of her life. This woman, who had written so eloquently that suffering really did not exist, spent the last two years of her life in the blackest psychotic depression I have ever witnessed . . . it was almost frightening to be with her.'[42]

Dr Schucman evidently felt that she could not change a word of the book, yet her great fear was that *The Course* would become a cult. 'Against Helen's better judgement, *The Course* was published first in a small private edition and then in a larger public edition. To her great discomfort Helen's identity became known.' But Father Groeschel did not see that Helen Schucman had the classic symptoms of demonic intervention, which did not become apparent until near the end of her life. He did not regard the entity that provided the information to Helen as demonic, perhaps because his frame of reference was psychology, which allows for fragmentation of the psyche without the intervention of evil. But one key factor remains glaringly obvious in illustrating the demonic: 'the blackest psychotic depression', which engulfed her, and the severity of it, which frightened those around her. This kind of psychological disintegration is to evil what malignant tumours are to cancer.

In every case of demonic oppression you will find a dark depression, usually dependent on the level of invasion – whether it is an entity acting through the person, whether it is invoked outside the consciousness through astrology or Tarot cards. Intervention of any sort through continued occult practices will cause devastating problems. The depression that Father Groeschel witnessed is confirmation of the demonic nature of the entity who cleverly claimed to be the Son of God. Again, the Christ entity was not Jesus of the Bible; sin was of no consequence and suffering was an illusion – concepts that are clearly in opposition to the biblical God. The fact that the information given to Schucman was not even close or similar to her own beliefs, and the fact that she grew to hate *The Course* while unwilling to change a word of it, indicates the likelihood that a controlling demonic entity was indeed at work.

Angels and channelling

The wave of books, information and even films that came out a few years back on angels fuelled the desire for an experience and understanding of the supernatural. I certainly agree that there are heavenly messengers who dispense God's graces and protection, and who are active on earth today, but they cannot be accessed through methods that God does not condone. The angels craze opened up a virtual Pandora's box of spirituality. In this unusual atmosphere, it is highly likely that the spiritual world is exploding with activity. If the Marian prophecy is accurate, we are entering a critical period in history, when it may be vitally important for people to be settled in their spirituality, reconciled with their beliefs and their conscience, so that if we meet God unexpectedly we are prepared. It would therefore make sense that the dissemination of information through the occult spiritual world would be brimming over and, as we can see, it is.

We see evidence of the popularity of occult techniques in the 'psychic hotline' business, which has successfully infiltrated television. It is not uncommon to see talk shows that feature monthly, or even weekly, psychic spots, with astrologers or even purveyors of Ouija boards (which will cause possession quicker than any other known method) appearing on-screen. People are encouraged to accept this entertainment as 'real'. Naturally, they are bound to think there is something to it.

Books on angels continue to be produced, but they have become more sophisticated in their approach. They provide information on how to contact your angel as a guide, and on the benefits derived from the wisdom received from these beings. I receive countless angel books and only one in ten is actually accurate. Experience has become the primary indicator for the reality of the supernatural, without any discernment or caution in this field of the unknown. The floodgates are open again.

In just one of many books, author Ruth White tells of her personal guide, Gildas, who claims to be a fourteenth-century Benedictine monk.[43] According to White, he is one of a group of guides who is trying to build a bridge of communication between their world and ours to aid our transition into the 'golden age'. She says that these discarnate communicators will appear in a manner which is either 'acceptable or attractive to us and [will] take on a personality in order to communicate with us'. She believes these guides are highly evolved beings, just as so many others have down the ages. White believes that it is possible for a grandparent or another relative to become a guide upon death, which is right in line with Dr Moody's practices.

White and others qualify their work with the notion that we were all brought up with the idea that we have a guardian angel. It is only social conditioning that has led us to dissociate ourselves from the whole concept of the supernatural, which in reality, she believes, is quite natural to us and should therefore be cultivated. This conditioning, she claims, blocks the path, diffusing awareness, and apparently this is why we need to learn how to contact our angel or guide.

Superficially, this sounds very convincing because we all want to better ourselves. The lure continues with the notion that self-empowerment is possible if we drop our present patterns of life. Then the perspective gained through this type of spiritual guidance will supposedly give life a sense of meaning. This, unsurprisingly, is where most people take the bait. The dangers here are many but the most immediate is that of establishing contact and believing these beings have a divine origin.

'Wise guides,' White says, 'channelled at a very high level may urge you to take calculated risks,' thereby acknowledging, 'to follow may mean hard lessons to be learned.'[44] The intent of these so-called guides, or demons, is to cultivate a dependence on their advice, which seems to be the case with White when she says, 'Guidance from Gildas and being there to receive it is a life's work.' Although she says 'surrender' may not necessarily mean for a lifetime. To me it sounds more like bondage as she talks about how disturbing it can be when the guides threaten to cut off all advice unless the victim follows faithfully.

These beings come in the guise of humanitarian virtue and, like many, White buys into their seemingly innocent agenda. There is a familiar ring in this dialogue with the enticement several thousand years ago in the Garden of Eden, when the serpent tried to seduce Eve to eat from the Tree of Knowledge, with the promise of wisdom and the power to become like God. It sounds a bit clichéd, but the similarities are overwhelming.

'Lucifer,' White says, 'is not a bringer of evil, but the closest companion to the human journey.' She believes Lucifer is rather selfless – 'as an angelic being, he made an important sacrifice to journey with us'.[45] Here is a woman who, like countless others, believes earnestly that she is imparting valuable information to the world from strange discarnate entities.

White also claims that it is important for the person channelling to be under full trance, otherwise the messages could be corrupted by the person's own belief system, implying that an independent belief system is less than preferable. Guides may refer to themselves as many things, such as Mary Magdalene, the Direct Voice of God, and the Virgin Mary. But White insists that one must be alert to the lower and higher types in the hierarchy, commenting 'by their fruits we shall know them'. It is similar to the entity who appeared to Dr Schucman as the Son of God and dictated *The Course in Miracles*, but whose teaching was in direct opposition to that of Christ. If you want to use scripture to support an argument, you must also accept references to what 'fruits' implies and what is considered demonic and off-limits like channelling, mediumship and necromancy. But White resists the Christian religion with its 'heavy morality . . . and judgemental god'. A concept which, no doubt, is reinforced by Gildas.

But the most revealing and blatant passage in her book is where she speaks of sub-personalities, and goes on to describe them as aspects of ourselves, individual talents we acquire in life such as becoming an artist or teacher. She claims these sub-personalities have a bearing on working with guides and angels and gives an exercise similar to her others, for making contact with these demonic beings. But again she makes reference to their controlling nature when she says, 'Sub-personalities can reveal themselves to you and what *they may require of you.*' While exploring this realm, White says, '*You may find you are legion.*'[46] Since most of the information in her book comes directly from Gildas or presumably other guides, this statement is of particular concern, especially in light of the most well-known reference to the term legion, in Mark 5, 1–9. It talks about a man who was so violent no one dared to go near him. 'When Jesus came upon him, the "unclean spirit" in him recognised Jesus and cried out in a loud voice, "What have you to do with me, Jesus, son of the Most High God?" Jesus commanded the "unclean spirit" to come out of him and then asked him, "What is your name?" He replied, "Legion is my name. There are many of us."

'Seeing a herd of swine on the hillside, they [the demons] pleaded with Jesus, "Send us into the herd of swine. Let us enter them." And He let them, and the "unclean spirits" came out of the man and entered the swine. The herd of about two thousand rushed down a steep bank into the sea, where they were drowned.' The man who had been possessed by the legion was now sitting there in his right mind and was grateful to Jesus for what he had done for him. And all around him were seized with fear.

White has no idea of the danger she is in, or of the nature of the entities who communicate with her, nor does she understand that these evil beings do not have to manifest themselves violently or destructively to be demonic. Books such as hers, while beautifully illustrated with the flowery language of fulfilment and truth, are in reality as dangerous as those on the black arts. They are simply a more conventional and attractive entrée into the spirit world of the demonic.

Kristina is a close friend of mine, someone I would call alive with the spirit – the Holy Spirit, that is. She found herself curious about her guardian angel and from a strange set of coincidences, it appears that she was warned of the menacing powers which came in the guise of angelic protection.

In the spring of 1990 she started thinking about the existence of angels, particularly guardian angels, and wondered what hers might be called. She recalled, 'Then the idea popped into my head, "Why not ask it?" So I did. Immediately, from nowhere, came the name Gregory. I didn't know any Gregorys and couldn't see where else it had come from, so I decided this must be it.'

Kristina was pleased to think that she had an angelic minder, whom she could call on when needed. Walking down a lonely street, for instance, she would ask him for protection. 'I liked knowing his name,' she said. 'It made him more real and I was intrigued to know about others, too.'

She went on to persuade a friend, Vivian, to discover the name of her guardian angel, telling her how to ask. The name Harold jumped into Vivian's mind, and the two women laughed about their angels having such ordinary names. But they began to adopt an extraordinary routine. Kristina said, 'Once Viv knew hers, I would sometimes ask Gregory to get Harold to give her a dig if I wanted her to ring me, and sometimes it worked. It was a kind of heavenly shortcut, which made me feel I had an inside edge on life. As far as I was concerned, the whole thing was innocent.'

Innocent? Later, Kristina was able to recognise that during that time she started to feel very tired. At first she put this down to having a stressful job. But it got worse. She was always tired, particularly in the morning: even if she had had a full night's sleep. All she could think of was going to bed. 'Eventually,' she said, 'I made an appointment to see my doctor as I suspected I might be anaemic. My blood test, however, was clear and I began getting really worried that maybe I had ME.'

Soon afterwards Kristina received an alarming phone call from Vivian, who had also reported feeling tired. A house guest had left her a book entitled *The Hot Line*, by an Anglican vicar called Peter Lawrence, in which he told of his work in casting out evil spirits. Page 146 was a real eye-opener. He related how he had cast out a spirit who called itself Gregory, and that the next spirit to appear claimed to be called Harold. Not quite being able to believe it, he asked the demons what symptoms they brought and they answered, 'Tiredness.' The man whom Revd Lawrence was trying to help confirmed that he had indeed been feeling very tired, particularly when he read the Bible or prayed. So the vicar prayed that this 'tiredness leave in Jesus's name', which it eventually did, accompanied by a wail and a bout of coughing.

Kristina said, 'The coupling of those two names and the tiredness, which both Viv and I had been suffering, was enough to make me feel more than uneasy. Fortunately, a day or so later, I was due for my regular visit with my spiritual counsellor and explained to him what had happened, before asking his advice.'

Kristina was lucky. Her counsellor Father Jim McManus, wise in spiritual matters, knew what to do. He asked her if she had been talking to her 'angel' and, when she admitted that she had, he laid his hands on her and prayed. 'If anything has come into Kristina,' he prayed, 'leave her in the name of Jesus.' Then they prayed together that the spirit of God would fill her with His power, energy and love.

'I didn't feel anything in particular as he prayed, and even afterwards I wasn't sure if I felt any different,' said Kristina. 'The following morning, however, when my alarm clock went off, I had no trouble getting out of bed and one of my flatmates even said, "You look awake this morning." Since then, although I get tired when I go to bed late, the chronic, inexplicable tiredness that dogged me for six months has never come back. And I have certainly not been speaking to Gregory or Harold, or whoever they were.'

After that episode, Kristina concluded, 'We may well have guardian angels, but I now think I should have questioned where that inner voice came from. Just because it claimed to be an angel certainly doesn't mean it was. Thank goodness God did expose what I'm sure was the danger, as bizarre as it may seem, and as unprovable as it undoubtedly is. Otherwise, I imagine I would still be having medical tests to find the cause of my lethargy and getting more and more depressed.'

A friend of mine, Michelle, a very sophisticated woman, had come to visit me in London from Los Angeles one summer about six years ago. She was suffering from emotional troubles as she was going through a divorce and I tried to console her. She decided to extend her stay for six weeks and naturally we became closer friends. This was about two years after my experiences in Medjugorje and my realisation of the danger in occult practices.

After a dinner party one evening, one of the group of friends commented on Michelle, saying that while she was quite beautiful they could not handle being around her. 'She is so heavy, how can you take it?' Anne asked. In my sympathetic mode, I failed to correlate the heaviness, similar to what Dr Peck had described in the exorcisms he witnessed, to anything more concrete.

I had noticed she was reading a book on how to get in touch with your higher self, but I didn't think too much of it. Then later one night I told her about my experiences with evil and what had happened in Medjugorje (see Chapter 4). I asked her about the book, and she explained that it was basically instructions on how to tap into your inner wisdom, who would then act as a guide and help you with problems in life. When she told me that she had been successful, an entity had revealed its name, alarm bells rang.

I told her about the consequences of guides and what, in reality, they were, even though they looked so innocent and useful.

Then she told me that she had carried Tarot cards with her for years, which increased the likelihood of an evil presence around her. I asked her if she would be willing to speak to someone before she left London. Feeling less certain than I do today about whether this woman was really in trouble, I hesitantly got in contact with the leading exorcist for the Westminster diocese, through an associate of mine. I told him of my experience and that, although I was not certain Michelle was in trouble, an entity had revealed its name and that made me feel uncomfortable enough to call. He chatted with her over the phone and said he could not be sure about anything, more than likely it was a false alarm, but to come in the next morning just to be safe.

The next day I took her round to his office. He told me to go and have breakfast while he spoke to her and, if need be, when I came back in forty-five minutes' time we would pray for her. I felt like an idiot, certain that I had overreacted. But I kept reminding myself that it was better to be safe than sorry.

When I knocked on the door, the priest immediately pulled me inside, with a sense of urgency that confirmed my suspicions. He said we would pray immediately. Michelle, of course, had only slight symptoms but still enough for others to notice the heaviness about her. This oppression would have plagued her for the rest of her life had she not agreed to consult an expert.

We went upstairs to a room where he conducted these meetings and told us to sit down. She sat next to me while he stood in front of her and began the ceremony. I closed my eyes and so did she; I prayed that God would help her and the priest. Ten minutes into it, I felt a presence similar to the one I describe in Chapter 4, when a woman manifesting demonic-like symptoms hugged me and I felt my consciousness being ripped from me. I have only had that feeling a couple of times in my life and it is something you do not forget. I opened my eyes in panic and at the same moment the priest turned to me as if he recognised something was wrong and made the sign of the cross in front of me, and it left. I was relieved. We finished the prayer, thanked him and left, a bit stunned. Later I could not help but recall the uncanny timing; just as I had opened my eyes in fear he turned before me, when he could not have been aware of my facial features. He must have sensed the thing leaving and trying to come towards me.

Afterwards I told Michelle she needed to throw the Tarot cards away and stop all psychic activity, otherwise it would come back and be far worse. (Remember that Pastor Kayiwa says the demons can come back and they will, as we shall see in the next story.) She understood and actually followed my suggestions. I was relieved to think this woman several years older than myself was trusting enough to accept my advice and accept the threat of danger and resulting problems. I suspect her depression was far worse at the time than she admitted, and she was ready to try anything.

While many of you will be suffering from the effects of the occult and will not have the chance to seek out someone skilled in this field for help, I suggest you turn to the appendixes for a prayer, to Defeat the Power of Evil, which I strongly advise for cutting all links with the demonic and the resulting symptoms.

The games evil plays

Evil is very cunning in its manifestations and unfortunately it continues to delude even the devout and the most knowledgeable. Myles Dempsey is one of a handful of people in England who specialise in deliverance ministry – healing people for whom occult activity is usually followed by frightening changes in behaviour. Often they will have tried all sorts of treatment or therapy. What starts as a bit of fun – a spot of fortune-telling, a seance or some spiritual healing – ends up going hideously wrong, leaving people with bizarre psychological and physical problems.

Spiritualists are of particular concern to Dempsey. Though he emphasises that many act in good faith, they often come to recognise that what they are involved in is not neutral. Spirits can give them the power to heal, but the person they are treating may receive a false healing. They may be freed of a condition or illness, but something far worse can happen.

'This is obviously not something in which you take a degree course. Deliverance,' Dempsey says, 'involves using special prayers to address spiritual oppression caused by occult activity.' He believes that this oppression is a result of a spirit that has entered a person's life, deceptively, through a forbidden act. The spirit then manifests itself in such unsettling ways as depression, financial and even physical problems. People active in this field believe that many diseases include a spiritual factor which is not apparent to most therapists and doctors, and consequently not dealt with medically. They believe that by praying for an individual suffering with symptoms associated with demonic oppression, total healing of body, mind and soul can result.

Dempsey stresses that exorcism is only part of his treatment. Exorcism, he says, is like surgery in medicine. 'I'm involved in the Church's healing ministry, which is much wider. It's concerned with broken bones, someone's history and their emotional and mental state. Exorcism is an important but small part of the ministry of healing. You can't be a surgeon and not know anything about health in general.'[47]

Dempsey, an Irishman, is a leader of the Charismatic Renewal Movement in England and has been active in the Catholic Church for forty-two years. Before retirement, he was director of a training establishment for the construction industry. Now his work echoes, to some extent, that of Jesus, where he meets a possessed and violent man in a graveyard and commands the demons out of the man into a herd of swine. I could see the parallel when Dempsey told me about a case early on in his work when one of his colleagues fell apart.

208

'When I worked with Tom he was in his late thirties. One morning his wife phoned to say he wouldn't be coming into work. He had hurt his back carrying a fireplace. I visited him and talked to the doctor, who said he would be in traction for three to six months. The next morning, he was back at work behind his desk.'

Dempsey asked him to explain and Tom said, 'After you left there was a knock at the door. When my wife answered, a man said, "You've got someone ill here." She thought he had come from the hospital, so she let him in.'

Dempsey goes on, 'Tom did not notice that the man was rather rough-spoken for a doctor or paramedic. But he told him what was wrong and the man put his hand on Tom's back. Tom felt an extraordinary suction and the pain vanished. He stood up, moved around and felt fine. Instinctively I said to Tom, "If I were you, I would have never allowed him to do that." '

After that, according to Dempsey, things took a dramatic turn. Tom's personality began to change. He became very disagreeable, and even his children did not like him. He ended up having to get another job and came down with all sorts of illnesses. His stomach was badly ulcerated and his duodenum closed almost completely. He developed a mania for speed and suicidal tendencies. 'He wasn't a particularly young man to be going 150 mph on the motorway,' Myles told me. Tom already had a fast car, but now he bought an expensive motorcycle. 'He even said he was hoping for a fatal accident.'

His daughter, who was highly intelligent, seemed to lose control of her life. His son suddenly developed acute learning disabilities. His wife started keeping cats, until they filled the house. Eventually the cats developed a disease that caused them to die howling. Then financial problems enveloped the whole family.

'Eventually,' said Dempsey, 'I left that company and went to work for another, where Tom lectured occasionally. One morning as I was at the blackboard, I felt this presence, a force, but I couldn't see anything. The ceiling began to vibrate and the entire building began to shake. There was no one in the room. The energy came flushing at me. I knew it was something spiritual in nature. By then I was well into the work I am doing now and the entity had recognised me as the enemy. [This happens to many people in the healing ministry, when they attempt to deliver someone from the clutches of evil spirits.]

'I had to stand against it and fight it. I began to pray and it was a terrible struggle. After a bit, it began to die down, and in walked Tom. He had carried it with him and didn't even know it. The nature of the problem was obvious to me. When Tom's problems began, I was unsure of the reason for his condition. But I was aware of the peculiar nature of the symptoms. I asked Tom if he had seen the man who was responsible for taking the pain away during his injury. He replied, "Oh yes, I saw him regularly. He told me my back would be healed, but I would suffer with my stomach. When I went back, it didn't work."

'I can be objective about this case because I didn't know anything about spiritualism at the time. This is what I mean by false healing. Tom was drawn back to this man on the promise of false hope. You always receive something far worse after the initial healing. His entire life was a catalogue of disasters.'

According to Dempsey, two main things happen when people get involved in spiritualism. They either fall into a deep depression or develop suicidal tendencies, or both. 'It's easy,' he says, 'to recognise the kind of depression that is due to a visit to a spiritualist. The person walks in and you immediately sense it. You can't define it in psychological or scientific terms. It isn't depression at all, but demonic oppression. This ability to determine whether it is demonic comes from discernment I have developed over the years. It need only take one visit to any type of spiritualist to become victimised by oppression. The more often someone visits, the worse it will be. Even if the spiritualist thinks he is acting in good faith, it means nothing at all. There is no grey area here.'

Dempsey illustrates this point with another case, from north London, in which a priest asked for his help. A woman in his parish who worked as a spiritualist medium was having problems, but failed to see anything wrong in what she was doing, even though the priest warned her that it was contrary to her faith in God. She eventually arranged to have counselling with Dempsey and it was organised that a group pray for her in an adjacent room, while he talked to her.

Dempsey said, 'When she came to the door, her legs were suddenly like lead. We could barely get her up the stairs. The resistance had begun. I explained that she had opened herself to the spirit world, how dangerous this was, and how these spirits were not of God but evil, in the disguise of good. I told her how harmful this was and how much God was against this type of activity. Finally, she acknowledged that what she had done was wrong and agreed to have the appropriate prayers said for her to be released from it.'

Once the prayers began, her eyes rolled, she began to froth at the mouth, she screamed and turned odd colours. 'Some of the more extraordinary deliverances I've seen haven't been characterised by this type of behaviour at all,' observes Dempsey. 'But this was a real spiritual battle. The spirit didn't want to give up control of her, though finally it broke.'

Afterwards the woman said, 'I feel so much lighter. I feel marvellous.' They went on praying for her for quite some time. Then they asked her about her family and she told them that she had involved them in spiritualism too. They warned her about how important it was to clear the family of the evil as well, and she agreed. She asked about what she should say to all her clients, and Dempsey told her to be straightforward and tell them she wanted nothing more to do with it. 'You have to make it very clear about the danger,' he told her. 'If you go back to it, the effects can be far worse.'

She went home, intending to act as they had advised. The next day her eighteen-year-old daughter exhibited the most extraordinary manifestations: crippling pain and contortions. The mother knew it was an evil spirit taking revenge on her daughter and, in her simplicity and ignorance, she spoke to the spirit, saying, 'Leave my daughter alone. You can come back to me.' The spirit stopped molesting the daughter and jumped back to her.

When the priest found out about it, he and Dempsey saw the woman again.

Dempsey says, 'I explained how foolish she had been and how very serious it was. She recognised that she had made a mistake, so we made arrangements to have the whole family come in. We had to get rid of what had entered her because, I must emphasise, when it re-enters, it is far worse. We repeated the same procedure and, although the opposition was much stronger, we finally broke it.'

But it was to no avail. Even though the woman had seen the harm done to her daughter, she could not give up her life as a healer, although she understood the source that was healing through her was not even human.

211

Dempsey concludes, 'People do not realise there is no neutral ground in the spiritual world. It is either God or the devil. These fallen angels or evil spirits have far greater intelligence than man. They are very clever and their work is to trick us into bondage without knowing it. People are unaware that they have given control of their lives to a negative spiritual entity. They can experience all sorts of misfortune and not realise what they have done to cause this kind of heartache for themselves.'

Raised to believe in the spirit world

For Dr Raphael Gasson there was little chance that he would escape from the effects of the occult. His grandmother was an ardent spiritualist, his grandfather also showed an interest, and his mother was influenced by spirits too. Their first exposure came when they tried to contact their relative, Gasson's aunt Rachel, known as Ray. It was during their contact with Ray's supposed spirit that she insisted that her new-born nephew should take her name. Hence the name Raphael. The connection did not end there.

As an infant, Raphael's bedroom was dominated by a large portrait photograph of Ray.[48] Dr Gasson recalls, 'Something sinister about it always puzzled me. One evening, when I was about five years old, the picture seemed to look back at me in a way it never had before. Ray's eyes became real, her features alive and, while I watched, it seemed as if she stepped straight out of the picture frame to my bedside. I screamed with fear. Nothing could shake my conviction that Ray actually moved. I was in total terror. Finally, the picture had to be hidden out of my sight.'

But this did not stop the spirit visitations, nor did his fears subside. His grandmother became convinced that the spirit of Ray was coming to him at night for a special purpose, and to discover why she visited a spiritualist medium. Through that medium she heard Ray was there only to watch over her nephew; she had never meant to frighten him. 'It should have made my grandmother wonder about all this activity,' said Dr Gasson. 'But it did the trick. The visits stopped.'

Born in 1920, Gasson grew up as an Orthodox Jew and was brought up according to Jewish ritual and Hebrew classes. The strictness of Judaism became irksome as he grew older. He began to study music and eventually broke from his religion. (He went on to earn nineteen academic degrees and diplomas, and to write twenty-three books on theology, music, calligraphy and education.) In his early life he also underwent a number of psychic experiences. 'One evening, when I was feeling disturbed and disheartened, I found myself walking around the streets of London. Suddenly I saw a replica of myself standing in front of me. Spiritualists would say that I saw my own etheric body. As I looked at this strange vision of myself, it told me to follow it. As I started to follow, my mind went completely blank, and the next thing I remember was sitting in a spiritualist church where a woman was speaking.

'After a hymn, the speaker pointed at me and told me my name. She went on to tell me that she knew about the strange experience I had undergone with my double, described one of my music professors and commented on the remark he had made recently about a piece of music I had just written. She told me I was a medium and that I had been watched by spirits all my life. She reminded me of the spirit manifestation of my childhood and told me I was now old enough to understand what they all meant. She told me God had seen the difficulties, and had sent the spirits to aid me in getting to the meeting.'[49]

To a young man with Gasson's background, this seemed plausible and he soon took up an interest in spiritualism, going to seances and developing various types of mediumship. Eventually, he became a deep trance medium. Many seriously ill people visited him and he really believed that, in healing them, he had found a knowledge of God. Visions and other psychic experiences became a natural, everyday occurrence to him and he was ordained a minister in a Spiritualist church.

Gasson then met a man claiming to be a Rational Spiritualist, who did not believe in a personal God. He boasted that he was a master of black magic and knew that the spirits controlling him were evil, but were doing good work. He said that people calling themselves Christian Spiritualists were dishonest: a spiritualist could not be a true Christian. Gasson says, 'He invited me to conduct a seance with him and I was convinced nothing would happen, because our viewpoints were so radically opposite. We would not be able to work in harmony.'[50]

He decided that their joint seance (in which neither man would be able to recall anything) should be witnessed. Once it was over he was amazed when everyone present said that it was an extraordinary event. 'I became very concerned. Here was a man who did not believe in God but believed only in dealing with evil spirits, producing definite phenomena and doing good works. On the other hand, I was spending a lot of time at prayer and devotion and producing no better phenomena. Was God answering my prayers or were they being answered by evil spirits? Was God working through this man, and not evil spirits, as he thought?'

We can get some indication of Gasson's confusion when he reveals one of his spirit guides: an African witchdoctor who told him that while on earth he used to eat white people. This resulted in his being taken prisoner, tortured, blinded and put to death. Now a feeling of repentance for past deeds made him anxious to do good.

According to Gasson, when the guide enters and speaks, it is invariably as a native of a different country. It often speaks a foreign language, which is interpreted into the language of those present by another spirit guide, who is controlling the body of another person.

He goes on, 'Many types of mediumship include healing: the blind are made to see, the lame walk, the deaf hear. Spiritualist healers believe in the laying-on of hands, as do Christians. The healer lays hands on the sufferer and they feel the power being transmitted from the medium. The congregation cooperates by concentrating on the patient and sending out love rays or healing thought rays. The healing is done by spirits, and the medium is the only vessel through which they work, and everyone – especially the medium – is aware of this.'

People want to believe. A young woman had approached Dr Gasson to say that she was extremely distressed to hear him say that the communicating spirits were demons, because they had given her back her sight. 'Surely demons would not do such things?'

He also received a letter from a man who worked as a medium, who was reading his book on mediumship in bed one night, but did not believe it. Suddenly his bed caught fire and he almost died. He now believes in the danger of the occult.

As Gasson observes, 'Something does happen at seances to convince even the most rational and intelligent people that spirit communication is not only possible but can become an everyday

214

experience. Communications do come through to earnest seekers into this system of teaching, which is bound to some extent to alter their outlook on life.'

Dr Gasson abandoned trance mediumship when he realised that the spirits really were demonic beings. Now disabled and living in retirement, he is active in eleven charities, mostly for the disabled, and continues to teach in two theological colleges.

The dangers of astrology

Astrology is undoubtedly popular. Millions of people on every continent read their horoscopes daily in newspapers and magazines. Gallup has estimated that between thirty and forty million Americans believe in astrology, a figure dwarfed by the 700 million adherents in India and close to one billion in China. No wonder the astrology industry is thought to be worth at least $1 billion a year. In the West, it is common for most readers of 'star guides' to excuse their habit by saying that they do not take it too seriously, claiming that it is just harmless fun. Even those who go deeper into the subject – having their birth charts compiled, for instance, or consulting astrologers before they make important decisions – maintain that there is no danger involved. They also take comfort from the fact that big business has begun to take astrology seriously, with CNN reporting recently that 300 companies listed in the Fortune 500 now make use of astrologers.

Astrology has a long history. In the ancient world, it became the strongest of all the various forms of 'deity' worship, infiltrating Greek paganism, influencing the peoples of Israel, Syria and Egypt, and eventually being proclaimed an official religion of the Roman Empire. The astrological system arose from the notion that the world was a living being, in which the events of a man's life could be interpreted by corresponding movements of the stars. The coming of Christianity killed off similar ancient beliefs, but it never quite defeated popular interest in astrology. It went underground for centuries, reviving in Britain more than 200 years ago. Since then, with more and more people seeking explanations for their existence outside the mainstream religions, particularly Christianity, its appeal has widened tremendously.

What modern practitioners fail to realise is that there are strong links between astrology and spiritism (or spiritualism). It

215

was in the late 1800s that Thomas H. Burgoyne is said to have started the Church of Light, an astrology-based occult group that remains popular. He was a Mason and a renowned psychic and medium, whose spirit guides instructed him to prepare a complete system of occult education. Of the 4,500 pages that were rapidly dictated, 1,800 pages were devoted to astrology and these documents, forming twenty-one courses, are still in use today. This doctrine on the occult is given to new initiates in astrology as 'a standard book of reference'.[51]

It appears that the spirits were determined that astrology should make a comeback among unsuspecting, naïve humans. For the truth is that astrology – along with Tarot cards, as we shall soon see – acts as a conduit to the demonic. It is a magnet or contact material which draws evil towards people. Not that astrologers themselves always realise this; they remain as susceptible as their followers. Many who do understand the link keep it secret from their clients. But there are some who readily admit to contact with the spirit world and, among them, are those who become wise enough to give up the craft. They include former astrologers Karen Winterburn and Charles Strohmer.

Ms Winterburn's signed statement, in which she rejected astrology, is acutely revealing. She wrote, 'In twelve years of serious astrological study and professional practice, I never met a really successful astrologer – even the most "scientific" ones – who did not admit among their professional peers that spiritism was the power behind the craft.'[52]

She admitted, 'I was convinced it [the astrological information] wasn't coming from me.' She took a familiar route, from humanistic psychology through spirit channelling to occult involvement. She explained, 'Astrology as a divination tool was the perfect entrance. It appeared to be secular, technical and humanistic, a "neutral" tool . . . Its occultic presuppositions were not immediately apparent . . . I became hooked . . . driven to find out the "hows" and "whys".'[53]

This led Ms Winterburn down the perilous path to channelling, which she now calls 'a sanitised term for spirit mediumship'. She later came to realise that all spirit beings were trying to influence human beings. She wrote, 'Once the astrologer becomes dependent upon one or more of them, these spirit intelligences . . . lead the astrologer into forms of spiritual commitment and worship. This is the worst kind of bondage.

Seasoned astrologers who have experienced fairly consistent and dramatic successes in character reading and prognostication invariably become involved in some form of worship of these demons.'[54] In other words, the better the astrologer, the greater the influence of the spirits.

Charles Strohmer points out how to recognise spirit involvement in the astrological chart, 'You have a new horoscope before you. You begin to notice that a certain item in the chart gets your attention. It sticks out in your mind, softly glaring at you. You begin to dwell upon its meaning. Perhaps a particular aspect of the chart pops into view, one you had not noticed before. It becomes difficult to shake off this impression that you "see". So you begin to discuss it with him or her [the client]. What is occurring? The [astrologer's] mind is becoming focused upon a portion of that client's life. [As a medium] this is a detail that a familiar spirit is privy to. It is the spirit that is somehow doing the focusing.'[55]

Strohmer illustrates how the spirit world interacts with the astrologer. 'As we look honestly at astrology, we begin to see that adherents of this system, without knowing it, are banging on the door through which communication is established with . . . deceptive spirit beings. Eventually that door opens. And the opening produces an appalling development in the adherent's life. He or she matures in the craft in a most unthought-of manner, as a spirit medium . . . In much the same way that the palm of the hand or the crystal [ball] is "contact material" for the fortune-teller, the horoscope chart is used by the astrologer.'[56]

According to Strohmer, once a person dispenses with that contact material, 'the spirits have no point of contact to make the psychic connection, to seep information through the spokesperson to the client . . . Without the contact with the spirit beings, there would be no astrological disclosures. Or, if they did come, it would be almost entirely from guesswork.'[57]

Gary Keen, a former Vice-President of the US-based Professional Astrologers Incorporated, echoes Strohmer's point. 'When the new astrologer reaches a point of perception – a sudden awesome insight, like a large wave engulfing him on the beach – the chart has talked, giving him a conclusive truth, he knows he has seen beyond himself. As the hair prickles his neck and coldness runs down his back, he knows he has stepped across a divide that separates the material from the mental or unknown (spiritual world) – the discovery of an unseen latent power that has been looming in existence for eons of time . . . He will attempt to develop some form of association with this unseen magical power that resides within, around and above the horoscope he holds in his hand.'[58]

This problem is exacerbated when people travel further afield for new astrological 'experiences'. Many Indian astrologers, for instance, believe that the planets are gods (living spirits) and are endowed with supernatural powers. Dr Gouri Kapoor argues that these planets can inflict either pain and disease or pleasure, helping or destroying. Therefore he considers it important for one's well-being to keep the planetary gods happy.[59]

Jung's views on astrology were not so very different. He claimed that whenever a case proved too hard for him, he would take out an astrological chart. 'The gods and goddesses are within us,' he said. 'These planets represent our contact with the sacred, so it's good to get to know them.'[60] But how can we get to know a planet?

A number of academics have become concerned at the way in which astrology has increased its hold on the population. (Even some of the so-called 'serious' newspapers in Britain now publish horoscope charts.) Among them is Allan Chapman, a Fellow of the Royal Astronomical Society and a historian of science at Oxford's Wadham College, who says, 'At the personal level I think it is dangerous. I don't know if you could call it a spirit, but there is something that makes a person turn towards what is, to me, a distracting evil force.

'Dealing with astrology in the context of Christianity is certainly opening the door to a whole car-load of spiritual mischief, because Christianity requires a recognition of our limitations as well as our God-given powers. To try to look into the future – especially with a defective intellectual tool like astrology – is a breach of our duty to submit to God's grace, rather than trying to steal Prometheus's fire. Making decisions that don't involve Christ is dangerous. For that reason it isn't just a bit of fun. Astrology is dicing with the devil. It's a malignant force. It's not just spiritually suspect, but spiritually malicious.'[61]

Yet this is so little recognised that people who should know better are quite happy to go on dabbling in astrology. I recall a lunch with Clive Thornton, the chairman until a year ago of *The*

Universe, England's largest-selling Roman Catholic newspaper, which is owned by the Bishops Conference. He told me that one of his interests was breeding cattle and he had won several awards. Many other breeders sought his advice because of his renown for accurately predicting the sex of offspring. How, I asked, was he able to achieve such success? His answer amazed me.

He explained that his daughter was an astrologer and that she would draw up horoscopes for him. I told him that astrology was an occult art and that its apparent success was achieved through spirit contact that was demonic. He scoffed at me and rejected my view. Here was the head of the largest religious newspaper in England taking part in practices directly opposed to the teachings of the Bible. The occult will weave its way into one's life at any opportunity.

Tarot cards: gateway to the occult

In my own misguided search for a non-religious spirituality, my problems with the occult started with astrology, then came mediums, but I moved on to something I thought altogether more intriguing: Tarot cards. These seemed to represent a gateway to knowledge, not accessible by ordinary means, through which I could obtain divine answers. How wrong I was. I never entertained the possibility of them leading me to evil. Although I grew up a Christian, I did not believe in the devil. In the beginning, I had no need for the Church, taking the view that their sermons did not 'speak' to me and were unable to tell me anything useful to guide me through my everyday life.

My mother tried to convince me to give up Tarot cards, using all sorts of persuasive tactics, but when I asked her for a clear-cut reason to explain what was wrong with them, even she, a devout Christian, was unable to give me one. She did not believe in the devil either, and when she asked religious sisters their views on the devil, they indicated they did not believe in him, either. That is how far removed the Church has been from doing its job. They should have been describing in detail the dangers of mystical activities such as Tarot-card readings.

It is thought that the Tarot originated with the Egyptian god Thoth, but this is contested by those who believe that the cards were created in fourteenth-century Italy and known as *Tarrochini*. One of the most prolific writers on the Tarot, called Papus, claimed it was originally connected with the esoteric Jewish Kaballa. In the mid-nineteenth century the French magician Eliphas Levi developed the Tarot's occult connection by associating the cards with the Kaballa, assigning each of the twenty-two trump cards to the Hebrew alphabet. (Due to secrecy, most of the Jewish community is unaware of the occult nature of the Kaballa.) Theosophists, Rosicrucians, Kabbalists and Freemasons have all incorporated Tarot symbolism into their systems, usually teaching that the Tarot carries with it a secret tradition or doctrine.

There are several different packs of Tarot cards designed by, among others, Aleister Crowley, Salvador Dali and a late nineteenth-century order known as the Golden Dawn. This order, which developed the Aquarian Tarot or the Tarot of witches, promulgated techniques for systematic conscious exploration of the mental realms, until then denied to all but those aware of Eastern occult tradition.[62]

But slowly the veil of secrecy shrouding occult mysteries is being stripped away and exposed for what it really is.

The occult's royal connections

Betty Palko, the medium who counselled the late Diana, Princess of Wales, uses the Tarot. Palko was drawn into the trade when a spiritualist put her in touch with a spirit who claimed to be her father. Then 'it' revealed information so close to her heart that she believed it had to be the truth. It obviously never occurred to her that 'it' could be the 'Father of all Lies' in disguise. Nor, of course, did it strike Diana that way. Unfortunately, her life was littered with emotional problems, such as eating disorders and depression, before its tragic end.

The type of problems Diana faced are characteristic of the effects of evil. Although experts claim there is no certainty about the cause of eating disorders, most authoritative studies suggest that they stem from abuse. Whatever the reason, Diana's avid interest in the occult could have opened the door to the demonic to create these problems and then left her without divine protection before her death.

Unfortunately she was far from alone in the royal family in taking a misdirected spiritual journey. Prince Charles was a long-time confidant of Laurens van der Post, a friend and disciple of Jung. Van der Post claimed that while he was out at sea he dreamed of Jung saying goodbye to him, only later learning that this had occurred at the time of Jung's death. Also coinciding with the moment of Jung's death was a bolt of lightning that struck his favourite tree in his garden near Zurich. Years later, in the same garden while speaking into the camera during filming of a documentary on Jung, van der Post was re-telling the tale of the uncanny coincidence when lightning again struck the garden.[63]

It has been rumoured that Prince Charles had spiritual experiences after the death of his favourite uncle, Lord Mountbatten, which could well have influenced him. It is also thought that the Queen Mother may have attended a seance or two in her day, while it is a matter of historical record that Queen Victoria routinely consulted mediums. Her most favoured servant, John Brown, allegedly kept the Queen in touch with her beloved husband, Prince Albert, after his death in 1861.

Given this kind of history, and Prince Charles's possible ongoing interest in spiritualism, Princes William and Harry have a greater than average chance of inheriting problems. I am certain that the demonic nature of the occult is not known to the royal family, but they should be made aware of it, particularly in view of their position as head of the Anglican Church.

The three principal monotheistic religions of the world, Judaism, Islam and Christianity, expressly forbid communication with the spirit world. And the reasons have been misunderstood for centuries. From as far back as the early days of the Old Testament the spiritual domain has held unparalleled intrigue for many, but the evidence for discerning the work of God from the reality and deception of Satan continues to be largely concealed. I hope I have illustrated for you a reasonable and accurate picture of the facts and the associated dangers of the occult. The wisdom of scripture may conclude it best:

'For the spirit scrutinises everything, even the depths of God. Among human beings, who knows what pertains to a person except the spirit of that person that is within? Similarly, no one knows what pertains to God except the spirit of God. We have

221

not received the spirit of the world but the spirit that is from God, so that we may understand the things freely given to us by God. And we speak about them not with words taught by human wisdom, but with words taught by the Spirit, describing spiritual realities in spiritual terms.

'Now the natural person does not accept what pertains to the Spirit of God, for to him it is foolishness, and he cannot understand it, because it is judged spiritually. The spiritual person, however, can judge everything but is not subject to judgement by anyone.' (1 Corinthians 2, 10–15.)

And it is this wisdom of the Spirit that will give you freedom from the realm of darkness, for ever.

Notes

1. *The Spear of Destiny*, Trevor Ravenscroft, Samuel Weisner, York Beach, Maine, 1982.
2. Reverend John Hampsch, interview, 1997.
3. *The Screwtape Letters*, C.S. Lewis, HarperCollins, London, 1942, p. 9.
4. *People of the Lie*, Dr M. Scott Peck, Arrow Books, London, 1990, p. 46.
5. Ibid., pp. 208–32.
6. Ibid., pp. 224–5.
7. 'Healing Your Family Tree', Revd Hampsch, audio tapes, Claretian Tape Ministry, Los Angeles.
8. Ibid.
9. Op. cit., note 4, p. 217.
10. *Aleister Crowley: The Nature of the Beast*, Colin Wilson, Aquarian Press, UK, 1987, p. 16.
11. *The New Spirituality*, Dave Hunt, Harvest House Publishers, Eugene, Oregon, 1988, pp. 172–5.
12. Ibid., quoting from *The Unexplained*, Allen Spragget.
13. Op. cit., note 11, p. 175.
14. Op. cit., note 4, p. 220.
15. *The Paranormal: An Illustrated Encyclopedia*, Stuart Gordon, Headline Book Publishing, London, 1992, p. 700.
16. *The Witch-cult in Western Europe*, Margaret Murray, Oxford University Press, 1921.
17. Op. cit., note 15, p. 700.

18. *The Kingdom of Cults*, Walter Martin, Bethany House Publishers, Minneapolis, Minnesota, 1985, pp. 229–30; op. cit., note 15, pp. 621–2; *The Challenging Counterfeit*, Raphael Gasson, Bridge Publishing, Plainfield, New Jersey, 1966, pp. 48–9.
19. Op. cit., note 10, p. 17.
20. Op. cit., note 18 (Gasson), pp. 48–9.
21. Op. cit., note 15, pp. 91–2.
22. *The Secret Doctrine*, Theosophical Publishing House, USA, 1988.
23. I am indebted to Dave Hunt's, *The New Spirituality* (op. cit., note 11, pp. 65–6, 111), for his revelations on Jung's involvement with the occult.
24. *Memories, Dreams and Reflections*, C.G. Jung, Pantheon Books, USA, 1963, p. 208.
25. *Psychology and the Occult*, C.G. Jung, Princeton University Press, Princeton, 1977, pp. 146–52.
26. *Collected Letters* (Volume 1), C.G. Jung, Princeton University Press, Princeton, 1973, p. 43.
27. Op. cit., note 24, p. 214.
28. *Do the Heavens Rule Your Destiny*, John Ankenberg and John Weldon, Harvest House Publishers, Eugene, Oregon, 1989.
29. Op. cit., note 3, pp. 39–40.
30. 'We Train the Psychics', Gillian Cribbs, *Miracles and the Extraordinary* magazine, London, Issue 3, 1995.
31. Ibid.
32. Ibid.
33. Ibid.
34. Ibid.
35. Ibid.
36. *Love, Medicine and Miracles*, Dr Bernie Siegel, Harper Perennial, USA, 1986, pp. 19–20.
37. Ibid.
38. Review of *Reunions; Visionary Encounters with Departed Loved Ones*, Raymond Moody with Paul Perry (Little, Brown, London, 1995) by Helmut Lutz, *Miracles and the Extraordinary* magazine, Issue 2, 1995.
39. *A Still Small Voice*, Father Benedict Groeschel, CFR, Ignatius Press, San Francisco, 1993, pp. 75–82, 163-5.
40. Ibid., p. 77.
41. Ibid., p. 79.

42. Ibid., p. 76.
43. *Working with Guides and Angels*, Ruth White, Piatkus, London, 1996, p. 6.
44. Ibid., p. 44.
45. Ibid., p. 24.
46. Ibid., pp. 48, 57–8.
47. Myles Dempsey, interviewed by author, 1994.
48. Op. cit., note 18 (Gasson), p. 14.
49. Ibid., p. 19.
50. Ibid., p. 21.
51. Op. cit., note 28, Ankenberg and Weldon provide a comprehensive account of astrology and spiritualism, pp. 201–20.
52. Ibid., p. 221.
53. Ibid.
54. Ibid., p. 222.
55. *What Your Horoscope Doesn't Tell You*, Charles Strohmer, Word Publishing, Milton Keynes, 1988, p. 69.
56. Ibid., p. 65.
57. Ibid.
58. *Spiritual, Metaphysical and New Trends in Modern Astrology*, Joan McEvers, Llewellyn Publications, St Paul, Minnesota, 1988, pp. 19–20; op. cit., note 28, pp. 227–8.
59. *Remedial Measures in Astrology*, Dr Gouri Shankar Kapoor, Ranjan Publications, New Delhi, India, 1985; op. cit., note 28, pp. 208–9.
60. Op. cit., note 28, p. 207.
61. Allan Chapman, interviewed by Patricia Miller, *Miracles and the Extraordinary* magazine, Issue 4, 1995.
62. Op. cit., note 15, p. 648.
63. *Jung and the Story of Our Time*, Laurens van der Post, Penguin Books, London, 1978.

Epilogue

'My people perish,' said the prophet Hosea, 'from lack of knowledge.' But readers of this book no longer lack knowledge. You have read a wealth of evidence, which proves conclusively that supernatural activity is not a figment of people's imaginations; it cannot be dismissed as the territory of cranks and fantasists. Along the way many cynics, sceptics and atheists have changed their minds. Once confronted by irrefutable proof, they discover that they cannot, after all, explain away extraordinary events by relying on their supposed rationality and the discoveries of science.

Miracles have happened, are still happening and, by God's grace, will go on happening. People have been cured of 'incurable' diseases and have witnessed 'impossible' phenomena. They have discovered that prayer works and that those who have religious belief are happier. Such believers find that they have a greater ability to fight disease. And couples who pray together are shown to have a far greater chance of staying together than those who do not. You have been able to share the lesson they have all learned: spirituality is good for you. This, truly, is the reason behind faith; and it is the *raison d'être* of this book.

Unfortunately, supernatural activity has been a secret for too long and is still not widely recognised. That is why spreading this knowledge is so important. This is not a book to read and then forget, or even one to stimulate your individual thoughts, merely to keep them to yourself. Instead it is a book that should engender action. Western society, despite its deep-seated trust in what it likes to imagine is man-made progress, may well have reached a critical turning point. According to prophecy, we are at the eleventh hour, and the situation that we face now begs the question: can we afford to go on ignoring the warnings that have been given to us so often?

'No man,' wrote the poet John Donne, 'is an island.' Whatever propaganda we may hear from modern economists and politicians who deify 'the individual' – thus denying the overriding importance of the community and of society – Donne undoubtedly got it right. We are bound together, every race and every country, like a cluster of grapes, one resting upon the next, creating an environment that is either wholesome or destructive. We are not isolated individuals competing with one another in a crude, unending war, which Charles Darwin called the survival of the fittest. As humans, we are connected to each other and are able to help the weak. The family is the foundation on which everything else rests, so our responsibilities begin with our children. But they do not end there: we have duties and obligations to our community, to the larger society of our country and then to other countries, eventually encompassing the whole world.

As has already been pointed out, we have for too long failed to fulfil that commitment, both to God and to ourselves, and millions have paid the price for that failure. Since the time of Moses we have been warned of the consequences of our actions, both individually and corporately – whether for good or for evil – and the results come back to haunt us over a period of three, four, sometimes ten generations. What we do today affects tomorrow, the day after and the year after that, down through time indefinitely. We owe it to our children and our children's children to cure our current spiritual sickness. Why should any of us want to cause suffering for future generations?

Fortunately, as we have seen, many people *are* responding to the spiritual void in today's world. But their reaction is laced with confusion, and even a denial of basic truths, as people seek a new path to a more fulfilled state of happiness. Right and wrong are not a matter of opinion. Rules are to be cherished, because they provide a moral grounding for society. Our mission should be to find our way back to that basic precept and to reintroduce the purity of those straightforward rules.

Given the evidence already presented, it would appear that the first sensible step we should take in rebuilding our society should be to rediscover God – the God we knew as children – and ask Him for the 'gift' of faith. It is difficult to overcome weaknesses by relying on our own will alone. Far better to begin the healing process with prayer, before it is too late and we are punished by God's divine justice.

One clear message repeated throughout this book has been the danger of taking the wrong path in our search for the sacred. It can be difficult to know which way to turn, because there are so many philosophies on offer masquerading as beneficial alternatives to God. But these are false. That is why exploring the realm of the supernatural is not for the naïve. For instance, just because alternative medicine offers hope, and can indeed help cure us, it does not mean that its claim to spiritual wisdom is valid.

In truth, even the most knowledgeable among us have to admit that we are humble: we cannot know what God does not wish us to know. That is why spiritual matters cannot be judged by human wisdom, but only by God's hidden wisdom, which is not confined to this age or the next. The human spirit (the spirit of this world) is not capable of understanding the mysteries of the unknown; nor can our scientific 'laws', such as they are, hope to comprehend the divine. It is only the spirit of God, which He gives us, that can judge that which is unseen.

Good, of course, is only one side of the coin. On the other side lurks evil. To believe in one is to believe in the other. Yet many find it hard to comprehend the continuous supernatural battle with the powers of darkness, in spite of the overriding proof. This is not archaic superstition, but fact. We have seen that there is significant evidence to suggest that we face a highly intelligent, deceptive spiritual enemy, which continually works against us and against God. But if we embrace God, we have protection from the devil. It is when we ignore Him that we face our greatest peril, especially if we invite evil into our lives, by taking up ungodly practices linked to the occult.

The real danger lies in keeping all this knowledge – about the upward path to good and the downward path to evil – to yourself. Now, armed with all that you have read, you have the chance to change your heart and your life. The next step is to save other people's lives. Faith is not embarrassing. It is a recognition that there is something beyond man, and we need to proclaim that to people everywhere. If this book makes a contribution, however small, to that enlightenment, then it will have justified its publication.

Appendix I

Prayer to Defeat the Power of Evil[1]

Heavenly Father, I love You, I praise You, and I worship You. I thank You for sending your Son Jesus who won victory over sin and death for my salvation. I thank You for sending your Holy Spirit who empowers me, guides me, and leads me into the fullness of life. I thank You for Mary my heavenly mother, who interceded with the holy angels and saints for me.

Lord Jesus Christ, I place myself at the foot of your cross and ask You to cover me with your Precious Blood which pours forth from your most Sacred Heart and your most Holy Wounds. Cleanse me, my Jesus, in the living water that flows from your Heart. I ask You to surround me, with your holy Light.

Heavenly Father, let the healing waters of my baptism now flow back through the maternal and paternal generations to purify my family line of Satan and sin. I come before You, Father, and ask Your forgiveness for myself, my relatives, and my ancestors, for calling upon any powers that set themselves up in opposition to You or that do not offer true honour to Jesus Christ. In Jesus' Holy Name, I now reclaim any territory that was handed over to Satan and place it under the Lordship of Jesus Christ.

By the power of your Holy Spirit, reveal to me, Father, any people I need to forgive and any areas of unconfessed sin. Reveal aspects of my life that are not pleasing to You, Father, ways that could have given or could give Satan a foothold in my life. (*Pause and wait for a moment*) Thank you, Father, for these revelations. Thank you, for your forgiveness and your love.

Lord Jesus, in your Holy Name, I bind all evil spirits of the air, the water, ground, underground, the netherworld below. I further bind, in Jesus' name, any and all emissaries of the satanic headquarters and claim the Precious Blood of Jesus on the air, atmosphere, water, ground and their fruits around us, the underground and the netherworld below.

Heavenly Father, allow your Son Jesus to come now with the Holy Spirit, the Blessed Virgin Mary, the holy angels and the saints to protect me from all harm and to keep all evil spirits from taking revenge on me in any way.

(*Repeat the following sentence three times: once in honour of the Father, once in honour of the Son, and once in honour of the Holy Spirit*)

In the Holy Name of Jesus, I seal myself, my relatives, this room (place, home, business, church, car, plane, and any specific friends, relatives or business partners etc.) in the Precious Blood of Jesus Christ.

(*To break and dissolve all satanic seals, repeat the following paragraph three times in honour of the Holy Trinity because satanic seals are said three times against the Holy Trinity*)

In the Holy Name of Jesus, I break and dissolve any and all curses, hexes, spells, snares, traps, lies, obstacles, deceptions, distractions, diversions, spiritual influences, evil wishes, evil desires, hereditary seals, known and unknown, and every dysfunction and disease from any source including my mistakes and sins. In Jesus' Name, I sever the transmission of any and all satanic vows, pacts, spiritual bonds, soul ties, and satanic works. In Jesus' Name I break and dissolve any and all links and the effects of links with: astrologers, fortune-tellers, mediums, psychics, channellers, clairvoyants, crystal healers; psychic healers, dowsers, occult seers, palm, tea leaf, or Tarot card readers, satanic cults, spirit guides, shamans, witches, witchdoctors, Voodoo, Santeria, numerology, the *I Ching*, the Runes (and any person you wish to name specifically). In Jesus' Name, I dissolve all effects of participation in seances and divination, Ouija boards, horoscopes, occult games of all sorts and any form of worship that does not offer true honour to Jesus Christ.

Holy Spirit, please reveal to me through word of knowledge any evil spirits that have attached themselves to me in any way. (*Pause and wait for words to come to you, such as anger, arrogance, bitterness, confusion, deception, fear, hatred, insecurity, jealousy, pride, resentment, etc. Pray the following for each of the evil spirits revealed*) In the Name of Jesus, I rebuke you spirit of —————. I command you to go directly to Jesus without harm and without manifestation to me or anyone, so that He can dispose of you according to His Holy Will.

I thank You, Heavenly Father, for your love. I thank you, Holy Spirit, for empowering me to be aggressive against Satan and all evil spirits. I thank You, Jesus, for setting me free.

Lord Jesus fill me with faith, hope, humility, kindness, joy, patience, peace, security, wisdom and understanding. Help me to walk in your Light and Truth, illuminated by the Holy Spirit so that I may share with others the gift of your Love. Glory be to the Father, to the Son and to the Holy Spirit as it was in the beginning as now and ever shall be, world without end. Amen.

Notes

1. MARY Ministries, Scottsdale, Arizona, USA.

Appendix II

For information on healing services

Holy Trinity Brompton (Anglican)
Brompton Road
London SW7 1JA
Tel: 0171 581 8255

Kensington Temple (Pentecostal)
Kensington Park Road
London W11 3BY
Tel: 0171 727 4877

Charismatic Renewal Centre (Catholic)
Allen Hall, 28 Beaufort Street
London SW3 5AA
Tel: 0171 352 5298

For referral

Anyone who would like information on any of the people written about in this book can contact me (see over). If you need help because of problems related to the occult, I can provide you with a referral.

Author's Request

I would appreciate hearing from anyone who would care to share their story of healing with me. Research into this field is very important and your contribution would be helpful. I am primarily concerned with psychological, emotional, physical or possibly financial problems that may coincide with occult activity or physical healings that can be properly documented.

Rochelle M. Gibler
Mail Box 2, 157 Gloucester Road
London SW7 4TH

Bibliography

Achterberg, Jeanne, *Imagery in Healing: Shamanism and Modern Medicine*, Shambhala, Boston and London, 1985.

Ankenberg, John, and Weldon, John, *Do the Heavens Rule Our Destiny*, Harvest House Publishers, Eugene, Oregon, 1989.

Benor, Dr Daniel J., *Healing Research* (Volumes 1 and 2), Helix Editions Ltd, UK, 1994.

Benson, Herbert, MD, *Timeless Healing: The Power and Biology of Belief*, Simon and Schuster, New York, 1997.

Boa, Kenneth, *Cults, World Religions and the Occult*, Scripture Press Publications, USA, 1977.

Brown, Michael, and Mariani, Drew, *A Bridge to Heaven*, Marian Communications, Lima, Pennsylvania, 1993.

Brown, Michael, *The Final Hour*, Marian Communications, Lima, Pennsylvania.
Trumpet of Gabriel, Faith Publishing Company, Milford, Ohio, 1994.

De Montfort, St Louis, *The Secret of the Rosary*, Montfort Publications, Bay Shore, New York, 1954.

Dossey, Larry, MD, *Healing Words*, HarperSanFrancisco, 1993.
Prayer Is Good Medicine, HarperSanFrancisco, 1996.

Gasson, Raphael, *The Challenging Counterfeit*, Bridge Publishing Inc., South Plainfield, New Jersey, 1966.

Gobbi, Father Stephano, *To the Priests*, The Marian Movement of Priests, St Francis, Maine, 1996.

Gordon, James S., MD, *Manifesto for a New Medicine*, Addison-Wesley Publishing Company Inc., New York, 1996.

Gordon, Stuart, *The Paranormal: An Illustrated Encyclopedia*, Headline, London, 1992.

Groeschel, Father Benedict J., CFR, *A Still Small Voice*, Ignatius Press, San Francisco, 1993.

Hampsch, Revd John, CMF, *Healing Your Family Tree*, Our Sunday Visitor, Huntingdon, Indiana, 1986.

Hunt, Dave, and McMahon, T.A., *The New Spirituality*, Harvest House Publishers, Eugene, Oregon, 1988.

Jung, Carl, *Collected Letters*, Princeton University Press, Princeton, 1973.
Memories, Dreams and Reflections, Pantheon Books, USA, 1963.
Psychology and the Occult, Princeton University Press, Princeton, 1977.

Laurentin, Father René, *The Apparitions at Medjugorje Prolonged*, The Riehle Foundation, Milfred, Ohio, 1987.

Lebar, Revd James J., *Cults, Sects and the New Age*, Our Sunday Visitor, Huntington, Indiana, 1989.

Lewis, C.S., *The Screwtape Letters*, HarperCollins, London, 1942.

McAll, Dr Kenneth, *Healing the Family Tree*, Sheldon Press, London, 1982.

Martin, Walter, *The Kingdom of Cults*, Bethany House Publishers, Minneapolis, Minnesota, 1985.

Moody, Dr Raymond, *Reunion: Visionary Encounters with Departed Loved Ones*, Little, Brown, London, 1995.

Parsons, Heather, *Man of Miracles*, Robert Andrew Press, Dublin, 1994.

Peck, Dr M. Scott, *People of the Lie*, Arrow Books, London, 1990.

Petrisko, Thomas, *Call of the Ages*, Queenship Publishing, Santa Barbara, California, 1995.

Ravenscroft, Trevor, *The Spear of Destiny*, Samuel Weisner, York Beach, Maine, 1982.

Siegel, Dr Bernie, *Love, Medicine and Miracles*, Harper Perennial, USA, 1986.

Strohmer, Charles, *What Your Horoscope Doesn't Tell You*, Word Publishing, Milton Keynes, 1988.

Trosclair, Margaret, M., SOSM, *Do You Believe That Jesus Can Heal You?*, Mary's Helpers Publishing Company, Marrero, Louisiana, 1996.

Van der Post, Laurens, *Jung and the Story of Our Time*, Penguin Books, London, 1978.

White, Ruth, *Working with Guides and Angels*, Piatkus, London, 1996.

Williamson, Marianne, *A Return to Love*, Thorsons/Harper Collins, London, 1992.

Wilson, Colin, *Aleister Crowley: The Nature of the Beast*, Aquarian Press, UK, 1987.

Index

241